Freud and the 20th Century

FREUD
AND
THE
20th
CENTURY

Edited and Selected
by BENJAMIN NELSON

MERIDIAN BOOKS, INC.   *New York*

Benjamin Nelson

Benjamin Nelson was born in New York City in 1911. He is
a graduate of the College of the City of New York and
received his doctorate at Columbia University. He is now
Professor of History and Social Science and Chairman of the
Department of Sociology at Hofstra College in Hempstead,
New York. He has previously taught at the College of the
University of Chicago, Columbia University, and the Univer-
sity of Minnesota. He has been awarded Fellowships by Co-
lumbia University, the Guggenheim Foundation, and the
Carnegie Foundation.

During 1955-1956 he served as Associate Editor of the *Journal
of the History of Ideas*. He is currently Advisory Editor of
Psychoanalysis. His publications include: *The Idea of Usury:
From Tribal Brotherhood to Universal Otherhood; Essays in
Medieval Life and Thought* (as co-editor); *An Introduction to
Social Science* (with collaborators); "The Future of Illusions;"
and other papers in scholarly reviews.

*A Meridian Books Original Edition
Published April 1957 by Meridian Books, Inc.
First printing March 1957
Second printing March 1958
Third printing April 1959*

Contents

PREFACE

It would be supererogation here to chronicle the career or detail the accomplishments of Sigmund Freud. The centenary of his birth (May 6, 1856) is continuing to be enthusiastically commemorated wherever civilized men remain free to express their minds on matters of moment. The neglect or oversight of this date in those lands where liberal institutions remain in abeyance is one more proof—as if any more were needed! —that those who present themselves as guides to a new Eden unclouded by the name of Freud live by sham and evasion, for which a terrible price will yet be paid.

Hardly more than Freud do the authors represented in the present symposium need either introduction or warrant. Each is known for his habit of candor, distinctive learning, and uncompromising integrity in championing the cultural values he prizes. Here they speak with their accustomed directness and clarity concerning the place of Freud in the life and thought of our era. The outcome, arranged by the editor into a six-part panel, is now presented as an historic contribution to our understanding of our natures and destinies, and to the help of psychoanalysis and its creator in exploring them, as we move unsteadily into a new millennium.

It is not pretended that every shade of opinion finds its spokesman here. Even the omissions which seem flagrant are likely to have accident rather than design for their explanation. Wherever possible, an effort has been made to amend this lack by appropriate matter in the footnotes and in the Selected References. Of this much the reader may be assured:

the authors hail from many lands, speak many tongues, espouse diverse—even contradictory—views, and are by no means committed to the promotion of psychoanalysis or the Freudian point of view. The spirit of dialogue and debate we have sought to evoke in these pages was not to be had by emulating the sectarian exclusiveness so frequent in the contrived "symposia" of these days of make-believe.

Three of our essayists—Abram Kardiner, Viktor von Weizsaecker, Erik Erikson—had close personal contact with Freud or his circle and write about him and his work with evident authority. (Kardiner and von Weizsaecker supply us with anecdotes or letters from Freud not previously available in English.) The contributions of Freud's thought to psychiatry, psychology, social thought, literature, the arts and philosophy are pungently evaluated by well-known workers in these fields —Gregory Zilboorg, Gardner Murphy, Frederick Hacker, Will Herberg, Stanley Edgar Hyman, Alfred Kazin, E. H. Gombrich, Abraham Kaplan and Jerome S. Bruner.

The centenarian here receives—and needs—no garland of praises. Hardly one of the symposiasts finds his teachings complete, without flaw. One—Nigel Walker—frankly doubts that his adulators are right to compare him to Copernicus and Darwin. Another, Jacques Maritain, acknowledges his genius in psychoanalysis but declares him victimized by a faulty philosophy far inferior in its fabric to that of St. Thomas, albeit free of some of the shortcomings of Descartes and Bergson. Reinhold Niebuhr—he is seconded in this by Herberg—proclaims Freud's abandonment of the sentimental rationalism of the Enlightenment and the Victorian gospel of the "certain evanescence of evil" and inevitable progress to illimitable perfection, but deems his view of man and polity less realistic and less comprehensive than that suggested by the Old Testament Prophets and the Epistles of St. Paul.

None denies his central importance for the way we have come to view man and the world. None would minimize his prime contribution to the achievement of a technique for the healing of mental ills. All, it happens, prefer him to other exponents of so-called dynamic psychologies, notably Adler,

Jung, and the American neo-Freudians and neo-Adlerians, Karen Horney, Harry Stack Sullivan, and Erich Fromm.

How different in this respect is the temper of the 1950's from that of the 1930's and 1940's, when formless clichés concerning his defects as man and scientist were on every tongue. One reason, surely not the most important, for this change of tone, may be found in the extraordinary materials made available to us during the last seven years. Three publications in particular deserve notice in this connection: Freud's intimate letters to Dr. Wilhelm Fliess, with his notes and drafts, dating from 1887 to 1902; the new edition of *The Interpretation of Dreams* by James Strachey which makes possible for the first time an informed reading *in any language* of that seminal work; the two volumes thus far issued of the life and work of Freud by Ernest Jones.

To the editor at least, one question seems to run through the present symposium like a haunting obbligato: Will the Twentieth Century go down in history as the *Freudian Century?* At one point in these pages, the famed German pioneer in psychosomatic medicine, Viktor von Weizsaecker, names the date 1900 the dawn of a new era in the history of science and cultural sensibility. That year saw the publication of *The Interpretation of Dreams,* which was followed in 1901 by the quantum theory and in 1905 by the theory of relativity.

Is it possible that the impact of Freud will in the end prove to be more decisive and far-reaching than the discoveries of Planck and Einstein? May not the new forms of awareness growing out of Freud's work come to serve as a more authentic symbol of our consciousness and the quality of our deepest experience than the uncertain fruits of the fission of the atom and the new charting of the cosmos?

None of the following writers addresses himself directly to this theme and none was asked to do so. Neither folly nor partisanship were the price of participation in the present symposium. Sole responsibility must rest with the editor for daring to tread in shoals so deep and treacherous. The following are his own views, here made known to his collaborators for the first time:

Freud seems destined to be the bridge from the Nineteenth to the Twenty-first Century. Properly to be understood, he needs to be seen against a number of backgrounds other than those of neurology and medical psychology, with which he is usually identified. Freud's journey within—the *Interpretation of Dreams* (1900)—parallels and goes beyond that of Marcus Aurelius, St. Augustine, Dante, Pascal, Kirkegaard, Rimbaud and other more recent explorers of the soul. None took soundings so deep as he, none focussed so unrelentingly and evolved such powerful resources for mapping the innermost labyrinths as he; none described the mind's itinerary with less resort to fable, fancy or despairing leaps into faith. The *Interpretation of Dreams* initiates the existentialist consciousness of the Twentieth Century. When his divine comedy was ended (Freud knew and even hinted at the connection of his pilgrimage with that of the Tuscan voyager), there was little life left in the gallery of guises—Byronism, Promethianism, Parnassianism, dandyism, diabolism, pietism, scientism, moralism and so many others—assumed by the philosophies and substitute religions of the modern era.

His *Civilization and Its Discontents* at the zenith of his career (1930) is the most distinctive statement in the philosophy of existence and civilization which has been produced in the present century. By contrast to it, naive rationalisms and naive romanticisms alike—philosophies *seemingly as diverse* as those of Comte and Spencer, Schopenhauer and Nietzsche in the Nineteenth Century; Dewey and Sartre, Spengler and Toynbee in the Twentieth—seem shades of yesteryear, without power to express our present experience of the condition of men or the designs of history. Too few years are left in the present Century to exhaust the dimensions of his message or to approximate the substance of his hopes.

The present writer will say no more, lest he outlast his welcome. For the clearer and wiser counsel the reader has every right to expect, he has only to turn now to the following pages.

B. N.

New York, February 9, 1957

PART I: *Mid-Century Perspectives*

ONE

THE FREUDIAN REVOLUTION ANALYZED

ALFRED KAZIN

It is hard to believe that Sigmund Freud was born over a century ago. Although Freud has long been a household name (and, in fact, dominates many a household one could mention), his theories still seem too "advanced," they touch too bluntly on the most intimate side of human relations, for us to picture Freud himself coming out of a world that in all other respects now seems so quaint.

Although Freud has influenced even people who have never heard of him, not all his theories have been accepted even by his most orthodox followers, while a great many of his essential ideas are rejected even by many psychoanalysts. In one sense Freud himself is still battling for recognition, for because of the tabooed nature of the materials in which he worked and the unusually speculative quality of his mind, Freud still seems to many people more an irritant than a classic.

On the other hand, Freud's influence, which started from the growing skepticism about civilization and morality after the First World War, is now beyond description. Freudianism gave sanction to the increasing exasperation with public standards as opposed to private feelings; it upheld the truths of human nature as against the hypocrises and cruelties of conventional morality; it stressed the enormous role that sex plays in man's imaginative life, in his relations to his parents, in the symbolism of language.

It is impossible to think of the greatest names in modern literature and art—Thomas Mann, James Joyce, Franz Kafka, T. S. Eliot, Ernest Hemingway, William Faulkner, Pablo Picasso, Paul Klee—without realizing our debt to Freud's exploration of dreams, myths, symbols and the imaginative profundity of man's inner life. Even those who believe that original sin is a safer guide to the nature of man than any other can find support in Freud's gloomy doubts about man's capacity for progress. For quite other reasons, Freud has found followers, even among Catholic psychiatrists, who believe that Freud offers a believable explanation of neurosis and a possible cure, and so leaves the sufferer cured to practice his faith in a rational way.

Many psychologists who disagree with Freud's own materialism have gratefully adopted many of Freud's diagnoses, and although he himself was chary about the psychoanalytical technique in serious mental illness, more and more psychiatrists now follow his technique, or some adaptation of it. For no other system of thought in modern times, except the great religions, has been adopted by so many people as a systematic interpretation of individual behavior. Consequently, to those who have no other belief, Freudianism sometimes serves as a philosophy of life.

Freud, a tough old humanist with a profoundly skeptical mind, would have been shocked or amused by the degree to which everything is sometimes explained by "Freudian" doctrines. He offered us not something that applies dogmatically to all occasions, but something useful, a principle of inquiry into those unconscious forces that are constantly pulling people apart, both in themselves and from each other.

Freud's extraordinary achievement was to show us, in scientific terms, the primacy of natural desire, the secret wishes we proclaim in our dreams, the mixture of love and shame and jealousy in our relations to our parents, the child as father to the man, the deeply buried instincts that make us natural beings and that go back to the forgotten struggles of the human race. Until Freud, novelists and dramatists had never dared to think that science would back up their belief that personal passion is a stronger force in people's lives than socially accepted morality. Thanks to Freud, these insights now form a widely shared body of knowledge.

In short, Freud had the ability, such as is given to very few individuals, to introduce a wholly new factor into human knowledge; to impress it upon people's minds as something for which there was evidence. He revealed a part of reality that many people before him had guessed at, but which no one before him was able to describe as systematically and convincingly as he did. In the same way that one associates the discovery of certain fundamentals with Copernicus, Newton, Darwin, Einstein, so one identifies many of one's deepest motivations with Freud. His name is no longer the name of a man; like "Darwin," it is now synonymous with a part of nature.

This is the very greatest kind of influence that a man can have. It means that people use his name to signify something in the world of nature which, they believe, actually exists. A man's name has become identical with a phenomenon in nature, with a cause in nature, with a "reality" that we accept—even when we don't want to accept it. Every hour of every day now, and especially in America, there are people who cannot forget a name, or make a slip of the tongue, or feel depressed; who cannot begin a love affair, or end a marriage, without wondering what the "Freudian" reason may be.

No one can count the number of people who now think of any crisis as a personal failure, and who turn to a psychoanlyst or to a psychoanalytical literature for an explanation of their suffering where once they would have turned to a minister or to the Bible for consolation. Freudian terms are now part of our thought. There are innumerable people who will never admit that they believe a word of his writings, who nevertheless, "unconsciously," as they would say, have learned to look for "motivations," to detect "compensations," to withhold a purely moralistic judgment in favor of individual understanding, to prize sexual satisfaction as a key to individual happiness, and to characterize people by the depth and urgency of their passions rather than by the nobility of their professions.

For much of this "Freudian" revolution, Freud himself is not responsible. And in evaluating the general effect of Freud's doctrines on the modern scene, especially in America, it is important to distinguish between the hard, biological, fundamentally classical thought of Freud, who was a determinist, a pessimist, and a genius, from the thousands of little cultural symptoms and "psychological" theories, the pretensions and self-indulgences, which are often found these days in the prosperous middle-class culture that has responded most enthusiastically to Freud.

There is, for example, the increasing tendency to think that all problems are "psychological," to ignore the real conflicts in society that underlie politics and to interpret politicians and candidates—especially those you don't like—in terms of "sexual" motives. There is the cunning use of "Freudian" terms in advertising, which has gone so far that nowadays there's a pretty clear suggestion that the girl comes with the car. There are all the psychologists who study "motivations," and sometimes invent them, so as to get you to buy two boxes of cereal where one would have done before.

There are the horrendous movies and slick plays which not only evade the writer's need to explain characters honestly, but, by attributing to everybody what one can only call the Freud-ian nightmare, have imposed upon a credulous public the belief that it may not be art but that it is "true"—that is, sex—and so must be taken seriously. And, since this is endless but had better stop somewhere, there are all the people who have confused their "urges" with art, have learned in all moral crises to blame their upbringing rather than themselves, and tend to worship the psychoanalyst as God.

The worst of the "Freudian revolution" is the increasing tendency to attribute all criticism of our society to personal "sickness." The rebel is looked on as neurotic rather than someone making a valid protest. Orthodox Freudians tend to support the status quo as a matter of course and to blame the individual for departing from it. Freud himself never made such a mistake, and no one would have been able to convince him that the Viennese world around him was "normal."

The identification of a military group, or a class, or a culture, with an absolute to which we must all be adjusted at any price is a dangerous trend. And the worst of it is that to many people psychoanalysts now signify "authority," so that people believe them on any and all subjects.

On the other hand, the greatest and most beautiful effect of Freudianism is the increasing awareness of childhood as the most important single influence on personal development. This profound cherishing of childhood has opened up wholly new relationships between husbands and wives, as well as between parents and children, and it represents—though often absurdly overanxious—a peculiar new tenderness in modern life. Similarly, though Freud's psychology is weakest on women, there can be no doubt that, again in America, the increasing acknowledgment of the importance of sexual satisfaction has given to women an increasing sense of their individual dignity and their specific needs.

But the greatest revolution of all, and one that really explains the overwhelming success of Freudianism in America, lies in the general insistence on individual fulfillment, satisfaction and happiness. Odd as it may seem to us, who take our striving toward these things for granted, the insistence on personal happiness represents the most revolutionary force in modern times. And it is precisely because our own tradition works toward individual self-realization, because private happiness does seem to us to be both an important ideal and a practical goal, that Freudianism has found so many recruits in this country.

Freud himself made his initial effect in the most traditional, the most rational, the most human kind of way; he wrote books; he presented evidence; he made claims and gave proofs. People read and believed. Many more did not read, and most of those who read Freud's first great work, *The Interpretation of Dreams,* did not believe any of it. But, after all, very few books ever have a decisive effect on the world. In Freud's case, what counts is that some of the people who read were so stirred that they went on to change other minds.

The only kind of change in life which means anything—because it transforms everything in its path—is that which changes people's thinking, their deepest convictions, that which makes them see the world in a different way. This does not happen often, and it is the effect of Freud's books and clinical papers, radiating from a small circle of fellow-doctors in Vienna, that made Freud's influence so impressive. Only the power of truth can explain it. For everything was against him.

He was a Jew in the obsessively anti-Semitic culture of Imperial Austria. He was working with names for things—id, libido, superego, Oedipus, complex, infantile sexuality—that required a special effort, a "suspension of disbelief," as Coleridge would have said, to believe in. Freud insisted that he had not looked for this kind of material.

He had been an extraordinarily able neurologist, was the greatest authority in Europe on children's paralyses, had independently discovered the anesthetic properties of cocaine, but in his usual fashion had impatiently gone on to other experiments before he could get independent credit for his discovery. Far from being flighty in scientific matters, he had been thoroughly trained by the prevailing school of physiology to think of the body as a machine, and in his own thinking he was a rigorous, old-fashioned rationalist whose only religion was science itself.

Freud even claimed that the evidence for his theories had been forced on him. But this was not quite true, either. Even when we remember Freud's rigid scientific training and his own utter honesty, it has to be made clear—not as a criticism of his method but as a characterization of his genius—that Freud was a "plunger," a highly speculative mind. It was the extraordinary combination of patience and daring, of method and radically new insight, that made him great.

Though his old teacher and colleague, Joseph Breuer, came upon the famous example of hysteria in a woman which was the first clinical source for the book they wrote together—

Studies on Hysteria, which is technically the first document in psychoanalysis—Breuer soon took alarm from the dangerously "sexual" interest of the material and withdrew. Freud went on; working alone, he pieced together, in his own thinking, the whole set of sexual motivations that no one else had faced so bluntly or had systematized so closely into a whole new field of active cause-and-effect in the inner life of human beings.

It was this kind of comprehensive insight, backed up on the one hand by the utmost boldness in thinking out his material to its logical conclusion, and on the other by an extraordinary literary gift for persuading readers of the reality of what he was writing about, that led to Freud's effect on so many intellectuals, starting in the exciting years just before the first World War.

Freud's work appealed to the increasing regard for individual experience that is one of the great themes of modern literature and art. The sensitiveness to each individual as a significant register of the consciousness in general, the artistic interest in carrying human consciousness to its farthest limits—it was this essential side of modern art that Freud's researches encouraged and deepened. He brought, as it were, the authority of science to the inner prompting of art, and thus helped writers and artists to feel that their interest in myths, in symbols, in dreams was on the side of "reality," of science, itself, when it shows the fabulousness of the natural world.

Even if we regret, as we must, the fact that Freud's influence has been identified with a great many shallow and commercially slick ideas, the fact remains that if Freud's ideas appealed generally to the inwardness which is so important to modern writers and artists, it was because Freud thoroughly won his case against many aggressive but less intelligent opponents.

The people whose lives were changed by such masterpieces as *The Interpretation of Dreams, The Psychopathology of Everyday Life, Three Contributions to the Theory of Sex, Totem and Taboo,* were honestly convinced that Freud spoke the truth. They saw in Freud that passionate conviction of the reality of his theories that is the very stamp of genius, and as they read, they were prepared to give up other convictions—a sacrifice that caused some of them the deepest anguish, but which their conviction of Freud's utter truthfulness and objectivity made necessary.

Now, if we look back for a moment, the impact of these theories seems all the more remarkable in view of the natural human tendency to suspect, to limit and to derogate sexual experience. What Freud proclaimed above all else was that "nature," which is nearest to us in the erotic side of man, and which culture and society are always pushing away as unworthy of man's "higher" nature, has constantly to be brought back into man's awareness. Freud saw in man's sexual instinct a force of profound natural urgency, a whole system of energies, which could be repressed and forgotten and pushed back into the unconsciousness only at the cost of unnecessary strain and even of self-destructiveness.

Yet far from preaching "sexuality" itself at any cost, Freud admitted that "civilization" requires the repression or at least the adaptation of sexuality. Civilization as we know it, Freud said, had been built up on man's heroic sacrifice of instinct. Only, Freud issued the warning that more and more men would resent this sacrifice, would wonder if civilization was worth the price. And how profoundly right he was in this can be seen not only in the Nazi madness that drove him as an old man out of Vienna, that almost cost him his life, but in the increasing disdain for culture, in the secret lawlessness that has become, under the conformist surface, a sign of increasing personal irritation and rebelliousness in our society. More and more, the sexual freedom of our time seems to be a way of mentally getting even, of confused protest, and not the pagan enjoyment of instinct that writers like D. H. Lawrence upheld against Freud's gloomy forebodings.

For Freud the continuous sacrifice of "nature" that is demanded by "civilization" meant that it was only through rationality and conscious awareness that maturity could be achieved. Far from counseling license, his most famous formula became—"Where id was, ego shall be"—the id representing the unconscious, the ego our dominant and purposive sense of ourselves. However, consciousness meant for Freud an unyielding insistence on the importance of sexuality. And it was just on this issue that, even before the first World War, his movement broke apart.

Jung went astray, as Freud thought, because he was lulled by the "mystical" side of religion; Adler, through his insistence that not sex but power feelings were primary. Later, Harry Stack Sullivan and Erich Fromm tended to emphasize, as against sex, the importance of personal relatedness to others, and nowadays many psychoanalysts tend to value religion much more highly than Freud ever could. But the root of the dissidence was always Freud's forthright insistence on the importance of sexuality and his old-fashioned, mid-nineteenth-century positivism. For Freud always emphasized the organic and the physical rather than the social and the "cultural."

In fact, it is now possible to say that it is precisely Freud's old-fashioned scientific rationalism, his need to think of man as a physical being rather than a "psychological" one, that explains the primacy of Freud's discoveries. Psychoanalysis, especially in America, has become more interested in making cures than in making discoveries, and it is significant that there has been very little original thought in the field since Freud.

Freudianism has become a big business, and a very smooth one. The modern Freudian analyst, who is over-busy and who rather complacently uses his theory to explain everything, stands in rather sad contrast to that extraordinary thinker, Sigmund Freud.

Perhaps it is because Freud was born a century ago that he had the old-fashioned belief that nothing—not even a lot of patients—is so important as carrying your ideas beyond the point at which everybody already agrees with you. Nowadays everybody is something of a Freudian, and to many Freudians, the truth is in their keeping, the system is complete. But what mattered most to Freud was relentlessly carrying on the revolution of human thought.

TWO

A NEW COPERNICUS?

NIGEL WALKER

The century that follows a man's birth is usually long enough to let him find his proper place in history. In Freud's case it is a little too short. The science of the mind is still a battle-field for rival empires of faiths, ideologies and academic theories; and a battle-field is no place for a monument until the fighting is over. What is more, one of the exceptional things about him was that most of his original thinking was done after his fortieth year, at a time of life when most men, whether they know it or not, are being carried forward by the intellectual momentum which they acquired in their twenties or thirties. Freud continued to produce new ideas until his seventies— some would say until his eighties. As a result, we are still too close to him to plan the scale of his monument.

Another difficult question to answer is "What should be inscribed on the monument?" With what victories should he be credited? Freud was not always modest in speaking about his contribution. He once referred to himself as the Copernicus of the mind, and on another occasion compared himself to Darwin.[1] But his achievement is not so easily defined as that of the great astronomer or biologist. His own followers, when they try to articulate on the subject, tend to be incoherent through enthusiasm or mysticism, while his enemies owe him more than they dare admit.

For example, he did not discover, or "invent," the unconscious. Herbart and Eduard von Hartmann did that. What he did discover—and here "discover" and "invent" mean the same thing—was a technique for alleviating certain kinds of disorder by making the patient talk. Mesmer, Charcot and Bernheim had shown how certain disorders could be alleviated if the physician talked to the patient; theirs was the technique of hypnotism and suggestion. Freud, who had studied under Charcot and Bernheim but was not a particularly successful hypnotist, achieved more permanent results than they did by making the patient talk to the physician: this was the psychoanalytic technique.

In some cases this technique worked only if the patient could be brought to talk about incidents which he could not normally remember, or about desires and feelings which he could not admit, even to himself. Freud found it easier to picture the state of affairs in his patients' minds if he visualized them as consisting not only of a conscious, introspectible mind but also of an unintrospectible, unconscious one. In doing this he made use of Herbartian psychology which he had learned at his Vienna school. The importance of this step was threefold. It was the first real use of the academic science of psychology in a therapeutic technique; hitherto psychologists had made their "discoveries" in their armchairs or their laboratories, and had neither helped nor been helped by the hospitals and clinics. Secondly, the technique itself was important because its very nature made it necessary to think of the mind in a new way. Hitherto it had been possible to conceive it as consisting simply of conscious processes—to see it in a two-dimensional way, as it were. Freud's technique forced him—and eventually most of Christendom—to think of it in a three-dimensional way. It was like the discovery of perspective by the early Italian painters.

But its real importance lay in the fact that it provided Freud with a method of making use of the close connection which he had observed between the experiences of the infant and the disorders of the adult. He was not of course the first person to discover that the child is father to the man. What he did discover was how to lessen the effects of childhood upon the mental health of the adult. His method was to treat the long-past experiences and emotions as if they were still present in the adult; and the concept of the unconscious was the only thing that made this possible. It enabled both analyst and patient to think of these experiences as being preserved underneath the latter's conscious thoughts. By inducing his patients to think in this way he made it easier for them to revive these experiences. I do not mean that he regarded the unconscious as simply a useful fiction; he believed in its reality. But whether he was right or wrong in this, its therapeutic value is beyond doubt.

Nor was Freud the first to make the distinction between what he called the "ego" and the "id"—between that collection of organized, more or less conscious and more or less consistent bunch of principles and prejudices that we loosely call the "self" and the unorganized, inconsistent, sometimes unrecognized and often anti-social needs and emotions with which our bodies are endowed. A good deal of the credit for this distinction, as Freud acknowledged, must go to the unpopular Nietzsche, and some of it to a little-known doctor called Grod-deck.[2] What Freud did, and what no psychologist, philosopher or psychiatrist had hitherto done, was to weld together all these notions—the unconscious, the ego, the id and one or two additions of his own, such as the superego—and make of them a diagram of the mind that was of practical value for therapeutic purposes. The history of psychology is full of psychological systems; every well-known name belongs to someone who drew a new diagram of our mental processes. Some of these were extremely useful for explaining and systematizing the phenomena studied in the laboratory; some of them even made our everyday behavior seem plausible. But when it came to sorting out the tangle of the disordered mind they proved useless, and the psychiatrist had to rely on trial and error with drugs and shocks and knives. Freud's diagram looked rather different from those of the laboratories; to some people it appeared gross and overcomplicated. But the technicians who used it in tinkering with the mechanism seemed to get results.

Freud's own explanation of the success of his technique was not necessarily the right one. Even his own latter-day followers think that he attributed too much virtue to the catharsis of the past, and not enough to the patient's relationship to the analyst —in technical terms, the "transference". But most psychiatric techniques—even such drastic ones as prefrontal leucotomy— have been introduced with even less idea of why they worked; and this has not prevented them from working, although it has made the task of improving them a slow and empirical one.

Like many great clinicians, Freud was an observant natural historian of man as an animal. As a clinician, he found that a large number of his patients suffered from some disturbance of normal sexual function. As a natural historian (and a father) he observed what had previously been revealed only to anthropologists and nursemaids—namely, sexual behavior among the young of the human species, who had hitherto been regarded as sexless by all right-thinking people. As a psychologist he therefore saw in the sexual instinct the physiological power-source for many adult drives. He was not the first psychologist to emphasize the importance of man's sexual behavior to an understanding of his whole complex personality. The Frenchman Charcot, although careful in his public utterances, had privately stressed this to the young doctors who understudied him in the Salpetrière, among them Freud. Meanwhile a contemporary of Freud, an Australian doctor called Havelock Ellis, was beginning the first volumes of his enormous *Studies in the Psychology of Sex*. Freud himself, although he began by attributing most neurotic disorders to disturbance of the sexual function, soon saw that this was much too simple to fit the facts, which pointed also to the importance of the other natural functions of the infant—feeding and excreting. As time went on his explanations were more and more frequently couched in terms not of sex but of a psychic force called the *libido,* which, coupled with the instinct of aggression, underlay the apparently diverse forms of human conduct.

Now that we have survived the initial shock to our prudery

and pomposity, we can see his notions not as a far-fetched piece of foreign dirty-mindedness, but as an attempt to reduce to the smallest possible number the principles underlying the multifarious pursuits of man. Although William of Occam was the first to put it into words, this has always been the aim of science—to explain with the minimum number of entities. This is what the physicists since Democritus have been trying to do for matter—to reduce it to the minimum number of homogeneous particles.

Many Freudian concepts—such as repression or the wish-fulfilment function of dreams—are such common intellectual coinage nowadays that they need no explanation or comment. What is not so commonly recognized is that underlying them is a startling anticipation of one of the most recently developed sciences—cybernetics. War-time advances in methods of designing automatic gun-aimers, electronic computers and other self-correcting devices have shown how the principle of homoeostasis can be used to explain many of the more complex ways in which the human nervous system operates. A homoeostatic device is one which automatically corrects or compensates for any deviation from a predetermined set of values—whether this is a temperature as in the case of a thermostat, or a height and compass bearing, as with an automatic pilot. Fifty years ago Freud saw that this principle could be used to explain the way in which human beings reacted to stimuli. At first sight they seemed to seek certain stimuli (such as food) and avoid others (for instance dangerous animals). Freud saw that it was possible to regard all reactions of this kind not as being of two kinds—positive and negative—but as consisting entirely of one kind—negative, that is avoidance, reactions. Even when we appear to be seeking the stimulus as we do with food when we are hungry, it is possible to regard this as the avoidance of the pricks of hunger. This point of view made it possible for him to interpret all the reactions of the human central nervous system as designed to protect it from stimuli. The infant cries to protect itself from hunger. In the same way, he thought, the central nervous system tries to protect itself from certain of its own processes which threaten it with distress, and this kind of avoidance reaction is called "repression." In the same way, too, when the nervous system is asleep it tries to protect itself from stimuli that threaten to awake it, and thus creates dreams which disguise the stimulus or delude the dreamer into thinking he has dealt with the stimulus. The hungry man dreams he is eating, and does not awake. This is what Freud called the wish-fulfilment function of the dream.

This explanation of phenomena such as dreams and repression led Freud to define the central nervous system as a mechanism of which the function is to reduce stimulation to its lowest possible level. This is of course a completely materialistic definition, and perhaps even more depressing and derogatory of human dignity than most materialism. But if you can overlook this for the moment, it is possible to see in it that profound kind of simplicity that characterized such great scientific thinking as, for example, Newton's Laws of Motion. Like Newton's Laws, Freud's definition is a little too simple to fit all the phenomena; but that is another story. The point is that this hardly recognized theoretical formulation of Freud's would have been a natural accompaniment to the development of cybernetics in the nineteen-forties: but Freud formulated it in 1915. This is, of course, of no more than historical interest, for the idea was not taken up and investigated, and it was left to the mechanically-minded neurologists and cyberneticists to rediscover it on their own.

It will be obvious that I am not concerned, except indirectly, with the practical therapeutic aspects of the technique which Freud evolved. Nor shall I try to deal with his excursions (and those of his enthusiastic followers) into the fields of anthropology and literature. Like many a recreational outing, these were not complete successes, but I do not think anyone will maintain that they were altogether unilluminating.

What I am trying to decide is whether the comparison of Freud to Copernicus and Darwin is justified.

Almost all scientific advances are of three kinds. They may be technical; a method may be discovered of doing some hitherto impossible thing, or of doing an old thing in a new and better way. They may be what are nicknamed "natural history" discoveries—that is, observations of a new phenomenon, or more accurate descriptions of one that is already known. Thirdly, they may be theoretical—a neater equation to describe magnetic phenomena, or an extension of Boyle's Law so as to include the behavior of gases at particularly low temperatures. This sort of advance going on all the time, and every few years, in some field or other, a sufficiently important one occurs to become headline news.

There is, however, a fourth kind of advance which is not nearly so familiar. Indeed in any single science it probably occurs only once in two or three hundred years. It consists of a thorough revolution in the way in which that particular science looks at its subject. Take the case of chemistry. By the end of the eighteenth century there had been a good deal of accurate observation, with precise measurements, of the ways in which various elements combined with each other or behaved under changes of temperature. These were in themselves scientific advances of the kind I have labelled "technical" or "natural history." There were also quite a number of explanatory theories of very limited utility, including the notorious phlogiston theory of combustion. In 1803, however, Dalton showed how the laws which explained these phenomena could be simplified by the assumption of the atomic structure of matter. This assumption did not make the observations of his predecessors any truer than they had always been; but without it very few of the subsequent observations and technical advances of the nineteenth and twentieth centuries would have taken place. Its original simplicity has now become complicated again by the assumption of a variety of sub-atomic entities; but it was the revolutionary step in chemical thinking which turned chemistry into a science.

Consider, too, one of the men with whom Freud compared himself—Copernicus. As every schoolboy knows, the Ptolemaic conception of a geocentric universe was the official theory of occidental astronomy until the enormous simplification made possible by Copernicus' heliocentric assumption was appreciated. Like Dalton, Copernicus was not the first to make his

revolutionary suggestion; he was anticipated by the Pythago-
reans just as Dalton was by the Epicureans. Copernicus' theory,
like Dalton's, did not go all the way; he did not, for example,
realize that the earth's orbit was an ellipse and not a perfect
circle. Some of his reasons for arriving at his theory were extremely unsound. Yet without it modern astronomy would not
have been a possibility.

As there is no handy name for conceptual advances of this
kind, I do not see why we should not call them "Copernican."
Other Copernican thinkers—for they are molders of thought
rather than discoverers of fact—were Newton, Einstein and
that other figure with whom Freud compared himself, Darwin. I do not want to suggest that such a revolution is entirely
the work of one man, or that a Copernican notion springs
fully grown from his head without warning. Most of those I
have mentioned owed a great deal to the work of their predecessors and even of their contemporaries, although Copernicus
himself is probably an exception. If any of the Copernicans
had been prevented by some accident from putting forward
his idea, someone else would have been bound to do so, sooner
or later. But none of these reservations lessens the achievement
of these men or their entitlement to a special place in the history of their science.

Was Freud a Copernican? I find this a difficult question to
answer. His influence on twentieth-century thinking about the
mind has certainly been immense. What is more, it has been
achieved almost entirely through his own writings, and owes
little to his followers. As I said at the beginning, we are too
close to his influence to assess it impartially. But I should like
to offer a guess at what people will say about him a hundred
years from now. By that time he will no longer be regarded
as the "discoverer" of the unconscious of the ego and the id.
His attempt to derive all instinctive behaviours from two basic
drives will be of purely historical interest. So will his homoeostatic account of the central nervous system, since it was
forgotten and the principle rediscovered in a more precise form
by the neurologists of the nineteen-forties.

He will be remembered for his achievement in selecting

from among the techniques for treating disorders of the mind, and from among the psychological systems of the academic psychologists, the only pair that would form a working team. This synthesis was of course partly due to a lucky combination of circumstances. A free-thinking Jew learns Herbartian psychology in the sixth form at a Vienna school. After becoming a neurologist and discovering the limitations of physical methods of treatment he studies the hypnotic techniques of the Paris school. Not being a particularly good hypnotist, he tries to achieve similar results by other means. Result—psychoanalysis.

It was this synthesis that transformed the treatment of mental disorders from a semi-religious, semi-empirical study into a systematic technique with rules and reasons. What Freud thought of, therefore, as a scientific revolution in our conception of the mind was rather a technical advance which, by its spectacular nature, popularized the three-dimensional conception already suggested by nineteenth-century German thinkers. In much the same way the circumnavigation of the globe did more to convince people of the earth's roundness than all the geographers' arguments. In comparing Freud to Magellan rather than Copernicus I am not devaluing his achievement. Technicians such as Watt and Marconi probably had a greater effect upon the next generations' way of life than Newton or Dalton. It is true that the number of patients treated by psychoanalysis or derivative methods is a negligible fraction of twentieth-century mankind, so that its direct effect has been less tangible than that of the steam-engine or the wireless set. But its indirect effects upon our approach to problems connected with the mind, whether therapeutic, legal or educational, has exceeded even the hopes of its discoverer.

THREE

THE CHANGING CONCEPT OF MAN
IN PRESENT-DAY PSYCHIATRY

GREGORY ZILBOORG

We may not overlook the fact that psychiatry was born out of medicine and matured by medicine. By the same token we may not overlook the fact that the psychiatrist, dealing more directly with the inner life of man than the doctor representing any other medical specialty, has always had to draw upon certain special prejudices concerning the human mind, or upon various philosophies prevailing at a given time, in order to create for himself a medicopsychological frame of reference usually not found in autopsy material or purely physiological observations or speculations.

The earliest attempts to form such a frame of reference go back to the thirteenth century and even earlier, when more and more frequent references were being made to human experience. These references to human experience came not from the medical men of the time, but from the theologians and philosophers who began to show an increasing interest in human psychology. It is clear therefore that psychology, even empirical psychology, was a product if not an integral part of philosophy. For many centuries it continued to be a fact that if and when a medical man espoused the cause of psychology, he would become a philosopher rather than a psychiatrist. John Locke is a case in point; as late as the seventeenth century psychology was much closer to philosophy than to medicine.

This tradition of thought is rather striking. Thus Pinel, an excellent empirical clinician and practical psychiatrist, himself the son of the rationalist eighteenth century, felt the above-mentioned tradition so deeply that he entitled his major work *Nosologie philosophique*. The same intellectual tradition remained in force till the end of the nineteenth and the beginning of the present century. William James went through what seemed to be natural evolutionary stages of medicine: physiology, psychology, and philosophy. And Freud, in connection with his gropings for an understanding of the working of the human mind, stated that he did not feel that medicine (i.e., purely biological medicine) interested him very much, that philosophy was a field to which he gravitated more, and he was therefore particularly glad that he developed an interest in psychology which he apparently considered to be intimately connected with philosophy.

In other words, less than sixty years ago the man who was destined to revolutionize our views on human psychology felt that medical psychology was perhaps closer to philosophy than to natural sciences. This, we must note again, came from Freud who did more than anyone else in the history of psychopathology to make psychology a biological discipline, an empirical, scientific system of investigation and understanding of man.

If we cast now a cursory glance at the psychiatrists of the end of the nineteenth century we shall easily notice that people like Meynert, Krafft-Ebing, or Moebius had to draw on the philosophers of their day, had to use them as props as it were to support their theoretical formulations of what they thought man really was. In some respects and in some quarters things are not very different today. Karl Jaspers is an excellent example of how the philosophy of existentialism affects the psychological concept of man—just as Brentano, when Freud was a college student, was an example of how *Gestaltpsychologie* began to show its earliest buds in the circles in which people were turning their attention to psychology.

Freud's was the first psychopathology that seems to have been created independently from a prevailing philosophy. Yet it only seems so. It is true, of course, that despite the apparent similarity of some of Freud's ideas to those of Herbart, Schopenhauer, and Nietzsche, Freud did not read those philosophers till sometime after his basic ideas had been formulated. However, there is incontestable evidence in all the writings of Freud that, while disclaiming any allegiance to any established philosophic system, Freud was a Darwinist; he was also deeply under the influence of physics as Helmholtz presented it. Therefore, particularly in his earlier writings, Freud seems to show the influence of physicochemical and biophysiological theories which were of his day.

There is nothing unusual about this, of course—except the paradoxical position into which psychoanalysis was put by its own creator: Freud, to whom we owe the knowledge of what Bleuler called depth psychology. This same Freud showed more than a mere tendency to place the understanding of the deepest subjective experiences of the individual into some sort of more or less mechanistic, "objective," disindividualized, scientific Darwinian mold. It is true, Freud never pressed the point so far, and ultimately he seems to have spontaneously liberated himself from the more rigid and more intolerant aspects of what is known as scientism.

To state what I have in mind briefly and without any further elaboration, I would say this: the search for human experience as the source of the understanding of man, a search which started vaguely and obscurely around the eleventh century and was clearly defined by the thirteenth century, reached its peak in the psychoanalytic study of man which I believe is the true successor of the sixteenth-century humanism minus the latter's cultivation of Greco-Roman erudition. This said, the major question or problem which was suggested in the title of this paper may now be approached.

The question is: what concept of man does the psychiatry of today have, if any, and how does the existence of this concept manifest itself in present-day psychiatry?

We need not go into the theological and purely philosophical concepts of man which dominated our thought before the establishment of the so-called scientific age, that is, the middle of the seventeenth century. Suffice it to say that man has been recognized as a person and a personality since the establishment of the Judeo-Christian tradition. But man as a living value in himself, man as a living unit who in addition to his obligations to God and society has rights which he may assert, man as a functioning unit of mankind—all this was not recognized until the eighteenth century which, through the assimilation of the humanism of the sixteenth century, established the concept of the human personality and man's value as a social particle, as a living individuality, as a moral unit, and as a carrier of life.

Scientific medicine was not much preoccupied with these changing tides of human thought, not because it had no interest in them but because its own tradition sufficed. It was the tradition of saving lives, relieving people from suffering, preserving the normal functioning of the body, preventing illness. All this was sufficient unto medicine, because medicine contained and carried within itself the eternal values of mutual assistance, preservation of life, alleviation of suffering, and rendering man a useful member of the community.

Psychiatry, as is well known, did not fare as well until it liberated itself from many theological preoccupations, until it learned to differentiate soul from psychic apparatus, and to understand that reasoning is not the only weakness of man, that will can be enslaved by a multitude of unconscious drives and emotions. This enlightenment came to us only recently, within our own lifetime. And because it came within our lifetime, it was accompanied by many and hectic battles between the old and the new. The scientific mind was anxious because it saw in depth psychology a possible return to the pre-psychiatric psychiatry of human abstractions. The theologian and the religious moralist were anxious because the new depth psychology seemed to threaten the very foundation of transcendental morality and faith. That a truth, particularly a psychological truth, is a truth and therefore cannot threaten but can only support scientific knowledge, that it cannot threaten faith and morality because neither is based on untruth about man—all this seems to have been forgotten during the battle.

The trouble is that a war of ideas, like a war of armies, is really not a contest of reason or reasons. Rather it is, as it probably always shall be, a true war—a combat which is considered really finished only if one of the combatants is destroyed or brought to his knees to ask for mercy. A war of arms cannot end in a draw and bring real peace; a war of ideas seemingly ending in a draw leaves a sense of ideational vacuum with the passions for mutual destruction temporarily in a faint of fatigue but potentially ready to resume the senseless battle of mutual annihilation any moment an opportunity arises.

We might say that one of the most regrettable human feelings is our inability to keep free from anxiety whenever we are confronted with a new idea, and that the most common defense against such anxiety is hostility, intolerance, incapacity to see the other person's point of view. The anxiety about anything new leads us inevitably to a sort of retreat or regression to older and therefore "safer" habits of thought, and the result is an inevitable loss of energy and creative vision. This I believe is what happened to psychiatry during the last quarter of a century or so. We reopened and reclosed a cycle of mental attitudes which bid fair to affect deeply not only our thinking but our clinical practice.

Some twenty-five years ago, after Freud had revised his hypothesis as to the origin of anxiety, the human personality seems to have been conceived of (whether a clear-cut formulation of it was made or not) as a complex system of ego defenses against anxiety, and against other noxious psychological agents which are forever interfering with the amorphous peace of the mind. The totality and the indivisibility of the human personality seemed then to have found its psychological, or in the broadest sense of the word its psychobiological, meaning. It did not matter whether one was an "orthodox," "liberal," "eclectic," "free," or "chained" Freudian. Whoever the given clinician was, his was the position that the human personality as

a unit and totality was the central point for clinical consideration.

The question, of course, might be raised whether one is justified in ascribing to Freud's influence alone the almost predominant role in the establishment of this twentieth-century
humanism in clinical psychiatry. I think we are, for no one
more than Freud in the scientific clinical world concentrated
our attention on the inner life of man. I have in mind humanism in its traditional historicopsychological sense, not phil-
anthropic humanitarianism—which is a different story and a
different department of human endeavor.

It is with the spirit of the new humanism that we entered the
last quarter of a century. The optimist had a great deal to be
pleased with; the pessimist had to wait a while before he could
legitimately raise his voice and point to the rumblings of totali-
tarian psychology, the mass movements, the almost complete
devaluation of human life in the cataclysm of militant fascism
and the ensuant world war.

As one reviews the major interests in psychology which developed as a result of these world-shaking events, one cannot
help but be impressed with the rather rapid progress of the
purely technological approaches to the problem of the functioning of the human personality.

From narcoanalysis (which was not really analysis but rather
a form of induced psychological catharsis) to electroshock and
cybernetics, the emphasis is laid on the grossly empirical and
mechanical and mechanistic. It is really not an exaggeration to
say that the process of scientific investigation in clinical psychiatry in the past twenty-five years has become more and more
a process of disindividualization. We have begun again to turn
to common denominators among individuals and to inventories
and questionnaires. It would be unfair to assume that the
above-mentioned procedures are superfluous or without any
value in clinical psychopathology; however, it is rather important not to overlook the meaning of the emphasis laid on this
or that procedure. In our days we witness the emphasis on inventories, tests, and questionnaires to the detriment if not at the
expense of the more direct study of the inner life of the person.

And by inner life I do not mean the scientifically undefinable spiritual life of man, but the workings of the psychological apparatus within the living person in the latter's totality.

I am aware that what I am now saying might be considered unjust by some, or plainly untrue by others. For, they might say, is not that which is known as dynamic psychiatry and the almost universal acceptance of the role of the unconscious and of emotions in our psychology—is not this all a true sign of progress? The answer is: it is a sign of progress, but it is not of progress that I speak here; I am speaking of humanism in clinical psychiatry. And it is a recession of our recently acquired humanism that I believe I see. Recession in which sense? Recession in the sense of our overestimation of averages at the expense of the individual; in our tendency to look upon the source of human troubles as lack of adaptation, and at the same time unwittingly but surely and as often as not to confuse adaptation with a sort of psychobiological and sociological conformism. It is a recession of humanism, if under the flag of strict scientific thinking we speak of reality as something which is nothing more than the total perceptual world of man and either overlook psychological reality or confuse it with fantasy, a sort of nonpsychotic delusion.

In the light of these our failings or propensities, we must admit that humanism in its true sense is served poorly or not at all when the individual becomes but a psychobiological adaptive molecule of society, when the individual seems to be looked upon as having been born to serve society, instead of society's having been developed to serve man.

Thus on the purely moral philosophical plane we witness and can recognize the rather sickening phenomenon of the disindividualization of man in favor of his serving the social, or mass machine. No wonder man as a person has been ground up in this machine and has so often come out as so much clay or cement for the use of the master builders of totalitarianism. But what appears to be just as sad, although not so conspicuous, is that on the plane of psychology and psychopathology we are falling victims of the same process of disindividualization, all this to such an extent that even our language has become

neologistic and rather mechanistic. We don't live with one another anymore, conveying to one another directly and indirectly our feelings and intuition; we "communicate" instead.
We don't talk to one another; we "communicate." We no
longer establish relationships to and with people; we "relate"
instead—well or badly as the case may be. We don't adjust ourselves to this or that situation; we merely "adjust" well or
poorly as the case may be—but intransitively, as it were. We
no longer put ourselves in the place of another person, we
don't identify ourselves by way of conscious or unconscious
psychological processes with this or that person; we omit the
word ourselves and we plainly "identify"—quite intransitively.

All this, I believe, is the penalty we pay for the mechanistic
and organismic point of view which took possession of us under the influence of world wars and global mass movements.
Whether this sacrifice of the individual is a temporary one or
not remains to be seen, but there is no doubt that the socialization and intellectualization of our attitudes toward man
have led to a disindividualized concept of the human personality, even though we might appear in our own eyes more
scientific and more accurate if and when we speak in terms of
physiology and sociology—as if semantic changes in our vocabulary really enhance our understanding of the meaning and
the value of man.

PART II: *Men and Times*

FOUR

A PREFACE *(1917)*[1]
SIGMUND FREUD

Psychoanalysis was born of medical necessity. It originated in the need of helping the victims of nervous disease to whom rest, hydropathy or electrical treatment could bring no relief. A striking case recorded by Joseph Breuer had aroused the hope that the amount of help that could be given to such patients might vary directly with the extent to which it might be possible to understand the genesis, hitherto unfathomed, of their symptoms. Psychoanalysis, therefore, though originally a matter of purely medical technique, was directed, from the first, towards new research, towards the discovery of mechanisms whose nature was concealed but whose effects were far-reaching.

Its further progress led away from the study of the physical conditions of nervous illnesses in a degree surprising to the physician, and gradually the whole mental content of human life came within its sphere, including the health—the normal as well as the super-normal. It had to concern itself with affects and passions, and above all, with those constant subjects of the poet's art and enthusiasm, the emotions of love: it learnt to recognize the potency of memories, the unsuspected significance of the early years of childhood in shaping the conduct of later life, and finally the strength of those wishes which lead men's judgements astray and prescribe the paths of human endeavor.

For a time it appeared to be the fate of psychoanalysis to be incorporated into the field of psychology without being able to indicate in what way the mind of the sick patient differed from that of the normal person. But in the course of its development it came upon the problem of the dream, which is an abnormal mental product created by normal people under regularly recurring physiological conditions. And in solving the enigma of dreams it found in unconscious mentality the common ground in which the highest as well as the lowest mental impulses are rooted, and from which arise the most normal mental activities as well as the strange products of a diseased mind. The picture of the mental mechanisms of the individual now became clearer and more complete: it was seen that obscure impulses arising in his organic life were striving to fulfil their own aims, and that controlling them was a series of more highly organized mental formations, acquired and handed on by man under the pressure of his cultural development, which had taken possession of parts of these impulses, developed them or employed them in the service of higher aims— had bound them fast, at all events, and utilized their energy for its own purposes. This higher organization, which we know as the ego, had rejected another portion of the same elementary impulses as useless, because these impulses could not accommodate themselves to the organic unity of the individual, or because they conflicted with its cultural aims. The ego was not powerful enough to exterminate those mental forces it could not control. Instead, it turned away from them, leaving them on the most primitive psychological level, and protected itself against their demands by means of energetic defensive or reactive mechanisms, or sought to compromise with them by means of substitute-gratifications. Unsubdued and indestructible, yet inhibited in every direction, these repressed impulses, together with their primitive mental content, form the underworld, the kernel of the true unconscious, ever on the alert to urge their claims and to find any means for gratification. Hence the insecurity of our proud psychical superstructure, the nightly emergence of proscribed and repressed things in dreams, and our proneness to fall ill with neuroses and psychoses as soon as the distribution of power between the ego and the repressed is altered to the disadvantage of the former.

It requires but little consideration to realize that such a view of the life of the human mind cannot possibly be limited to the sphere of dreams and nervous diseases. If it be a justifiable view, it must apply also to normal mental phenomena, and even the highest achievements of the human mind must have some relation to the factors recognized in pathology—to repression, to the strivings for mastery of the unconscious and to the possibilities of gratification which are open to the primitive impulses. And now it became an irresistibly tempting task, indeed, a scientific duty, to extend the psychoanalytical methods of investigation from their original field to more distant and diverse spheres of mental interest. The psychoanalytical treatment of patients also pointed insistently in this direction, since it became evident that individual forms of the neuroses showed a marked correspondence with the most highly valued products of our civilization. The hysteric is undoubtedly a poet, though he represents his phantasies essentially by mimicry, without considering whether other people understand them or not. The ceremonials and prohibitions of obsessional patients force us to conclude that they have created a private religion for themselves; and even the delusions of the paranoiac show an unwelcome external similarity and inner relationship to the systems of our philosophers. We cannot get away from the impression that patients are making, in an asocial manner, the same attempts at a solution of their conflicts and an appeasement of their urgent desires which, when carried out in a manner acceptable to a large number of persons, are called poetry, religion and philosophy.

In an extremely brilliant and suggestive monograph, O. Rank and H. Sachs have collected the results which have so far been accomplished by the application of psychoanalysis to the fields of mental interest.[2] Mythology and the history of literature and religion appear to furnish the most easily accessible material.

The final formula which shall assign to the myth its particular province has not yet been found. But in a large work on the incest complex, O. Rank reaches the remarkable conclusion that the selection of subject matter, particularly in dramatic poetry, is limited chiefly by the range of the Oedipus complex, as it is called in psychoanalysis.[3] Through the elaboration of this complex into the most manifold variants, distortions and disguises, the poet seeks to elucidate his most personal attitude to this effective theme. It is in the mastery of his Oedipus complex, i.e. his affective attitude toward his family, and in its narrower sense his father and mother, that the individual comes to grief, and therefore it is this complex which regularly forms the kernel of his neurosis. It owes its significance not to any unintelligible concatenation of events. The importance of the parental relationship springs naturally from the biological fact of the long helplessness and slow maturing of the young human being, and the complicated development of his capacity for love; and furthermore guarantees that the lines on which the Oedipus complex is overcome shall run parallel with those on which the archaic and animal inheritance of mankind is most successfully brought under subjection. In this inheritance are contained all the energies necessary for the later cultural development of the individual, but they have first to be sorted out and elaborated. In the form in which the individual brings it with him into the world it is useless for the purposes of social life.

One step more is necessary before we reach the starting point for a psychoanalytical consideration of religious life. What is now the heritage of the individual was once, long ago, a newly acquired possession, handed on from one generation to another. The Oedipus complex itself must therefore have its own process of development, and the study of prehistory can help us to find out something about it. Such a study leads us to assume that the human family as we know it today was organized differently in remote primitive times, and this surmise is supported by data obtained from primitive races of the present day. If we submit the prehistoric and ethnological material relating to this archaic heritage to psychoanalytical elaboration, we come to an unexpectedly definite conclusion—namely, that god the father at one time walked incarnate on the earth and exercised his sovereignty as leader of the hordes of primitive men until his sons combined together and slew him; and further, that the first social ties, the basic moral restrictions, and the oldest form of religion—totemism—originated as a result of, and a reaction against, this liberating misdeed. Later religions are filled with the same content and with the endeavor to obliterate the traces of that crime, or to expiate it by substituting other solutions for the conflict between father and sons; while, on the other hand, they cannot refrain from repeating anew the removal of the father. As a result we can recognize in myths the echo of that occurrence which throws its gigantic shadow over the whole development of mankind.

This hypothesis, founded on the views of Robertson Smith,[4] and developed by me in my "Totem und Taboo" in 1912, has been taken by Th. Reik as the basis for his studies on the problems of the psychology of religion. . . .

FIVE

FREUD: THE MAN I KNEW,
THE SCIENTIST, AND HIS INFLUENCE
ABRAM KARDINER

My license for writing under the present title lies in the circumstance that I happen to be one of the few—namely, about
ten—Americans who had the opportunity of being associated
with Freud directly, between the end of World War I, that is,
about 1919, and 1925, when he acquired the illness which first
rendered him increasingly inaccessible and then ultimately
caused his death. The experience of having known him is unforgettable and I am certain that my memories of him have
suffered little distortion. Neither time's passage nor the
familiarity of our contact have tarnished his splendor.

It might be well, at the outset, to recount in anecdotal
fashion the story of my own association with Freud. In 1909 I
was a sophomore in college. The climate of psychological
opinion in America at that time was dominated by William
James and Titchener, a follower of Wundt, who represented
the so-called scientific dimension of psychology. Few outside of
highly specialized professional circles had heard of the Austrian
doctor who had been invited in that year (1909) to lecture at
Clark University in Worcester, Massachusetts. I was not even
aware that Freud was a visitor to these shores. Occasionally, in-

deed, one might hear mention, in departments of psychology, of the name of Freud, but whenever it came up it was inevitably accompanied by the observation, "Oh, he's crazy!" By contrast to departments of psychology, those of physics and chemistry referred to him respectfully.

Like many other Americans, I did not come to Freud directly. My acquaintance occurred in roundabout fashion through a dubious offshoot of his work, Otto Weininger and his book, *Sex and Character,* then popular in this country. *Sex and Character* was a garbled version of Freud's views on the male-female dichotomy, which Weininger had formed into a very fanciful, but not unattractive, theory of the evolution of the character of man and of the great personalities of the past and the present. Some years later, in Vienna, I told Freud about this. He replied that he knew Weininger, that, in fact, Weininger had brought his manuscript to him and asked him to find him a publisher. I asked Freud what he thought of Weininger. "Oh," he replied, "a sick genius and greatly misguided about what I was teaching."

My first actual clinical contact with Freud and Freudian views did not occur until I was a junior in medical school. Here I had the good fortune to meet a man who has had a permanent influence on my life, namely, Horace Westlake Frink. I can never forget how one Saturday morning Dr. Frink presented to his students a fireman with paralysis of both arms and a few weeks later brought the fireman back with the paralysis gone. Dr. Frink then explained to us the mechanism of the illness and its treatment. He had cured the stricken fireman by unravelling his unconscious motivation. This was the first time that I had directly encountered the name of Freud in connection with a clinical experience of a cured case.

On completion of my internship, I immediately sought out Dr. Frink and asked his advice about the future possibilities of psychiatry as a field of endeavor. He encouraged me to enter upon it because, he said, this could be a central field of the future. It will grow, Dr. Frink declared, adding: "Anybody can make a great discovery in it." I think it was the latter assurance that attracted me more than anything else to the study of psychology. Such opportunities for path-breaking research did not seem to exist in surgery and in medicine. I then asked him how to proceed. He gave me the requisite advice, advising me to get a job at Manhattan State Hospital, to learn something about mental disorders, and to submit to analysis.

After about a year of my analysis, Dr. Frink interrupted the proceedings and told me that he himself was going to Freud. "While I am there," he said, "I will talk to Freud about you and recommend that you continue with him." And so it was. In February of 1920 I wrote to Freud, received a reply, and engaged to see him in Vienna in September of 1921.

I must also mention who my nine colleagues in "Freud's group" were at that time: Dr. Leonard Bloomgart, Dr. Clarence Oberndorf, Dr. Monroe Meyer, Dr. Polon, and myself formed the American contingent. The British contingent was composed of the two Stracheys, James and Alix Strachey, Dr. John Rickman, and a Swiss doctor by the name of Philip Sarasin. This was the class of 1921-22, as we came to call ourselves.

My first interview with Freud was a disappointment. I was surprised when I first saw him. I had expected to meet a much taller man; his portraits seemed to give him a commanding height. Nor did I expect that his voice would be strident and rough. The greatest shock came toward the close of the interview. He was very glad that I had made arrangements to come, but he was very sorry to have to report that he had made a serious miscalculation. He had engaged to take six of us but had time for only five. He asked if I would mind going to Dr. Otto Rank in Vienna, and added the inducement that it would cost only half as much. Needless to say, he repeated this invitation to all my colleagues, and we all jointly refused. Whereupon we each spent a very bad night, because we didn't know what Freud intended to do. Was he actually going to seize one of us and throw us out, or would he hit upon a more amicable arrangement? We all returned the next day at three o'clock. He convened us and announced that he had found a happy solution. His daughter Anna, he said, had proved herself a mathematical genius. She had discovered that five times six was thirty, and that six times five was thirty, so that if each of us would renounce one hour a week he could accommodate all six of us. This was the beginning of the five-hour week.

The great paradox about Freud was that this man, against whom the world was arrayed for the license he had presumably encouraged and the iniquities he had allegedly unleashed upon it, was an ideal *paterfamilias,* a very modest man, living simply and quietly in Vienna and working twelve hours a day—not in the least a libertine. Disciplined dedication to his labors was his most conspicuous characteristic; he used in fact to boast about it. He took off only one Sunday afternoon a month. Unlike most Viennese, he had no interest in music, and told me that the only opera he had ever heard in his life was *Don Giovanni.* Otherwise he seemed a very kind, sweet gentleman. The discrepancy between his personality and gigantic achievement seemed enormous. On several occasions, I said to him: "You can't possibly be the man who wrote those great books."

Among the things that impressed one about Freud was his extraordinary facility of speech. He spoke English perfectly, and only occasionally would he get stuck on an English word that would have to be translated. He was, moreover, the greatest orator I have ever heard in my life. I would favor him over Winston Churchill in that regard. Freud possessed the ability of visualizing very concretely what he wished to say, and he knew how to plan his speech accordingly. Everything he said was practically fit for print; it was incisive, imaginative, filled with metaphors, analogies and stories—particularly Jewish ones—and it was not wordy. Freud talked like a book. His manuscripts had the same character: he almost never crossed out a line. One ought not to forget that the single distinction that Germany bestowed upon Freud was not a prize or an honor for his scientific achievement: it was the Goethe Prize for Literature.

Freud was a different man to everybody who knew him. My version of what he was to me does not presume to exhaust what he was to others. I recall an anecdote which will serve to show how Freud acted toward his followers. One evening there was a great discussion at the Society—that is, the Vienna

Psychoanalytic Society—concerning one of the members who had been guilty of what was euphemistically called "unconscious plagiarism." There was a great deal of debating to and fro—for about an hour and a half, I would say—during which Dr. So-and-So would quote what Dr. Freud had said in such-and-such an article, and somebody else would reply by quoting what Freud had said in another article on page so-and-so. Freud himself was sitting at the head of the table. After listenening to this for a considerable length of time, Freud tapped for order, his patience apparently at an end. He said, "Gentlemen, you do me a great dishonor. Why do you already treat me as if I were dead? Here you are debating among each other what I had said, and I sit at the head of the table, and not one of you thinks of asking me, 'What do you think now?'" He added, "If this is the way you treat me while I am still alive, I can well imagine what will happen when I am really dead."

Freud refused to put up with nonsense from his followers. On one occasion a member of the Society presented a paper on chess. Freud commented at its end, "This is the kind of paper that will bring psychoanalysis into disrepute. You cannot reduce everything to the Oedipus Complex. Stop!" He was an implacable enemy of cant and formula.

Despite his genius, Freud was an unknown man in Vienna. One incident should suffice to illustrate this. While I was there I lived with a family by the name of Frankel. The Frankels had been a very well-to-do family, but like all well-to-do groups who had invested their money in Austrian bonds, they became bankrupt after the war and had to let rooms to fellows like me. I received two huge furnished rooms, along with service, for about the equivalent of three dollars a month. After I had lived with the Frankels several weeks, the old Mr. Frankel thought it was part of his duty as a host to come and ask me how I was enjoying my sojourn in Vienna. He asked, "What are you doing here?" And I told him I was studying with Professor Freud. He said: "Professor Freud? Never heard the name." And he added: "Moreover, I should know, because my son-in-law is a professor at the University, and I know all the professors in the University of Vienna. But on the other hand, that name does sound familiar." Then he disappeared for a minute or two and came back with a little book, the pages of which he was fumbling and reading down the line: "F, F, F, Freud, Freud, here he is, Freud, Sigmund, Berggasse 19, a lodge brother of mine!" Mr. Frankel was reading from the Vienna catalogue of the members of the B'nai B'rith Abraham. When I told Freud this story, he was greatly amused. "You see," he said, "a prophet is never known in his own country."

2

I am sure that I may safely assume that you are very much interested to know what kind of an analyst Freud was. This is not as easy a question to answer as you might think. Times have changed, and the standards of 1921 are not the standards of today. But insofar as one can make any comparisons at all, I can report that he was incisive, sure, bold, possessed of tremendous empathy, and had no sentimentality at all. I have yet to meet his equal as an interpreter of dreams. He had an uncanny feel about symbols; and as far as tracking down character traits or infantile roots was concerned he was without peer. I learned techniques from him that have stood me in good stead for a lifetime. On the other hand, I cannot conceal from you the fact that occasionally some of his insights sent shivers down my spine because they stirred up so much trouble. In sum, when one saw Freud in harness, one beheld a genius in action.

Freud was not, however, a man who spent his attention lavishly or gratuitously. One had to earn it. In fact, I am very flattered by an observation that he made to me at the end of the very first hour that I spent with him. He said, "Did you prepare this speech?" I said, "No. Why do you ask?" He answered, "Because it was fit for printing (*druckfertig*)." He was apparently fascinated by what I had told him. And this, it proves, was quite a feat for anyone to accomplish. I came to realize this by comparing my experience with that of others who were also in contact with Freud at the same time. One had to interest and engage Freud; otherwise one might put him to sleep. Another notable characteristic of his was: if Freud felt sure of your interest and loyalty his generosity was unlimited. If, however, Freud had reason to distrust one, he could become very hostile if he thought that you were.

In what way did Freud's method of analysis differ from the course of treatment today? His answer to my question concerning myself as an analyst is pertinent: "I have many limitations as an analyst. In the first place, I get tired of people. Secondly," he said, "I am not basically interested in therapy, and I usually find that I am engaged—in any particular case—with the theoretical problems with which I happen to be interested at the time." And then he added, "I am also too patriarchal to be a good analyst"—that is, he demanded too much obedience.

I am not aware of what he did with some of his other students, but with me he talked quite freely. Among other issues he disclosed what some of his great fears were. He feared for the future of his work; he feared that it would be known to posterity as a Jewish science. To insure against this contingency, a large organization was evolved. Whether or not it fulfilled Freud's hopes still remains debatable. Also, Freud feared differences of opinion. He worried that lack of unanimity would destroy the value of his contribution. His fears have proven ill founded. His influence has persisted because man needed what he taught.

3

I come now to the final question I have put to myself: How shall we evaluate Freud's influence? Freud's work has survived and grown in significance because it has been socially relevant. Psychology is not quite like the other natural sciences. Man behaves toward psychology very much as children do toward syntax. They use it but they do not want to know about it. They can talk sentences, but they prefer not to study grammar. Thus, when man turns his eye inward (this in itself is unusual) it must mean that something very urgent is bothering him. In my view, it is social distress that underlies the intensification of the interest in psychology at the end of the nineteenth century. The development of psychoanalysis was a symbol of and a response to this malaise. The genius of Freud lay precisely in that he was aware of some of the things that were disturbing humanity. He seized upon one particular symptom of the aggravation, namely, the existence of neurosis.

Freud was not the first to turn the attention of man to motivation. In fact, the novelists had been doing so for a long time: George Eliot, Turgenev, Tolstoy, and, most of all, Dostoyevsky. All of these were occupied with motivations in human relations. Freud made this study systematic, not intuitive —made it rational and not inspirational.

What happened in this nineteenth century to promote this turn of events? What was there toward the close of the century that made the study of adaptation so imperative?

This remarkable century opened with the Napoleonic wars. Having succeeded in liquidating the remnants of feudalism in Europe and having destroyed all its political bulwarks and appurtenances, the French Revolution put into effective power the middle classes who had taken over the church, the culture, and finally the state. This is the group whose values and social goals were now accepted as the common pattern. Their influence had been increasing slowly for over two and a half centuries, and the political philosophy of this group is known to us as liberalism. Liberalism succeeded because it created and satisfied an ever-increasing ambit of human needs. Liberalism grew because it *hurt* nobody. Our interest in liberalism lies not in its historic, political or social forms, but in the new opportunities it created for the individual in contrast with the outlook of the previous era. It created the machinery for implementing freedom and social mobility. Above all, liberalism created the opportunity for man to have the voice to decide his own fate. The same wave that started at the beginning of the nineteenth century has now passed far beyond Western society, and has reached the backward peoples of the earth. It is the same movement, however, regardless of place.

Liberalism gave the individual the freedom to decide his own fate, to choose among many alternatives, to have as a goal new types of experience and enjoyment, as well as responsibilities. This movement of self-realization was ushered in between 1770 and 1850 by a movement commonly known by the now sentimentalized euphemism "the romantic movement." The "romantic movement" was in fact the emotional expression of a great social upheaval. In this movement the lowly, the ugly, and the heretofore disenfranchised acquired a claim to recognition. One's fate no longer depended on birth, but on character and ability. In the feudal ethos not happiness but salvation was the acknowledged goal.

The nineteenth century made happiness, enjoyment here and now, the legitimate goals of the age. Men provided themselves with the implements of its accomplishment through the development of industry, manufacture, and invention. Character and personality became recognized as the implements of social inter-action. In this atmosphere, neurosis could not be considered, as it had generally been stigmatized by the church, prior to the nineteenth century, as the work of the devil. Once again, as in classical cultures, neurosis came to be considered a disease. In the nineteenth century neurosis was interpreted as an impediment to happiness and effectiveness. The nineteenth century invented the social approval of neurosis.

The right to have a neurosis may be a great freedom, deserving of protection by international charter. The Nazis presumed to outlaw neurosis; the Russians are attempting the same now; and the Japanese acted in the same manner during their occupation of the Philippine Islands. The Japanese accomplished the liquidation of neurosis by saying that anybody in the Philippine Islands caught running amok—which was a kind of neurosis—would be shot. This stopped neurosis.

Men of the nineteenth century did not think to wait for epidemics or dancing tics to express suppressed difficulties. People felt freer to express neurosis and to seek help for it. The only technique of assistance available at that time was hypnosis.

The man who performed the social and political task of liberating neurosis from ecclesiastical opprobrium was Jean Charcot, one of the teachers of Sigmund Freud. His clinic became the Mecca for hysterics the world over. He compelled the recognition of hypnosis as a natural phenomenon and demonstrated the connections between hypnosis and hysteria. He even hinted at the presence of unconscious factors by telling his pupils that hysteria always involved a sexual component. From this point forward, it was only a question of how and when the rational approach to neurosis would become possible. It became possible in the brief span of time that described the difference of age between Charcot and Sigmund Freud. Charcot accomplished the socio-political objective; Freud the scientific.

It must be emphasized that the work of Freud was in harmony with the new ethos of liberalism. He destroyed the tyranny that accompanies the hypnotic procedure and substituted for it a more democratic, pedagogic method in which both physician and patient were, by the conclusion of the treatment, on a more or less equal level. In this Freud is the heir of nineteenth-century liberalism. It was liberalism which gave suffering a voice and neurosis an opportunity for expression. Freud merely invented the implement for liberating the energy that neurosis impounded and putting it to the service of the goals that liberalism had legitimated.

It is for this reason that I believe that Freud's work will remain socially relevant as long as man cherishes freedom, and as long as the goals of liberalism enjoy favor. So long as individuality, and not institutional pressure, is the decisive instrument of social inter-action, so long will Freud be deemed useful. When the individual becomes socially irrelevant, and individuality and emotions cease to be significant in one's life, then our present conceptions of character will become meaningless, and Freud will be forgotten. Freud's survival, in other words, the survival of the Freudian outlook, is contingent upon what happens to society.

Having noted the social influences that made Freud's work possible and relevant, I should like now to discuss very briefly the significance of his work itself. I shall, in the course of the succeeding observations, take no cognizance whatsoever of all the divisions that have appeared in the ranks of Freudian pupils. I do this for the reason that not one among the dissidents would have had a chance for emergence or survival were it not for Freud. Moreover, a method such as Freud's encounters the reaction of many minds, and there are bound to be differences of opinion. When I refer to the significance of his work I mean to make reference to the totality of what he brought into the world. It would be superficial simply to say that Freud invented a cure for neurosis. To say only that would do Freud a great injustice! Freud did much more than that. He invented a device of self-critique and self-correction, both for the individual and for society. He discovered the motions and the maneuvers of the mind in response to alterations in himself—that is, his needs and his wishes—and alterations in the external world, in his natural and human environment. He discovered these quite incidentally to the quest for the cure of neurosis.

One of the achievements of Freud, namely, the self-examination to which he subjected himself, is sometimes overlooked. This adventure of self-discovery, recorded in *The Interpretation of Dreams,* has, to my mind, been equalled in human history only a few times. It is an odyssey of far greater intensity than is recorded in the *Confessions* of St. Augustine, and much more sincere and modest than those that are contained in the *Confessions* of Rousseau. *The Interpretation of Dreams* is restrained; yet it ranks in intensity with the kind of inner self-encounter and honesty that must have preceded the creation of Kant's *Critique of Pure Reason* and Einstein's general theory of relativity.

I do not believe that Freud himself fully realized the implications of his own discoveries in *The Interpretation of Dreams.* In fact, we are still reflecting upon them now. He formulated some of the basic laws of mental functioning and discovered the reality of the integrative character of the human mind. With such discoveries he brought into the world a new definition of human fate, because he placed in the hands of man the means with which to alter impediments which were previously considered irremediable. "You need not be the victim of your own past," said Freud, "or of your own environment." And he discovered a new kind of freedom. And this is really what is meant when one talks about curing neurosis.

More than all of this, Freud defined a powerful instrument of social critique and self-direction. He did this by his astute analysis of the family constellation and his theory of repression, both of which enabled us to examine with greater accuracy and candor our customs and our mores, from which all the incentives for repression come. One of the first adventures that Freud had in this connection was to hit upon the sexual etiology of neurosis. He came in time to stress this strongly. Today, we no longer accept this emphasis without qualification.

What Freud was doing, however, was to provide a new critique of the mores and customs of Western society. I need not mention what constructions were placed on Freud's discovery of the sexual etiology of neurosis; he was taken to say that freedom from the restrictions of the Victorian sex morality would liberate mankind from all its ills. The fact is that he said nothing of the sort; rather, he adopted the emphasis on sexual elements in order to define a new kind of critique of society. He succeeded in fixing some guideposts on the basis of which we can judge the effectuality or the ineffectuality of our own mores. We are not now at the mercy of the momentum of institutions; we can pause, we can criticize and direct ourselves. This part of Freud's work has yet to be developed. The public has very little interest in the task. Most men remain interested in the alteration of personal fate, not of the fate of society.

At this moment in history the question arises: Can we, do we want to, employ the instrument that Freud made possible? Thus far, we have used it in a rather restricted sense, confining it to the treatment of neurosis and to those directives in connection with child-rearing that are supposed to prevent neurosis. The social applications of Freud's teachings yet remain to be realized; they still await public interest, and they confront us with a difficult task of public education. In this connection, many prejudices will have to be overcome. We have been trained in the past to see the discomforts of society largely in terms of economics, in terms of international conflict. Freud has given us a much broader frame of reference. Do we want to exploit this new conception? This is the aspect of Freud that has always engendered violent reaction. It would require an enormous amount of effort in public education to make Freud's implement of social critique available to many. Indeed the Freudian social critique may be too little and too late.

We are in fact in a race against time. If Freud's teachings can remain relevant only under the aegis of liberalism and the freedom of the individual, then there is no certainty whether time remains to implement his teachings. As the world turns and as the incalculable social pressures continue to mount, as a result of the surge of historical imperatives that we cannot control, time runs out. Freud has charted a course for the enhancement of our freedoms and happiness. Let us hope that those social conditions will prevail which should make possible the continuation of the work he began.

SIX

REMINISCENCES OF FREUD AND JUNG
VIKTOR VON WEIZSAECKER

1
27TH OF SEPTEMBER, 1939 (A FEW DAYS AFTER THE DEATH OF FREUD IN ENGLAND) [1]

Under the fresh impression of Freud's death in England and with the continual rejection by National Socialism of everything Jewish, I hope I will succeed in describing my meeting with Freud as independently as the matter requires. Here, too, an effort must be made to bring nearness and distance into correct proportion. Not only great nearness, but also too great distance cause the image of things to seem flat and distorted. Unlike mechanical explanation, historic evaluation is determined not only by the antecedents, but also by what comes afterwards. The question here is: What will be the outcome? Now, fifty years after the inception of psychoanalysis,[2] this has become fairly discernible. With the death of Freud, the man and the work have now finally become separated.

Freud's appearance was that of a scholarly man of the world from the era of the high middle-class culture. He showed not a trace of academic pedantry, his conversation passed easily from serious and difficult topics to a light and graceful *causerie*. But the aura of an outstanding man was always present. When I saw him the restraint of one who is undergoing bodily suffering was evident, but it was not oppressive. The agility of his mind was not affected. But once, though only for a second, the uncompromising wrath of the bearer of a spiritual mission burst forth almost terrifyingly.

In Freud's waiting room at 19 Berggasse, Vienna, one found the dark red plush-covered furniture of the 1880's. Several diplomas, framed under glass, of honorary membership of foreign, particularly English, societies were hanging on the walls. To the right of the entrance into his office by the window, there was a French print, showing a nude unconscious woman. She was stretched out and in the power of a demonic incubus, suggesting, as it were, the subject of psychoanalytic therapy. To the left of the door on top of a cabinet there stood a big simple antique urn. Its concentrated stillness might have expressed something of Freud's yet unrevealed philosophy.

In the spacious consulting and working room itself I remember only the long gallery of antique statuettes, bronzes, terracottas on his desk. Thus, when he looked up, the eye of the professor viewed these satyrs and goddesses. They revealed him as a collector of precious pagan art. However, only the main subject, the man himself, absorbed my attention.

Freud was very slim, but of at least medium height. The painful action of his mouth was by that time already marked by a prosthesis of the jaw. Some years earlier, he had been operated on for a sarcoma of the upper jaw with permanent success, incidentally. But he often suffered pain. The eyes were black, less looking out than sucking in, like a bottomless abyss. His face in old age proclaimed him one in the midst of battle. The deep wrinkle of the nose and cheek continued over the right eye like a streaming war standard, producing the effect both of beauty of the eyebrows and watchfulness of the hero who had devoted himself to works of peace, but has encountered deadly powers. Evidently he had learned to play with the extremes. Portraits from his early years show nothing of this. In these one sees a ruddy, vigorous and buoyant man. In a letter to me which draws a parallel between physiognomy and handwriting, Freud wrote that his handwriting had changed in the course of his life to such a degree that he could not recognize the identity of the writer. Apparently, both his facial expression and his handwriting underwent a like change: only slowly but ever more and more insistently he was gripped by the entanglement in a painful struggle. The handwriting of his old age seems to me like the dense but gracefully designed texture of a carpet. Both the simple basic directions, the vertical and the horizontal, are predominant. No letter, no word can be detached from the close connection with its surroundings, everything moves along like the serried ranks of a marching column. The impression of simultaneous agitation of many parts is repeated if one looks at each stroke. They are of fair length and straightness and always slightly swung or as though faintly trembling.

The literary style of Freud's writing belongs as well in the field of personal expression. I do not know if it will be admitted that, since the aged Goethe, Ranke, and the Humboldts, the German language has continued to decline from its height. Helmholtz and Hering still write in an impeccable style. But then the language of the men of science and scholars grows increasingly careless. In spite of his mastery of effects, Nietzsche had an unhappy influence. Thus, it has come to pass, that a great thinker like Scheler or an exemplary medical scholar like Krehl write in an outright poor style. Good language is no longer of any concern, the end of the classic manner has arrived.

In this Freud is an exception. His language, though no longer classic, is guided by artistic principles. They are: strict limitation to essential words; a certain ethereal lightness, even grace, eschewing emphatic phrases and superlatives, which had then begun to be used; observation of the logic inherent in our civilized languages; avoidance of the metaphor and of the merely atmospheric; a balance between scholarly objectivity and human subjectivity, the ego of the author always breaking through the detachment of the presentation. There is still another thing, to be praised or blamed according to one's point of view: a charm which verges on seduction, a noncommittal attitude which might be put down for modesty or for decadence.

But all these matters are of no weight against his observance of the duty to write in plain good form.

That the latter was entirely natural to him is proven by the private letters from his last decade which I possess. Even to the postcard they show a high level of culture which appears at one and the same time improvised and matured. It is impossible not to praise the style of Freud highly.

Even so, it is false when Freud is called an artist, as it were, a frustrated poet. It has in truth, it seems to me, been Asian wisdom which has come to us with him, in order now to shine brightly, now again to be rejected as un-European. As with Spinoza, his work centers on the analysis of passion—and analysis means almost the neutralizing, the dethronement, of the demons. The means to his end is insight. It is intelligence which Freud is proud of, and in his last work he praises it as a characteristic of his race. "You surely agree that most people are stupid," he said to me.

I will not pursue the background of this passion for thinking. The right way may be to renounce seeking to settle anything by thinking alone; true thinking unfolds itself only in the encounter with being. In *Studies on Hysteria,* which Freud published together with Breuer in 1895, one already finds the specific manner in which Freud himself seems to transform things sensually perceived into things analytically thought. Here, Freud *thinks through* the phenomena which others sought only to describe, to empathize with, to understand, or to explain causally. They are the expressions of the soul. The analyst divines in them a hidden and yet clear meaning. I have no better word for it than *psychic logic.* Freudian analysis is, therefore, neither a true nor a false explanation. One might best call it an application of perspicacity. Breuer's speculative neurological attempts at explanation differ characteristically from Freudian sagacity. Breuer seeks to give a hypothetic material explanation. Freud seems to say only once more what he had observed, namely the utterances and actions of the patients, but precisely in the *psycho-logical* way which is indeed the Freudian way.

The later separation of the two men was not to be avoided.

But the misunderstanding which divided them has generally persisted and has its roots in the unrelatedness of psychoanalysis to the thinking of the natural sciences and medicine as a whole. Those of its followers who, like Schilder and H. Hartmann reaffirm psychoanalysis to be a pure natural science, do not know what physics and even biology really are. They are right in one respect only, that psychoanalysis also initially perceives, observes, and describes before it explains. Psychoanalysis begins empirically. And now, the strange fact is that just this aspect has been overlooked by its psychiatric opponents. One did not take the pains, great indeed, required for verification, but condemned the theory out of hand; yet what these critics called the "theory" of psychoanalysis was for the most part observation! I cannot be shaken in this belief. At this point it must be stated that it is the utterances of patients which Freud reports in his *libido* "theory," in his "theory" of the *complexes,* and so on, including the metapsychology. It is this which has been designated as "his theory" by the ill-informed.

To justify this sentiment, I can relate that it was the ever surprising confirmation of his data concerning the psychology and the clinical treatment of neuroses which impelled me to ever more intense concern with psychoanalysis. Of course, there is always something of an attempt at systematical ordering in dream interpretation, in the motivation of symptom formation in hysteria, in the dynamics of the compulsion neurosis. But only the confirmation of observations in countless cases has been decisive for me. Freud, I realized, had always remained a clinical researcher. Indeed, his was the most accurate, most faithful and most objective examination and description of neurosis which existed. One might perhaps reproach Freud that he could have expressed this fact more strongly and more exclusively. But then one must add, too, that most of his opponents seemed to care still less.

On the whole, it has now become manifest that an upheaval has come about, which has changed the standards not only of clinical research but of scientific and cultural life since the turn of the century. *The Interpretation of Dreams,* the quantum theory, and the theory of relativity were all published in the first six years of the twentieth century, 1900, 1901, and 1905 respectively.[3] It soon became obvious that not only were the psychology and the clinical treatment of the neuroses at stake but that the contradictions that paved the way for the twentieth century had become manifest. The problem of neurosis was merely the storm-center where the prognosis for the science of medicine was decided. The consequence was that the style of inquiry, which had begun in the nineties, has spread since 1920 over a world which already wore an entirely new face.

If one follows this observation farther, another peculiar complication appears. Two matters attracted attention during the first decade of psychoanalysis: the unconscious and the increased importance of sexuality. As to the unconscious, the world had been prepared for it by the post-idealistic philosophy of irrationalism, above all by the philosophies of Schopenhauer, Feuerbach, Eduard von Hartmann, Nietzsche, but also by the novels of Dostoyevsky. The unveiling of sexuality, on the other hand, coincided with the crisis of the age of plush, the long coats and the corset, a crisis of the mores. Although the candor of Freud in sexual matters and his scepticism toward the evidence of the consciousness were revolutionary in that non-revolutionary time, they did not produce a very notable public effect. They merely aroused a sensation in an immediate circle. One should have expected that in the postwar period in which both great sexual freedom and great indulgence toward irrational tendencies prevailed, all doors should have been opened for the acceptance of an outlook like psychoanalysis. This was certainly the case to a large extent. However, precisely because the world was beginning to put somewhat into practice what psychoanalysis seemed to demand, namely the elimination of inhibitions, very soon—according to historic law—the reaction set in and on this occasion with passion and militancy.

I see in this occurrence a general law. If psychoanalysis, as a method of treating the sick, somehow bore within itself the ideal of how the healthy man might be formed, then psychoanalysis was bound to meet with the fate of all human ideals. The realization belies the intent and expectation. Hence what was argued about in Germany until 1933 was something other than the old psychoanalysis.

The false impression has arisen, therefore, that Freud, when recommending elimination of inhibitions, was advocating sexual license. This was a lie. On the other hand, Freud had not spoken enough of another psychic force, namely, the will, to satisfy the longing of the younger generation. Indeed, I believe that Freud unconsciously took for granted more of the established order of life and cultural forms than actually existed in the reality of the postwar era. Freud's abandonment of religion, his continual criticism of the consciousness, his stern demand to renounce every illusion, even where indeed no illness was involved, but where the value of life as such had been called into question—these all could really lead up over the path of psychoanalysis into the desperation of emptiness, were a man no longer so firmly rooted in the soil of high intellectual culture and civil order as was the author of this corrosive method of purgation himself.

This subject reminds me of a long conversation I had with Freud in his home in 1926. This visit took place at my initiative and was prompted by my wish to express my gratitude to the man by whose help the medical profession had become enriched for me in a way which seemed to inspire it with life at a time when it otherwise threatened to become numb and stagnant. As I intimated earlier, I refer to the psychic side of the living phenomena. But this by no means obvious step meant also interferences with a private, personal and vulnerable domain of the patient, who might offer resistance, even take revenge for the unwanted intrusion. No standards for the manner and limits of such a procedure could be obtained from academic medicine. Instead one came into conflict with authorities like the church, philosophy, or society. This may help to explain what remained in my memory of this conversation.

Freud did not consider it tragic when I declared that I myself had never undergone an analysis. I said that I might as well retain that bit of neurosis that I probably had. He answered that not every case had to be analyzed anyhow. Many people derived benefit from association with an eminent man and it was known that many a neurosis healed through the experience either of great luck or of misfortune. But the physician, having no control over that, had, therefore, to choose a different way. When the extent of the application of psychoanalysis came up, Freud implied that psychoanalysis would have interesting material for about another fifty years. He mentioned, for example, the psychology of the African matrilineal tribes where the Oedipus complex is directed, not against the father but against the brother of the mother, since he represents the authority of the family.[4]

Freud seems to have given me an evasive reply to my question about conflicts of psychoanalysis with binding ties, in particular of the Catholic religion. He said: "We (that is, the psychoanalysts) believe we have always found the way to respect and to spare these spheres in the patient." Freud's *The Future of an Illusion* appeared only a year later,[5] and I cannot believe that his views on the neurotic and illusionary character of religion had not yet been formed at that time. Also, attempts in my letters to get him to speak on this subject remained without success. Yet I could bring him in another way to a point where he faced problems otherwise kept secret. I asked him whether psychoanalysis was a finite or infinite process. After a pause he said hesitatingly and in a low voice: "I believe--an infinite one." This was truly to say more than he said in his questionable assertion that one always could spare the religion of the analyzed patient. This answer seems to me to imply that psychoanalysis transcends the temporary life of the soul. Religion does that, too, and consequently one can no longer evade the question whether psychoanalysis has substituted for religion. But Freud had no difficulty in abandoning the controversial area once more by saying he would confide to me the fact that some of his disciples, when "neuroticized," as it were, by the excess of neurotic material absorbed in their therapeutic work, themselves undergo analysis once again, and that such happened every few years. There was more benevolence than respect in the way he spoke of his followers. On the whole, he seemed weary of his school and not in need of it any longer.

At the parting, however, it became apparent that our encounter had not entirely passed over the more stormy depths of spiritual struggle. As it happens, when one is standing, on point of leaving, one cannot always find the concluding word; I broke an ensuing silence by a remark, perhaps more honestly felt than in good taste. I said somewhat abruptly that it seemed to me a strange coincidence that my visit had chanced to fall on All Souls' Day, for indeed that was the date. The unexpected result of this remark was that Freud asked in astonishment: "What do you mean?" I became a bit confused and tried to explain that I was "perhaps something of a mystic on the side." Whereupon he turned to me quickly and said with an openly horrified glance: "That is terrible." I said, yielding, "I meant to say there is also something which we don't know," to which he replied: "Oh, in that I more than match you." His tormented tone and the quick change of subject proved in my opinion that this time he was very serious about the matter, and perhaps also that he loved me a bit. He must have said then something about the unassailableness of reason. I did not hear it or else forgot it. There followed a handclasp, executed with a beautiful swing of his whole arm. A sympathy had been founded that never afterward altered.

At the time of this meeting with Freud not much of what I later learned to regard as the fruit of experience with psychoanalysis could yet have come forth. At least I do not remember having spoken then to its creator on the origin of bodily illness and its pathogenetic analogy to the analytic approach. Later, when this subject had been occupying me for years, I decided to publish the result. I sent Freud a rather extensive study on "Body Processes and Neuroses." This gave occasion to an exchange of letters, which might certainly anticipate greater interest among medical men, than the conversation reported above. I am, therefore, including the letter in which Freud defined his attitude regarding this study.

19 Berggasse,   16 October 1932
Vienna IX.

Dear Professor:

Sending your manuscript requires no excuse. It invites gratitude since I derived rare satisfaction and inspiration from it. I
am impatient to share both of these reactions with my friends
and shall accordingly strongly endorse the publication, in our
journal if you wish, of your study—edited and shortened, with
your consent. As to your scruples, which I might scold as
opportunistic, I can neither appreciate nor understand them,
but it occurs to me that on this point you did not request my
open criticism. I shall, therefore, not press you to take a step
which you do not take willingly.

I cannot doubt the correctness of the analytic solution of
your case. As the excessive homosexual component indicates,
your patient is paranoid—certainly less easily to be seen
through than a pure "transference neurosis." But precisely such
patients are frequently distinguished by their capacity for
psychic self-perception and for expression in "organ language,"
hence they are particularly instructive. The elucidation of the
disfunction, here micturition, caused by erotization imposed on
the genito-urinary organs, is in complete accord with the analytic theory, which I once tried to illustrate by the banal comparison that this was so, as if the master of the household had
entered a love affair with the cook, surely not to the advantage
of the kitchen. You show, further, the finer mechanism of the
disturbance, pointing out the opposing innervations, which
must cancel out or confuse each other.

I had to restrain the analysts from investigations of this kind
for educational reasons. Innervations, enlargements of blood
vessels, and nervous paths would have been too dangerous a
temptation for them. They had to learn to limit themselves to
psychologic ways of thought. But we can be grateful to specialists in internal medicine for the broadening of our insights.

The other part of your study, in which you try to determine a common point of view for psychic and organic illness,
contains new matter and makes us listen attentively, precisely
because through occasional observations we have drawn nearer
to the boundaries of this unexplored field. We have paid attention to the psychogenic factors in organic diseases, have learned
to understand that neurosis can often be replaced by a disease;
neither did the strange immunity of some neurotics against
infections and colds and its loss after psychic improvement
escape our notice. The points of view common to all diseases

like the interruption, the turning point, the crisis, etc., prepare us for important innovations.

Perhaps it cannot be avoided that we are more perplexed than convinced by the highly speculative train of thoughts, which you unfold, and that some of your abstractions give the impression of a provisional character to which one need not cling. I would venture some objections in details also. Scheler's dictum that psychology is unlogic cannot impress me. It is one of those ambiguous *aperçus* in consequence of which I always have borne a grievance against the philosophers. The fact behind it seems to be that the law of contradiction does not exist for the unconscious and that only the thinking of the ego has to create a synthesis. Likewise I must defend the symptomatic conception of the actual neurosis against your criticism. We are glad to have advanced here for once to direct toxic causation and would emphatically disagree if somebody should expect us to give, in the name of psychoanalytic consistency, a psychic explanation for the headache and stomach trouble of someone with a hangover. Strange that one is dissatisfied with us when once we strive to make allowance for direct organic influence.

I do not wish to pursue these small divergences any further. Your work, indeed, the entire direction of your research, opens to us perspectives which are so helpful that I should be disappointed, if they would lead only to an exchange of letters and ideas between us.

Very respectfully yours,
Freud

P.S. Please decide concerning the disposal of your manuscript.

Upon receiving this letter I did not revise the manuscript, but added the twelfth chapter which contains a collection of cases of angina in brief observation. When I was sending the enlarged manuscript to Vienna for a second time to be published in the journal issued by Freud, I seem to have written something about the anxiety connected with the production and publication of my study. A second short letter, which I am also inserting here, refers to this. Something in this letter, I believe, is suggestive of Freud's own experience.

19 Berggasse,
Vienna IX.
3 November 1932

Dear Colleague:

Taken ill by a tiresome grippe I only confirm today the receipt of your manuscript and express my satisfaction at the passage in your letter which confesses to the anxiety during your labor for the new bit of truth. No other utterance could have won so much respect and sympathy from me. As soon as I am capable again of company, I shall get in touch with the editor concerning your study.

Sincerely yours,
Freud

The following pages will reveal how I fared with the fulfillment of the expectations which had been aroused on both sides. Whenever I had printed something that could find Freud's interest, I would send it to Vienna and every time I received a cordial response, for the last time on occasion of his eightieth birthday. The events of the years 1933 and 1939 had no influence on my inward relation to him; however, they disturbed the outward contact. And as it was to be the lot of Freud to emigrate at his advanced age to England and to die there, it was mine to participate in the fate of my native land.

However, I have yet to recall a woman for whose acquaintance I am indebted to my connection with psychoanalysis: it is Lou Andreas-Salomé.[6] Around Christmas 1931 her book *My Gratitude to Freud (Mein Dank an Freud)* written in honor of Freud's seventy-fifth birthday, came into my hand. The impression it made on me was such that I wrote her a letter, though she was not known to me, a letter which later gained me a correspondence, a visit to her home, and a measure of encouragement which gave me real support at the very time of that anxiety I mentioned earlier. Lou was then seventy years old, quietly carrying on a psychoanalytic practice in Goettingen, and living the mysterious life of a *sibyl* in our intellectual world— for it is generally known that, as a young girl, she had been loved by Nietzsche, who had repeatedly asked to marry her. Her book on him has remained one of the best on his thought and his personality. Later she had been very close to Rilke for many years. She also wrote a beautiful book about Rilke. Finally, she had won the friendship and advice of Freud. Her letters were marked by an unequalled flair; from the first moment she knew with whom she had to deal and where the roots of my troubles lay. Perhaps she could not help me, but she understood how to love the spirit and was experienced in the worlds of loneliness. Her freedom toward the school psychoanalysis, which also had been manifested in her tribute to Freud and by the strength of her own originality, her highly individual transformation of the doctrine itself, had a refreshing effect upon me. Here one saw that one could translate what is true in a theory into other languages.

Gratefully I received the womanliness and warmth of her nature. It is perhaps no fault, though surely a loss, that the correspondence, so intense at first, later declined. She had fulfilled a mission with me and there was nothing I could have offered her in turn, that she could have needed at her old age. This extraordinary woman was still blond and had the swinging gait, as it were, of a swaying tree. She was less monumental than Gertrud Baeumer or Ricarda Huch, but possessed the gift of a charming, searching or groping understanding of human beings, without the all too virile imbalance of the productive and systematic intellectual woman. My reverence for Freud and my admiration for his work never needed confirmation. But the effect of psychoanalysis has something of an inexorably tightening noose. One cannot engage in it without, as it were, crying for help or at least struggling with it incessantly. The rare instance that somebody might conceive this science deeply enough and yet remain a personality has occurred to me never before or since in such a helpful way. I cherish her letters and her memory as one of the treasures of my recollections.

2
FREUD AND JUNG[7]

Only two of Freud's disciples have established schools of their own. Of these I never met Adler. He should not be named in the same breath with Freud, as has often been done. Neither did I frequently meet with Jung and, in spite of a certain sympathy, I never warmed up to him. This belongs, however, more in the chapter on "elective affinities" than in that on medical science.

C. G. Jung was the first to understand that psychoanalysis belonged in the sphere of religion, more accurately, to the dissolution of religion in our time. To him neurosis was a symptom of the man who loses his support in religion. Publicly he spoke about that only later, but once he said to me in conversation, "*All* neurotics seek the religious." At first, he may have been under the sway of scientific psychology and the curiosity of the researcher in the history of religion. Later he was prevented from speaking more openly about it by an old resentment against Christianity (he was the son of a parson) and probably also by tactical consideration—he was afraid of being identified with a superficial pastoral attitude.

He was deterred from professing atheism openly, as Freud did, by the realization that a man must never do that. He was deterred from professing a religion by the insight that all of us had been thrown into such a deep crisis of the religious that, in this sphere, there was no longer a word in the language which had not become ambiguous. Thus he really found himself in an insoluble situation. In his book on *Psychology and Religion* his attitude was speculative, not professing. He said something like the following: There may still be men who have or who believe they have the support of religion; in the case of the others, among whom he seemed to reckon himself, the situation is different; they must pay a price for it if they abandon themselves to illusion. The consequence of the loss of support, the loss of the center, is neurosis.

One may perhaps say: while Freud was discovering and building up psychoanalysis, he still was under the illusion that it was a medical task, the task of a physician, which could be founded on scientific truth. Once Jung had discovered the religious core, he could no longer keep up this illusion, but he needed to preserve it outwardly in order not to be misunderstood. He befogged his ultimate thoughts in a certain way, but it is not certain whether these ultimate thoughts were clear. This resulted in a sort of honorable mystification and insecurity of his behavior, which I felt distinctly. I respected it at bottom, because it had in a way its good reason and was more honest than a forced decision, which would have been insincere and not been believed. Moreover, he was neither a fanatic nor a genius of absolute consequence. This is again no reason to blame a man. Unlike Freud, he was in that sense, so to speak, a man like others, even though he surpassed most men in intelligence, talents, and personal vigor. He certainly has been one of the most eminent Swiss of his time, sharing the peculiar fate of his country, which has been spared by the storm and later by the hurricane of our era.

If I examine the reasons for aversion to him which at times has cropped up in me, I am broaching a rather insignificant subject, and its discussion serves only as a kind of justification of myself. Above all, I have been and remain bound up with Freud and had no reason to participate in the improvements that Jung applied to Freud's theory. I am still of the opinion that all the essential discoveries and intellectual achievements of psychoanalysis go back exclusively to Freud. But even among Freudians the insufficient depth-psychological distinction between the male and the female psyche has been regarded as a weak point of psychoanalysis. According to a widely held judgment, Jung has achieved progress in this respect. I cannot pretend to a judgment of my own in this matter and have no reason to dispute it.

The bridge to psychosomatic medicine was to be built from Freud's psychology, certainly not from what was specifically Jungian. For that reason and especially later when the Jewish question came to the foreground, it grieved me when Jung included in his writings ungrateful and questionable clichés which did not bespeak good character. As the situation of the German psychotherapists grew difficult, Jung helped them also only as long as it was convenient to himself.

Further, one misses a quality in Jung which must not be lacking in a classic. He has not been a good writer. His style is uneven and rather impersonal, and that seems to point to a lack of depth in his thinking and of decisive clarity at the base of his character. This is more of a statement of a fact than a reproach, and one would not make it if one were not impressed by him and prepared to expect something superior. Jung speaks better than he writes, but he writes about many things which it is better to speak about than to write. Finally, the personal entourage and followers of Jung are a motley crowd. While some of Freud's adherents have something sectarian and dogmatic about them, the men around Jung have been a curious mixture of inconsequential and somewhat mercurial individuals.

While these defects are on the all too personal side, Jung has after all done an extraordinary service to psychotherapy. He has humanized and freed it from the psychoanalytic scientific pretensions. He made it clear what crisis of culture really was about. For that very reason he had still to depart farther from medicine, and he could not possibly have a stronger interest in those problems, which occupied me, than in the unity of medicine and the somatic-psychic borderline question. Moreover, Jung's concept of neurosis is so overwhelmingly preoccupied with the calamity of the human soul that one feels rather moved by him to see a fault in confounding it with scientific and psychological questions. But neither he nor I understood clearly this serious problem at the time of our personal relations.

Subsequently Jung has, as far as I know, only kept company and exchanged ideas with representatives of the humanities. Thus his work is today a very serious occasion for me to re-examine my entirely different endeavors as a whole. While the physician and medical scientist get into a dilemma because from behind the natural side of man, the more essential and more important one of his spiritual destination breaks forth, Jung is in the dilemma of having to employ psychology both as a science and as a divining rod of faith. If the patient suffers from not believing in anything, what *shall* he believe in? To convey a faith to him would mean transgressing the competency of the physician or the psychologist. And although the psychotherapist advances nearer to the realm of religion and faith than the physician does, both can merely clear a space to be filled by the transcendental. In order to fill this gap, Jung did not entirely refrain from reviving in more intimate circles certain occultist or para-religious traditions. Indeed, the Jung circle itself has served as a surrogate for the objective religious community which had been abandoned. He paid his tribute to the catastrophe of European liberalism—by giving the diagnosis of a disease which could not be cured. *Ultra posse nemo obligatur.*

After what I have indicated, the question can never be "Freud or Jung?", but only "Freud or Freud *and* Jung?" [8] Altogether, the prominent men of the third generation I have mentioned elsewhere in these memoirs gave no reason to reproach psychotherapy for dogmatism. Each of them went his personal way and all tried to learn, wherever they could. I can offer proof in regard to all of these I have known.

The Sciences of Mind and Health

Part III. The Science of Good and Right

SEVEN

THE FIRST PSYCHOANALYST
ERIK H. ERIKSON

It is a solemn and yet always a deeply incongruous occasion when we select an anniversary to honor a man who in lonely years struggled through a unique experience and won a new kind of knowledge for mankind. To some of us, the field created by Sigmund Freud has become an absorbing profession, to some an inescapable intellectual challenge, to all the promise (or threat) of an altered image of man. But any sense of proprietary pride in the man to be honored this year should be sobered by the thought that we have no right to assume that we would have met his challenge with more courage than his contemporaries did in the days when his insights were new. It seems fitting to use his centenary to review some of the dimensions of lonely discovery.

It is not easy (unless it be all too easy) for a "Freudian" to speak of the man who *was* Freud, of a man who grew to be a myth before our eyes. I knew Freud when he was very old, and I was young. Being employed as a tutor in a family befriended to him I had the opportunity of seeing him on quiet occasions, with children and with dogs, and at outings in the mountains. I do not know whether I would have noticed Freud in a crowd. His notable features were not spectacular: the

79

finely domed forehead, the dark, unfathomable eyes, and certain small indomitable gestures—they all had become part of that inner containment which crowns the old age of good fighters.

I was an artist then, which is a European euphemism for a young man with some talent, but nowhere to go. What probably impressed me most was the fact that this doctor of the mind, this expert of warped biography, had surrounded himself in his study with a small host of little statues: those distilled variations of the human form which were created by the anonymous artists of the archaic Mediterranean. Certainly, of Freud's field, of conflict and complaint and confession, there was no trace in their art. This respect for form, so surprising in a man who had unearthed mankind's daimonic inner world, was also obvious in his love for proud dogs and for gaily bright children. I vaguely felt that I had met a man of rare dimensions, rare contradictions.

When I became a psychoanalyst myself, this same old man—now remote from the scene of training and gathering—became for me what he is for the world: the writer of superb prose, the author of what seems like more than one lifetime's collected works: a master, so varied in his grandiose one-sidedness that the student can manage to understand only one period of his work at a time. Strangely enough, we students knew little of his beginnings, nothing of that mysterious self-analysis which he alluded to in his writings. We knew people whom Freud had introduced into psychoanalysis, but psychoanalysis itself had, to all appearances, sprung from his head like Athena from the head of Zeus.

The early Freud became better known to us only a very few years ago, through the accidental discovery of intimate letters written before the turn of the century.[1] They permitted us to envisage Freud the beginner, the first, and for a decade, the only, psychoanalyst. It is to him that I would like to pay homage.

For orientation and comparison, let us consider the circumstances of another discovery of the nineteenth century, the discovery of a man who also was lonely and calumniated, and eventually recognized as a changer of man's image: Charles Darwin. Darwin came upon his evolutionary laboratory, the Galapagos Islands, on a voyage which was not part of an intended professional design. In fact, he had failed in medicine, not for lack of talent, it would seem, but partially because of an intellectual selectivity which forbade him to learn passively —a self-protective selectivity of the kind for which old Bernard Shaw, in retrospect, patted himself on the back when he said, "My memory rejects and selects; and its selections are not academic. . . . I congratulate myself on this."

Once embarked on the "Beagle," however, and on his way to his "laboratory," Darwin showed that dogged, that prejudiced persistence which is one condition for an original mind becoming a creative one. He now fully developed his superior gift, namely, "noticing things which easily escape attention, and observing them carefully." His physical stamina was inexhaustible. His mind proved ready for the laboratory, as the laboratory seemed to have waited for him. He could fully employ sweeping configurations of thought which had ripened in him: cutting across existing classifications, which assumed a parallel, linear origin of all species from a common pool of creation, he saw everywhere transitions, transmutations, variations, signs of a dynamic struggle for adaptation. The law of natural selection began to "haunt him." And he perceived that man must come under the same law. "I see no possible means of drawing the line and saying, here you must stop."

Darwin, at the age of twenty-seven, went home with his facts and theory, and traveled no more. He gave the scientific world a few papers primarily on geological subjects; then he withdrew to the country, to work, for twenty years, on *The Origin of Species:* he *made* it a long and lonely discovery. He now became physically incapacitated by insomnia, nausea, and chills. His father-doctor could not diagnose his disease, but declared the son too delicate for a career out in the world. The son became a life-long invalid. If his hypersensitivity was a sign of hereditary degeneracy, as some doctors believe, then there never was a degenerate guided more wisely in the utilization of his degeneracy by an inner genius of economy. For "I could . . . collect facts bearing on the origin of species . . . when I could do nothing else from illness." Not that Darwin did not realize what this restriction of his lifespace did to him: when, at the end, even Shakespeare seemed so "intolerably dull" as to nauseate him, he deplored the "curious and lamentable loss of the higher aesthetic tastes" and spoke of an "enfeeblement of the emotional part of our nature."

I do not wish to speculate here on the dynamics of a psycho-neurosis in a man like Darwin. But I do know that a peculiar malaise can befall those who have seen too much, who, in ascertaining new facts in a spirit seemingly as innocent as that of a child who builds with blocks, begin to perceive of the place of these facts in the moral climate of their day. "We physicists have known sin," Oppenheimer has said; but it does not take the use of scientific data for mankind's material destruction to make a scientist feel or behave as if he had sinned. It is enough to have persisted, with the naïveté of genius, on the dissolution of one of the prejudices on which the security and the familiarity of the contemporary image of man is built. But a creative man has no choice. He may come across his supreme task almost accidentally. But once the issue is joined, his task proves to be at the same time intimately related to his most personal conflicts, to his superior selective perception, and to the stubbornness of his one-way will: he must court sickness, failure, or insanity, in order to test the alternative whether the established world will crush him, or whether he will disestablish a sector of this world's outworn fundaments and make place for a new one.

Darwin only dealt with man's biological origins. His achievement, and his "sin," was a theory that made man part of nature. In comparing Darwin's approach to nature with his approach to a man, a recent biographer remarks half-jokingly, "In any case, no man afflicted with a weak stomach and insomnia has any business investigating his own kind."

As we now turn to Freud the psychological discoverer, I hope to make the reader wonder whether anybody *but* one at least temporarily afflicted with psychosomatic symptoms, one temporarily sick of his own kind, could or would investigate his own species—provided only that he had the inclination, the courage, and the mental means of facing his own neurosis with creative persistence. A man, I will submit, could begin to study man's inner world only by appointing his own neurosis that angel who was to be wrestled with and not to be let go, until he would bless the observer.

What was Freud's Galapagos, what species fluttered what kinds of wings before his searching eyes? It has often been pointed out derisively: his creative laboratory was the neurologist's office, the dominant species hysterical ladies—"Fräulein Anna O.," "Frau Emmy v. N.," "Katarina" (not a Fräulein, because she was a peasant).

Freud was thirty when, in 1886, he became the private doctor of such patients. He had not expected to be a practitioner; he had, in fact, received his medical degree belatedly. His mind, too, had been "selective." At the age of seventeen he had chosen medicine in preference to law and politics, when he heard Goethe's "Ode to Nature": the unveiling of Nature's mysteries, not the healing of the sick, provided the first self-image of a doctor. Then came *his* professional moratorium: as in an ascetic reaction to a nature-philosophic indulgence he committed himself to the physiological laboratory and to the monastic service of physicalistic physiology. What geology was to Darwin, physiology was to Freud: a schooling in method. The ideology of the physicalistic-physiologic method of the time was formulated in an oath by two of its outstanding teachers, DuBois Reymond and Brücke: "to put in power this truth: No other forces than the common physical chemical ones are active within the organism. . . . One has either to find the specific way or form of their action by means of the physical mathematical method, or to assume new forces equal in dignity to the chemical physical forces inherent in matter." *New forces equal in dignity:* we will return to this phrase.

When Freud exchanged the academic monastery for the

medical parsonage, he had fully developed a style of work which would have sufficed for an impressively productive life-time. He had published many papers on physiological and neu-rological subjects, and had two major works in preparation. Thus, when he became a practicing neurologist, he left a fu-ture behind him. But he had married the girl who had waited for him, and he wanted a family, in fact, a large one; he had earned the right to have confidence in himself.

Yet, a future anticipated in a man's configurations of thought means more than time not yet spent. To give up the laboratory meant to relinquish a work-discipline and a work-ideology to which Freud had been deeply committed. The work of a specialist catering to the epidemiological market was lacking in what Freud nostalgically called an inner tyrant, i.e., a great principle. Luckily, he had met an older practitioner, Dr. Joseph Breuer, who had shown him that there was a laboratory hidden in the very practice of neurology.

Freud's new laboratory, then, were patients, mostly women, who brought him symptoms which only an overly-serious and searching observer could accept as constituting a field ac-tivated by dignified forces. These ladies suffered from neural-gic pains and anesthesias, from partial paralyses and con-tractions, from tics and convulsions, from nausea and finicki-ness, from the inability to see and from visual hallucinations, from the inability to remember and from painful floods of memory. Popular opinion judged these ladies to be spoiled, just putting on airs—"attention-getting" some of us would call it today. The dominant neuropathology of the day, however, as-sumed some of their disturbances to be a consequence of hereditary degenerative processes in the brain. Freud, too, had learned to treat these patients like partially decerebrated bun-dles, or like children without a will: he had learned to apply massage and electricity to the affected body part and to domi-nate the patient's will by hypnosis and suggestion. He might, for example, order the hypnotized patient to laugh out loud when encountering in the future a certain thought or person or place, the sight of which had previously caused a fit or a paralysis. The awakened patient did laugh out loud, but more often than not, she would become afflicted again, and in connection with something else.

But Freud, like Darwin, could not believe in linear descent —in this instance, of isolated symptoms from defects of the brain. In an array of symptoms he, too, looked for a common principle, a struggle for equilibrium, a clash of forces. And he was convinced that challenging phenomena must have a hidden history. As Freud listened to his hypnotized patients, he realized that they were urgently, desperately offering him series of memories which, seemingly fragmentary, were like variations in search of a theme—a theme which was often found in a historical model event.

Here no detail could be too trivial for investigation. A patient suffers from a persistent illusion of smelling burned pancakes. All right, the smell of burned pancakes shall be the subject of exhaustive analysis. As this smell is traced to a certain scene, the scene vividly remembered, the sensation disappears, to be replaced by the smell of cigars. The smell of cigars is traced to other scenes, in which a man in an authoritative position was present, and in which disturbing subjects had been mentioned in a connection which demanded that the patient control her feelings.

It fits our image of those Victorian days—a time when children in all, and women in most circumstances were to be seen but not heard—that the majority of symptoms would prove to lead back to events when violently aroused affects (love, sex, rage, fear) had come into conflict with narrow standards of propriety and breeding. The symptoms, then, were delayed involuntary communications: using the whole body as spokesman, they were saying what common language permits common people to say directly: "He makes me sick," "She pierced me with her eyes," "I could not swallow that insult," or, as the song has it, "I'm gonna wash that man right out of my hair." Freud the neurologist now became "haunted" by the basic conviction that any neurotic symptom, traced along a path of associated experiences (not of neurological pathways), would lead to the revival in memory of earlier and earlier conflicts, and in doing so would yield a complete history of its origin.

As Freud proceeded with his reconstruction of the past of his patients, a dangerous insight dawned on him: such conflicts as his patients revealed were, in principle, shared by all men. It would be hard, indeed, "to draw the line and say here you must stop." He became aware of the fact that man, in principle, does not remember or understand much of what is most significant in his childhood, and more, that he does not want to. Here, a mysterious *individual prehistory* seemed to loom up, as important for psychology as Darwin's biological prehistory was for biology.

But Darwin had at his disposal the whole tradition of an ancient science. For Freud's psychologic findings, there were, at first, only physiologic methods, his own speculations, and the sayings of writers and philosophers, who, in their way, it seemed, had known it all. Yet, it appears to be part of a creative man's beginnings that he may change his field and yet maintain the manner of work which became part of his first identity as a worker. Freud had investigated the nature of brain lesions by slicing the brains of young animals and foeti. He now investigated memories as representative cross sections of a patient's emotional condition. In successive memories, he traced trends which led, like pathways, to the traumatic past; there experiences of a disruptive nature loomed like lesions interfering with growth. Thus, the search for traumatic events in the individual's forgotten prehistory, his early childhood, replaced the search for lesions in early development.

Psychology, of course, is the preferred field for a transfer of configurations of thought from other fields. The nature of things, or better, man's logical approaches to things is such that analogies—up to a point—reveal true correspondences. But the history of psychology also reveals how consistently neglectful and belated man is in applying to his own nature methods of observation which he has tried out on the rest of nature. That man, the observer, is in some essential way different from the observed world, is clear. But this difference calls for a constant redefinition in the light of new modes of thought. Only thus can man keep wisely different rather than vainly so. Before Copernicus, vanity as well as knowledge insisted that the earth must be in the exact nodal center of God's universe. Well, we know now where we are. Before Darwin, man could claim a different origin from the rest of the animal world with whom he shares a slim margin of earth crust and atmosphere. Before Freud, man (that is, man of the male sex and of the better classes) was convinced that he was fully conscious of all there was to him, and sure of his divine values. Childhood was a mere training ground, in charge of that intermediary race, women.

In such a world female hysteria was implicitly acknowledged by men and men doctors as a symptom of the natural inferiority, the easy degeneracy, of women. When Freud presented to the Vienna Medical Society a case of *male* hysteria, the reaction of his colleagues convinced him that years of isolation lay ahead of him. He accepted it then and there: he never visited that society again. Yet, their reaction proved to be only one small aspect of a memorable crisis in which a new science was almost stillborn, by no means only because of professional isolation, but also because of disturbances in the instrument of observation, the observer's mind. Freud's early writings and letters permit us to see a *threefold crisis:* a crisis in therapeutic technique; a crisis in the conceptualization of clinical experience; and a personal crisis. I shall try to indicate in what way all three crises were, in essence, one, and were the necessary dimensions of discovery in psychology.

First, then, Freud's change in technique. The textbooks describe it as the replacement of the cathartic and the suggestive methods by the psychoanalytic one. In Freud's *Studies on Hysteria,* however, a pervasive change in the doctor-patient relationship is clearly described. Freud judged some of his patients to be outstanding in character and talents, rather than degenerate. He began to let himself be led by the sequence and the nature of their communications. With amused surprise he would admit that a hypnotized patient, in suggesting to him that he should stop interrupting her with his authoritative suggestions, had a point. She fortified her point by unearthing memories which he would not have suspected. He realized that in hypnosis the patients had at their disposal a depth of understanding and a freedom of affect which they did not marshal in normal life. This he had not imposed by suggestion: it was their judgment and their affect, and if they had it in hypnosis, it was part of them. Maybe, if he treated them like whole people, they would learn to realize the wholeness which was theirs. He now offered them a conscious and direct partnership: he made the patient's healthy, if submerged, part his partner in understanding the unhealthy part. Thus was established one basic principle of psychoanalysis, namely, that one can study the human mind only by engaging the fully motivated partnership of the observed individual, and by entering into a sincere contract with him.

But a contract has two partners, at least. The changed image of the patient changed the self-image of the doctor. He realized that habit and convention had made him and his fellow physicians indulge in an autocratic pattern, with not much more circumspection or justification than the very paternal authorities who he now felt had made the patients sick in the first place. He began to divine the second principle of psychoanalysis, namely, that you will not see in another what in principle you have not learned to recognize in yourself. The mental healer must divide himself as well as the patient into an observer and an observed.

The intellectual task faced here, namely, psychoanalytic insight and communication, was a massive one. Today, it is difficult to appreciate the psychosocial task involved. Freud had to relinquish a most important ingredient of the doctor role of the times: the all-knowing father role, which was safely anchored in the whole contemporary cult of the paternal male as the master of every human endeavor except the nursery and the kitchen. This should not be misunderstood: Freud did not, overnight, become a different man. Indeed, there are many who will see nothing in the nature of renunciation of paternalism in him. But we are not speaking here of opinions and roles in the modern sense, of personalities subject to change like the body styles of automobiles which retain little logical relation to the inner motor of the thing, nor to the laws of the road. True roles are a matter of a certain ideologic-esthetic unity, not of opinions and appearances. True change is a matter of worthwhile conflict, for it leads through the painful consciousness of one's position to a new conscience in that position. As Justice Holmes once said, the first step toward a truer faith is the recognition that *I*, at any rate, am *not* God. Furthermore, roles anchored in work-techniques are prepared in the intricacies of a man's life history. Whoever has suffered under and identified with a stern father, must become a stern father himself, or else find an entirely different measure of moral strength, an equal measure of strength. Young Martin Luther's religious crisis is a transcendent example of the heights and the depths of this problem.

Freud, as we have seen, had sought a new inner tyrant in a work-ideology shared with esteemed minds. He had relinquished it. Now, he discarded the practicing neurologist's prevailing role of dominance and of license. This, then, is the first aspect of Freud's crisis: he had to create a new therapeutic role, for which there was no ideological niche in the tradition of his profession. He had to create it—or fail.

The *second* problem which isolated Freud in those years was the course taken by his search for the "energy of equal dignity" which might be the power behind a neurosis; for the mental mechanisms which normally maintain such power in a state of constancy; and for those inner conditions which unleash the destructiveness of that power. The power, as we saw, was first perceived as "affect," the disturbance in the machine, as a "damming up." A long treatise recently found with some of Freud's letters reveals the whole extent of Freud's conflict between the creative urge to say in psychological terms what only literature had known before him, and on the other hand, his desperate obedience to physiology. The treatise is called "A Psychology for Neurologists." [2] Freud introduces it thus: "The intention of this project is to furnish us with a psychology which shall be a natural science: its aim, that is, is to represent psychical processes as quantitatively determined states of specifiable material particles and so to make them plain and

void of contradictions." Freud proceeds to develop a model of
organization of these "particles," a sensitive machine for the
management of qualities and quantities of excitation, such as
are aroused by external and internal stimuli. Physical concepts
are combined with histological concepts to create a kind of neu-
ronic Golem, a robot, in which even consciousness and thought
are mechanistically explainable on the basis of an over-all principle of inner constancy. Here, Freud, at the very beginning of
his career as a psychologist, tried to create a mind-robot, a
thinking-machine, in many ways related to the mechanical and
economic as well as the physiological configurations of his day.
As Freud wrote triumphantly to his friend: "Everything fell
into place, the cogs meshed, the thing really seemed to be a
machine which in a moment would run of itself." But one
month after Freud had sent this manuscript to that friend, he
recanted it. "All I was trying to do," he writes, "was to explain
defense (against affect), but I found myself explaining something from the very heart of nature. I found myself wrestling
with the whole of psychology. Now I want to hear no more
of it." He now calls the psychology a "kind of aberration." This
manuscript, found only accidentally, documents in a dramatic
way the pains to which a discoverer will go *not* to haphazardly
ignore the paths of his tradition, but follow them instead to
their absurd limit, and to abandon them only when the
crossroad of lone search is reached.

In the meantime, clinical work had brought Freud within
sight of his crossroad. His patients, he had become convinced,
were suffering primarily from the "damming up" of one ir-
repressible "affect," namely, sexual sensuality, the existence of
which had been consistently denied by their overclothed parents, and suffered only with furtive shame and anemic degrada-
tion by many of their mothers. In the epidemiological fact of
widespread female hysteria, Freud faced the specific symptoms
of the Victorian age, the price paid, especially by women, for
the hypocritical double standard of the sexes in the dominant
classes, the masters or would-be masters of industrial power.
However, the most glaring epidemiological fact (compare
poliomyelitis, or juvenile delinquency) does not receive

clarification until a seasoned set of theoretical configurations happens to suggest a specific approach. In introducing the energy concept of a sexual libido, which from birth onward is the fuel in everything we desire and love, and which our mind-machine must learn to transform according to our goals and ideals—in this concept Freud found at once the most fitting answer to the questions posed by his patients' memories, and the theory most consistent with his search for a "dignified force." But alas, it was also the most irrationally repugnant solution thinkable in his prudish times, and a solution of emotional danger to the observer. For, indeed, where "to draw the line"?

Here Freud's genetic fervor led to a faulty reconstruction. In the certainty of being on the right track, and yet shaken by inner and outer resistances, he overshot the mark. In search for a pathogenic Ur(-primal)-event, he was led to regard as historically real the patients' accounts of passive sexual experiences in the first years of childhood, and to consider the fathers of the patients the perpetrators of such events. He later confessed: "The analysis had led by the correct path to such infantile sexual traumas, and yet, these were not true. Thus, the basis of reality had been lost. At that time, I would gladly have dropped the whole thing." But finally, "I reflected that if hysterics trace back their symptoms to imaginary traumas, then this new fact signifies that they create such scenes in phantasy, and hence psychic reality deserves to be given a place next to actual reality." Freud would soon be able to describe psychic reality systematically as the domain of phantasy, dream, and mythology, and as the imagery and language of a universal unconscious, thus adding as a scientific dimension to the image of man what had been an age-old intuitive knowledge.

In the meantime, had his error detracted from the "dignity" of sexuality? It does not seem so. Knowing what we know today it is obvious that somebody had to come sometime who would decide that it would be better for the sake of the study of human motivation to call too many rather than too few things sexual, and then to modify the hypothesis implied by careful inquiry. For it was only too easy to do what had become civilization's "second nature," that is, in the face of the man's sexual and aggressive drives ever again to beat a hasty retreat into romanticism and religionism, into secrecy, ridicule, and lechery. The patients' phantasies were sexual, and something sexual must have existed in those early years. Freud later called that something *psychosexuality,* for it encompasses the phantasies as well as the impulses, the psychology as well as the biology in the earliest stages of human sexuality.

Today one can add that Freud's error was not even as great as it seemed. First of all, sexual seductions of children do occur, and are dangerous to them. But more important, the general provocation and exploitation of the child by parent and grandparent for the sake of petty emotional relief, of suppressed vengefulness, of sensual self-indulgence, and sly righteousness must be recognized not only as evident in case histories, but as a universal potentiality often practiced and hypocritically rationalized by very "moral" individuals, indeed. Samuel Butler's *The Way of All Flesh* is probably the most forceful statement on record. What today is decried as "momism" in this country, existed in analogous form in the father's role in the Victorian world: it is only necessary to think of Hitler's official account of his father-hate and the appeal of this account for millions of young Germans, to know that here is a smoldering theme of general explosiveness. In finding access to the altogether fateful fact of man's prolonged childhood, Freud discovered that infantile man, in addition to and often under the guise of being trained, is being ruefully exploited, only to become in adulthood nature's most systematic and sadistic exploiter. Freud's search thus added another perspective of as yet unforeseeable importance to the image of man.

Yet, this discovery, too, had to pass through its lonely stage. Freud had made a significant mistake, and he was not one to shirk the responsibility for it either publicly or privately. He made it part of his self-analysis.

About the first self-analysis in history we know from the letters, already mentioned, which Freud wrote to Dr. Wilhelm

Fliess of Berlin. The extent and the importance of Freud's friendship with Fliess was not even suspected until the letters revealed it.

The two doctors met for what they called their "congresses," long weekends in some European city or town. Their common heritage of education permitted them to roam in varied conversations, as they vigorously perambulated through the countryside. Freud seems to have shared Nietzsche's impression that a thought born without locomotion could not be much good. But among the theories discussed by the two doctors, there were many which never saw the light of publication. Thus, Fliess, for many years, was the first and only one to share Freud's thinking.

Psychoanalysts do not seem to like this friendship much; Fliess, after all, was not even a psychoanalyst. Some of us now read of Freud's affection for this man wishing we could emulate that biographer of Goethe who, in the face of Goethe's claim that at a certain time he had loved a certain lady dearly, remarks in a footnote: "here Goethe is mistaken." Freud, we now say, must have overestimated this friendship in an irrational, almost pathological way. But what, after all, do thinkers need friends for? So that they can share speculations, each alternately playing benevolent authority to the other, each be the other's co-conspirator, each be applauding audience, and cautioning chorus. Freud calls Fliess his *"Other one,"* to whom he can entrust what is not ready for "the *others*." Fliess, at any rate, seems to have had the stature and the wide education which permitted Freud to entrust him with "imaginings, transpositions, and guesses." That Freud's imaginings turned out to be elements of a true vision and a blueprint for a science, while Fliess' ended in a kind of mathematical mysticism, provides no reason to belittle the friendship. The value of a friend may sometimes be measured by the magnitude of the problem which we discard with him.

The friendship seems to have been unmarred by irrational disturbances, until, in 1894, Freud consulted Fliess in regard to his own symptoms and moods, which he condenses in the word *Herzelend*—something like "misery of the heart." Fliess had cauterized swellings in Freud's nose and had urged him to give up his beloved cigars. Suddenly, the intellectual communication appears jammed. "I have not looked at your excellent case histories," Freud writes, and indicates that his latest communication to Fliess "was abandoned in the middle of a sentence." He continues: "I am suspicious of you this time, because this heart business [*Herzangelegenheit*] of mine is the first occasion on which I have ever heard you contradict yourself." At that time, Freud speaks of his discoveries with the anguish of one who has seen a promised land which he must not set his foot on: "I have the distinct feeling," he writes, "that I have touched on one of the great secrets of nature." This tedium of thought seems to have joined the "heart misery" and was now joined by a mistrust of the friend. He wrote, "Something from the deepest depths of my own neurosis has ranged itself against my taking a further step in understanding of the neuroses, and you have somehow been involved."

Freud, at this point, had developed toward Fliess what later, when he understood it, he called a transference, that is, that peculiar mixture of overestimation and mistrust, which man is so especially ready to bestow on people in significant positions such as doctors and priests, leaders and kings, and other superiors, competitors, and adversaries. It is called transference, because, where it is neurotic, it is characterized by the blurring of an adult relationship through the transfer upon it of infantile loves and hates, dependencies and impotent rages. Transference thus also implies a partial regression to childish attitudes. It was this very area which, at that time, Freud was trying to understand in his patients. Yet, in Freud, it was quite obviously related to the processes of creativity. We have seen how young Freud, in his student days, had subdued an almost incestuous eagerness to "unveil nature" by the compensatory concentration on laboratory work. He had thus postponed a conflict by realizing only one part of his identity. But when, in his words, he "touched on one of the secrets of nature," he was forced to realize that other, that more creative identity. For any refuge to the established disciplines of scientific inquiry was, as the project proved, forever closed. It is in those moments when our divided selves threaten to drag each other down, that a friend, as Nietzsche said, becomes the life-saver which keeps us afloat and together; no wonder that here we can experience a desperate dependency comparable to that of a child on his father.

Freud thus discovered another principle in his new work, namely, that psychological discovery is accompanied by some irrational involvement of the observer, and that it cannot be communicated to another without a certain irrational involvement of both. Such is the stuff of psychology; here it is not enough to put on an armor of superiority or aloofness in the hope that, like the physicist's apron, it will protect vital organs against the radiation emanating from the observed. Here, only the observer's improved insight into himself can right the instrument, protect the observer, and permit the communication of the observed.

In his transference to Fliess, Freud recognized one of the most important transferences of all: the transfer of an early father-image on later individuals and events. And here we can recognize the pervasiveness in these crises of the great father theme. We saw this theme in Freud's determination not to play autocratic father to patients already crushed by autocracy; we recognized this theme as the core of his tendentious error in the genetic reconstruction of his patients' childhood; and we observe it in his filial reactions to Fliess. A dream, he now reported to Fliess, had clearly revealed to him the fact and the explanation for the fact, that an irrational wish to blame the fathers for their children's neuroses had dominated him.

Having established, then, both the actual and the fantastic aspects of a universal father-image, Freud now could break through to the first prehistoric Other of them all: the loving mother. He was free to discover the whole Oedipus complex, and to recognize it as a dominant theme in world literature and in mythologies around the world. Only then could he understand the full extent to which he, when sick and bewildered, had made a parent-figure out of Fliess, so that that mystic Other might help him analyze himself "as if he were a stran ger." He concluded that "self-analysis is really impossible, otherwise there would be no illness. . . . I can only analyze myself with objectively acquired knowledge." This insight is the basis for what later became the training analysis, that is, the preventive and didactic psychoanalytic treatment of every prospective psychoanalyst.

The friendship, for other reasons too, had outlived itself. It ended when Freud, in a way, could least afford to lose it. It was after the appearance of *The Interpretation of Dreams.* Freud then, as later, considered this book his most fundamental contribution; he then also believed it to be his last. And, as he wrote, "not a leaf has stirred": for months, for years, there were no book reviews, no sales to speak of. Where there was interest, it was mostly disbelief and calumniation. At this time, Freud seems temporarily to have despaired of his medical way of life. Fliess offered a meeting at Easter. But this time Freud refused. "It is more probable that I shall avoid you," he writes. "I have conquered my depression, and now . . . it is slowly healing. . . . In your company . . . your fine and positive biological discoveries would rouse my innermost (impersonal) envy. . . . I should unburden my woes to you and come back dissatisfied . . . no one can help me in what depresses me, it is my cross, which I must bear. . . ." A few letters later, he refers to his patients' tendency to prolong the treatment beyond the acquisition of the necessary insight. "Such prolongation is a compromise between illness and health which patients themselves desire, and . . . the physician must therefore not lend himself to it." It is clear that he has now recognized such "prolongation and compromise" in his friendship as well, and that he will refuse to permit himself a further indulgence in the dependence on Fliess. But he will sorely miss him—"my one audience," as he calls him.

In the course of this friendship a balance was righted: "feminine" intuition, "childlike" curiosity, and "artistic" freedom of style were recognized and restored as partners of the masculine "inner tyrant" in the process of psychological discovery. And Fliess? According to him the friendship was shipwrecked on the age-old rock of disputed priorities: Freud, he said, envied him. And, indeed, Freud had expressed envy that Fliess worked "with light, not darkness, with the sun and not the unconscious." But it does not seem probable that Freud would have changed places.

These, then, were the dimensions of the crisis during which and through which psychoanalysis was born. But lest anyone form the faulty image of a lamentably torn and tormented man and physician, it must be reported that the Freud of those years was what today we would call an adjusted individual, and what then was a decent and an able one: a man who took conscientious care of all the patients who found their way to his door, who with devotion and joy raised a family of six children, who was widely read and well-groomed, traveled with curiosity, walked (or, as we would say, exercised) with abandon, loved good food and wine wisely, and his cigars unwisely. But he was not too adapted or too decent to approach a few things in life with decisive, with ruthless integrity. All of which in a way he could ill afford, for the times were bad for a medical specialist; it was the time of the first economic depression of the modern industrial era, it was a time of "poverty in plenty." Nor did the self-analysis "reform" or chasten Freud. Some of the vital conflicts which pervaded the friendship with Fliess remained lifelong, as did some of the early methodological habits: in *Totem and Taboo,* Freud again reconstructed—this time on the stage of history—an "event" which, though an unlikely happening in past actuality, yet proved most significant as a timeless theme. But that early period of Freud's work gave to the new science its unique direction, and with it gave its originator that peculiar unification of personal peculiarities which makes up a man's identity, becomes the cornerstone of his kind of integrity, and poses his challenge to contemporaries and generations to come.

The unique direction of the new science consisted of the introduction into psychology of a system of coördinates which I can only summarize most briefly. His early energy concept provided the *dynamic-economic* coördinate. A *topological* coördinate emerged from the refinement of that early mind-robot; while the *genetic* coördinate was established on the basis of the reconstruction of childhood. This is psychoanalysis; any insight and only insight traceable in these coördinates is psychoanalytic insight. But these coördinates can be understood only through systematic study.

Since those early days of discovery, psychoanalysis has established deep and wide interrelationships with other methods of investigation, with methods of naturalist observation, of somatic examination, of psychological experiment, of anthropological field work, and of scholarly research. If, instead of enlarging on all these, I have focused on the early days, and on the uniqueness of the original Freudian experience, I have done so because I believe that an innovator's achievement can be seen most dramatically in that moment when he, alone against historical adversity and inner doubts, and armed only with the means of persuasion, gives a new direction to human awareness—new in focus, new in method, and new in its inescapable morality.

The dimensions of Freud's discovery, then, are contained in a triad which, in a variety of ways, remains basic to the practice of psychoanalysis, but also to its applications. It is the triad of a *therapeutic contract,* a *conceptual design,* and *systematic self-analysis.*

In psychoanalytic practice, this triad can never become routine. As new categories of suffering people prove amenable to psychoanalytic therapy, new techniques come to life, new aspects of the mind find clarification, and new therapeutic roles are created. Today, the student of psychoanalysis receives a training psychoanalysis which prepares him for the emotional hazards of his work. But he must live with the rest of mankind, in this era of "anxiety in plenty," and neither his personal life nor the very progress of his work will spare him renewed conflicts, be his profession ever so recognized, ever so organized. Wide recognition and vast organization will not assure—they may even endanger—the basic triad, for which the psychoanalyst makes himself responsible, to wit: that as a clinician he accept his contract with the patient as the essence of his field of study and relinquish the security of seemingly more "objective" methods; that as a theorist he maintain a sense of obligation toward continuous conceptual redefinition and resist the lure of seemingly "deeper" philosophic short cuts; and finally, that as a humanist he put self-observant vigilance above the satisfaction of seeming professional omnipotence. The responsibility is great. For, in a sense, the psychoanalytic method must remain forever a "controversial" tool, a tool for the detection of that aspect of the total image of man which at a given time is being neglected or exploited, repressed or suppressed by the prevailing technology and ideology—including hasty "psychoanalytic" ideologies.

Freud's triad remains equally relevant in the applications of psychoanalysis to the behavioral sciences, and to the humanities. An adult studying a child, an anthropologist studying a tribe, or a sociologist studying a riot sooner or later will be confronted with data of decisive importance for the welfare of those whom he is studying, while the strings of his own motivation will be touched, sometimes above and sometimes well below the threshold of awareness. He will not be able, for long, to escape the necessary conflict between his emotional participation in the observed events and the methodological rigor required to advance his field and human welfare. Thus, his studies will demand, in the long run, that he develop the ability to include in his observational field his human obligations, his methodological responsibilities, and his own motivations. In doing so, he will, in his own way, repeat that step in scientific conscience which Freud dared to make.

That shift, however, cannot remain confined to professional partnerships such as the observer's to the observed, or the doctor's with his patient. It implies a fundamentally new morality in the adult's relationship to childhood: to the child within him, to his child before him, and to every man's children around him.

But the fields dealing with man's historical dimension are far apart in their appraisal of childhood. Academic minds whose long-range perspectives can ignore the everyday urgencies of the curative and educative arts, blithely go on writing whole world histories without any women and children in them, whole anthropologies without any reference to the varying styles of childhood. As they record what causal chain can be discerned in political and economic realities, they seem to shrug off as historical accidents due to "human nature" such fears and rages in leaders and masses as are clearly the residue of childish emotions now under study. True, these scholars may have been repelled by the first enthusiastic intrusion of doctors of the mind into their ancient disciplines. But their refusal to consider the historical relevance of human childhood can be due only to that deeper and more universal emotional aversion which Freud himself foresaw. On the other hand, it must be admitted that in clinical literature and in literature turned altogether clinical, aversion has given place to a faddish preoccupation with the more sordid aspects of childhood as the beginning and the end of human destiny.

Neither of these trends can hinder the emergence, in due time, of a new truth. The stream of world events, in all its historical lawfulness, is fed by the energies and thoughts of successive generations; and each generation brings to the existing historical trends its particular version of an inescapable conflict: the conflict with its individual "prehistories." This conflict helps to drive man toward the astonishing things he does—and it can be his undoing. It is a condition of man's humanity—and the prime cause of his bottomless inhumanity.

Freud not only revealed this conflict by dissecting the strains of its pathological manifestations. He also pointed to what is so largely and so regularly lost in the conflict: he spoke of "the child's radiant intelligence"—the naïve zest, the natural courage, the unconditional faith of childhood which are submerged by fearful teachings and by limited and limiting information.

Now and again, we are moved to say that a genius preserved in himself the clear eye of the child. But do we not all too easily justify man's ways and means by pointing to the occasional appearance of genius? Do we not know (and are we not morbidly eager to know) how tortured a genius can be by the very history of his ascendance, how often a genius is driven to destroy with one hand as he creates with the other?

In Freud, a genius turned a new instrument of observation

back on his childhood, back on all childhood. He invented a specific method for the detection of that which universally spoils the genius of the child in every human being. In teaching us to recognize the daimonic evil in children, he urged us not to smother the creatively good. Since then, the nature of growth in childhood has been studied by ingenious observers over the world: never before has mankind known more about its own past—phylogenetic and ontogenetic. Thus, we may see Freud as a pioneer in a self-healing, balancing trend in human awareness. For now that technical invention readies itself really to conquer the moon, generations to come may well be in need of being more enlightened in their drivenness, and more conscious of the laws of individuality; they may well need to preserve more childlikeness in order to avoid utter cosmic childishness.

Freud, before he went into medicine, wanted to become a lawyer and politician, a lawmaker, a *Gesetzgeber*. When, in 1938, he was exiled from his country, he carried under his arm a manuscript on Moses, the supreme law-giver of the people whose unique fate and whose unique gifts he had accepted as his own. With grim pride he had chosen the role of one who opens perspectives on fertile fields to be cultivated by others. As we look back to the beginnings of his work, and forward to its implications, we may well venture to say: Freud the physician in finding a method of healing himself in the very practice of emotional cure has given a new, a psychological rationale for man's laws. He has made the decisive step toward a true interpenetration of the psychological with the technological and the political in the human order.

EIGHT

THE CURRENT IMPACT OF FREUD ON AMERICAN PSYCHOLOGY[1]

GARDNER MURPHY

When George Kelly asked me to speak to you on this topic, my first impulse was to ask if the word "current" might be omitted. I have so long dealt with everything in developmental terms that I have lost the capacity to see things as they are at any given time. On second thought, however, I began to like this word. The term "current" means flowing; so I *can* have my time dimension, if I wish. This is likewise the word used to describe the flow of electricity, and it is the electrical kind of flowing with which we are dealing in this instance; not with the gentle rippling of water, but with the tingling or shocking effects of electricity. Third, the word "current" is followed in this title by the enormous hammer blow of the word "impact," one of the finest words in English. The impression is thus correctly given that all flows smoothly until you strike a wall, or a thunderhole, as they say on the Maine coast, where the dead heave of the wave strikes that which it cannot move; or, as my mother used to say, an irresistible force strikes an immovable object. That is Freud! And if you will look at the psychology of 1900—that was psychology! The result of such successive impacts, of course, is that the coastline of Maine is gradually eroded; if not according to the heart's desire, at least according to an orderly, natural law regarding the interaction of profound realities in this world with which it may be our job to come to terms.

I am grateful indeed to have this opportunity to attempt an assessment of a great germinal influence and a great human being. Some of the Executive Committee may well have made a mistake in voting to invite me, perhaps being under the delusion that I am non-partisan. "What," they may feel today, "are you *really*, then, a Freudian?" Indeed, I am! Likewise, a Darwinian, a Pavlovian, an Adlerian, a Sullivanian, a Thurstonian, a Tolmanian. I conceive no disloyalty in resonating intensely to the great visions of these men. I shall not be frightened by those who say that an eclectic like myself snips from the system a bit of fabric which he then joins in the manner of a crazyquilt to all which has a semblance of likeness to it. I shall go on believing that the integrity of the living system is maintained, although the ideas that we use at any given time in trying to understand it are borrowed from very different cultural epochs and very different human individuals. And I believe that the insights of Freud, with reference to human motivation, impulse control, reality testing, and much else besides, are among the most profound ever vouchsafed to an investigator.

Despite Freud's long and arduous training under Brücke and his extraordinary capacity to observe, to develop and to test hypotheses, my reverence for Freud is in the first instance the reverence for a tremendous dream, a magnificent obsession which, after the icy reception in Vienna in the early nineties, led him unswervingly to the development of an epic view of human nature. The epic, whether it be the *Odyssey, The Divine Comedy, Paradise Lost,* or *Faust,* is a way of looking at man, in which artistic congruity and power are even more important than internal consistency or detailed conformity to fact; and while I reverence Freud as a contributor of many facts of major importance, I believe just as important is an assessment of his role as epic poet. He had at times the relentless logic of inductive and deductive method, but even when he failed here, he had the artistic feeling for the integrity of a dynamic whole.

While I should be abusing my privilege here to take much time to tell you what I accept and what I reject in Freud's vast system, I would name as an illustration of a specific contribution, which I believe to be of enormous value to all psychologists, his conception of the deterministic processes which appear in the psychopathology of everyday life, and his analysis of the role of internalization of the parents in the development of conscience. I believe that time will show that the central place in the Freudian epic is given to the doctrine of the unconscious, as first developed with respect to the conversion of latent to manifest dreams.

This Freudian epic is simply the most recent of a series of evolutionary epics of which the first in our Western tradition is that of Epicurus and Lucretius. With them the world is a system of material particles spinning and coalescing, forming ever more complex patterns which reach great power and beauty without guidance of any forces outside of themselves. This conception, remade out of the scientific materials of the seventeenth century by Hobbes and La Mettrie, found a poetic expression in the pantheistic monism of Spinoza, and underlay the cosmologies of the eighteenth century intellectualists. Within the bosom of such intellectualism, however, come to life again the doctrine of instinct implicit in the older theories; and this in the French evolutionist school and in German romanticism, as well, gave a drive-directed, and a goal-directed quality to the blind drifting processes of a mechanistic era. Darwinian evolutionary theory showed a way in which the life drives and the mechanical principles could be seen as two aspects of the same reality, with adaptation to environment as the result.

Evolutionism entered deeply into Freud. The ground was laid for a conception of life as struggle, and the struggle as essentially related to the life-generating processes. His exposure to Brentano's *act psychology* probably carried him further still toward mental life as an active quest rather than a sheer concatenation of associations. The medical stage had been set by the investigations of hypnosis and the first tentative discoveries of subconscious mental processes. This brought to fruition Freud's magnificent conception of the drive-directed conflict-born effort of animality in the direction of humanness, a struggle between unconscious instinctual trends and the socially-responsible ego. From this emphasis upon the conversion of animality to humanness there developed, after the paper on Narcissism in 1914, more and more concern with the nature of such humanness as related to parental identifications, impulse control and the more refined forms of reality testing. At the time of Freud's death, psychoanalysis was a balanced system, a tripod of id, ego, and superego.

This epic of love and death remains a lineal descendant of Lucretius and Spinoza; it declines to accept the optimistic conclusions of a philosophy of eternal improvement, and rejects all temptations in the direction of theocratic dualism or perfectionism. The respects in which this Freudian epic transcends the earlier versions of this cosmic drama are these: first, the specification of drive; second, the conception that life tendencies are deeper, more primordial than the phenomenon of consciousness, which is at best an elaboration or screening technique which can in no way obliterate or weaken the basic drive modulations; third, as James Harvey Robinson said, the discovery that, "as children, we are at our most impressionable age"; fourth, the conception that the ego is a derivative rather than a primary expression of life; and fifth, most general of all propositions, that all psychological activity is motivated, driven, guided, directed by life tensions seeking resolution. It is in this latter sense that psychoanalysis is a consistently dynamic psychology. It begins with force and ends with the dissipation of force through a tension-reducing process, always to be followed by fresh tension accumulations and further discharges. Every idle fancy, every quick calculation, every odd remark, every whim and every great decision alike, spring basically from the tensions of the tissues within us.

2

Now, to try to evaluate the impact of the epic as a whole or of the specific methods and doctrines involved within it, we must ask ourselves first what the evidence may be regarding the actual impact of Freud's ideas upon the various aspects of contemporary psychology and, second, how a psychologist today who *uses* Freud differs from one who *does not* use him. I state the issue this way because I cannot, with any enthusiasm, try to say what would have been if something else had not happened. I cannot tell you what psychology would have been like if there had been no Freud. I can, however, attempt in a groping way to differentiate between a psychologist who makes avid use of Freud and one who makes little or no use of him. I am, therefore, using a crude rating scale which may, I hope, give some first approximation to a guess as to the impact of Freud on the various specialized divisions of modern psychology. I will suggest various topics or divisions within which psychologists make specialized studies. In attempting to evaluate Freud's impact, the scale reads as follows: None = 0; slight = 1; limited = 2; moderate = 3; considerable = 4; great = 5; very great = 6. I will now attempt, in what I hope is not too dogmatic a fashion, a summary of what I believe these influences to be. I start from zero and work up to six.

Physiological Psychology—0. If this appears arbitrary, I can perhaps justify it by noting that when an extraordinary volume appeared three years ago on human biology and pathology, by 108 authors and investigators, the name Freud did not appear in the index. This may seem odd in view of the basic physiological nature of Freud's conception of drives. You will perhaps recall that he took his conception from the biology of the late nineteenth century, adding to it as he saw fit, for example, from L. L. Woodruff's study of protozoa, in a fashion to suit his purpose, but not in a fashion likely to have repercussions upon the exact laboratory methods of this discipline.

His biochemical conception of the nature of the erotic impulse appears to have evoked no interest among physiologists. The physiological psychology of today, as I scan it, is literally and completely non-Freudian; it is not even anti-Freudian.

Intelligence—o. This may puzzle you. Do we not have mounting evidence that intelligence is a very complex dynamic process; that, as Wechsler points out, there are non-intellectual components in intelligence; that intelligence is a complex expression of biological individuality; that it is, in Freud's sense, dynamic? Well, I suppose much of that is true. But I cannot see in the specialized literature of intelligence or intelligence-testing any evidence of Freudian influence at all, except that the so-called projective uses of intelligence tests, which carry us away from research studies of intelligence as such, do very definitely show a Freudian influence. My point, rather, is that the conceptual system which comes down to us from Spearman, and from Thurstone, looks for empirical cross-relationships between various types of abilities, and that, in spite of a certain bias toward purposivism evident in the thinking of many factor analysts, I cannot see that Psychoanalysis directly influenced their work. Perhaps I should say 1 rather than o, the

FREUD'S IMPACT ON THE DIVISIONS OF MODERN PSYCHOLOGY	
Physiological Psychology	0
Intelligence	0
Learning	1
Thinking	1
Perception	1
Comparative Psychology	1
Vocational Psychology	1
Drive, Feeling and Emotion, and Memory	2
Child and Adolescent Psychology	2
Social Psychology	3
Industrial Psychology	3
Imagination	4
Abnormal Psychology	5
Clinical Psychology	6
Personality	6

Index: o = None; 1 = slight; 2 = limited; 3 = moderate; 4 = considerable; 5 = great; 6 = very great. Scaled by G. Murphy, 1956.

purpose of such a chart being simply to draw a contrast, anyway. If you compare the use of a person-drawing test by Florence Goodenough with its use by Karen Machover, you will have the contrast which I hope to bring out.

With the rating of 1 on my scale there is included *learning, thinking, perception,* and the fields of *comparative* and *vocational psychology. Learning* theory is still primarily Pavlovian with rich embellishments, though some remnants from Thorndike and even from Ebbinghaus are still evident, and the main dissenter from the current primary doctrines, namely, Tolman, has been mainly influenced by Gestalt psychology and purposivism. It is nevertheless Tolman's vigorous defense of the concept of cathexis and his emphasis upon conflict that leads me to make the score 1 rather than 0. The comprehensive volumes on learning theory seem to vindicate this judgment. I am sure there would be some who would agree that the Yale efforts at integration of psychoanalysis and Hullian learning theory are of major weight, in which case you should probably shove this 1 up to 2.

The compendia now available on the *psychology of thought and judgment* do not seem to have much place for Freud. Thinking is still treated for the most part, and treated systematically, as a special case of associative process involving stimulus, set, inhibition, and other earlier concepts. Those of you familiar with the analytic material on creative thought will be surprised, but I shall ask you only to check with those studies in which thinking itself, rather than its relation to personality expression, is involved (a topic reserved for consideration later).

I note that *comparative psychology* has made some use, here and there, of Freudian ideas, but in most instances it appears to come to the same types of events through different paths—note, for example, the work of Hebb, and of the ethologists Lorenz and Tinbergen—rather than directly deriving ideas from Freud. One might think of the efforts to document psychoanalytic principles by the use of animals; I think here of J. McV. Hunt's and Alexander Wolf's studies of infantile inhibition as related to adult functioning. I cannot see, however, that ethologists derive their ideas in any sense from Freud.

Rather, I think it is extraordinary that Freud, after seventy-five years of discussion of such functions, could not make himself heard, and that the new studies of "imprinting" are not bracketed together with rather similar phenomena described by Freud in the case of the human young. I have given *vocational psychology* a 1 because of the use by some vocational counselors of conceptions of unconscious dynamics.

Now, with a value of 2, I have included the specialized topics of *drive, feeling and emotion,* and *memory,* and the areas known as *child and adolescent psychology.* In nearly every treatise on *drive theory,* of course, and on *feeling and emotion,* there is some reference to Freud, but usually simply as one of the theorists rather than one whose data are easily assimilated into what the author is trying to do. Drive theory, as we shall see, is used in a special way when one is dealing with personality theory as a whole. But when dealing simply with the analysis of drives, as such, the orientation is likely to be mainly physiological and, to some degree, comparative; but in these fields, as noted, Freud has made but little headway. The physiologists, notably Cannon, still continue to dominate the study of *emotion,* as such. *Memory* is perhaps the clearest example thus far considered of the genuine impact of Freud upon a standard laboratory subject-matter within the accepted field of experimental psychology. Though often somewhat misdirected through lack of orientation as to what Freud's theory of repression entails, there is nevertheless much interest in the role of affectivity in relation to memory processes, and these do indeed appear to owe much to Freud. In the case of *child psychology,* of course, some systematic treatises are almost wholly Freudian. I refer, of course, to such authors as Susan Isaacs. But you would instantly think of these authors as psychoanalysts, and if you looked to the systematic books on child psychology as such, you would find, I think, variations in warmth or coolness toward Freud, but none which actually give Freud's emphasis the cardinal position in the system. I admit that I was rather amazed to notice the huge Carmichael *Manual of Child Psychology* almost completely innocent of reference to Freud's concepts, but my amazement is a purely personal matter, and the record here and elsewhere would appear to show that child psychology cannot be graded at a point higher than 2 on my present scale.

The story is not very different with reference to *social* and *industrial psychology,* but may warrant a score of 3. While some outstanding social psychologists still align themselves with an individualistic position, emphasizing the powers and capacities and limitations of individuals in their social responses, and others go far afield in quest of man's richer social relationships and the study of culture, while a third group attempt to find a language which will do justice both to individuality and to group membership, I find no social psychology with any considerable influence which could be considered primarily Freudian. The cross-cultural material, especially from preliterate societies, is ordinarily used freely or even abundantly nowadays in the teaching of social psychology, and it is through this material from the anthropologists who are already deeply steeped in Freud that a considerable amount of Freudian material gets into our social psychology. A strictly Freudian social psychology, written thirty-six years ago by Everett Dean Martin, has remained almost without influence. There is a huge psychoanalytic literature on myth, ritual, group and crowd phenomena, sifted and resifted until very little has gotten into the standard social psychology of today. The same would be true for *industrial psychology,* except that perhaps the unconscious motivations found in industrial conflict might warrant a slightly higher Freudian score.

I think *creativeness* and *imagination* generally, as contrasted with the more ritualized flow of association in ordinary associative tasks, would warrant a score of 4. This field is, however, very rapidly undergoing change, owing to the vigorous large-scale research enterprises in creative fantasy now being undertaken. Here the Freudian impact seems to be very considerable and increasing.

Certainly, with this audience, it is hardly necessary to labor the point that *abnormal psychology* deserves a score of five or six. Despite a few successful approaches still current which belittle or ignore Freud, Freudian ideas are, in general, coming to be used more and more by non-Freudians. Many specialized research studies and many textbooks are almost wholly Freudian, except for chapters on mental defect and organic psychoses, which present rather limited opportunities as yet for such treatment. *Clinical psychology,* I think none would deny, certainly shows a very great Freudian impact, as does the *psychology of normal personality* in its developmental and structural aspects, and to these I give a 6.

3

I come now to a very difficult task. I promised to attempt a rough control on the influence of Freud by comparing those psychologists who use him with those who, on the contrary, refer to him only in a distant way, with threadbare references suggesting their unfamiliarity with the fiber of his thought, or those by whom he is not mentioned. From such a point of view we may discuss for a moment the kinds of psychological impacts that have definitely been present since the early twentieth century, which we shall assume to have been present in the environment of all psychologists. In spite of all complication, we shall use the pretense, then, that an independent variable—namely, familiarity with Freud—differentiates the group who display the impact and those who do not.

But in order to attempt such a comparison, we need some reckoning of the major forces at work in psychology aside from Freud which presumably exerted some sort of effect on *every* psychologist since the early years of this century. Perhaps we can learn a little about what these forces could do *without* Freud. What are these forces? First, evolutionary biology, as represented in the studies of reflex action and tropisms and, of course, the individualizing method of Francis Galton; the role of the central nervous system (especially as studied by Sherrington); the autonomic nervous system and glands of internal secretion (especially as studied by Cannon); the experimental psychology of perception (as dominated by Helmholtz, Wundt, and Titchener), upon which was grafted, after 1912, Gestalt psychology; the experimental psychology of learning and memory (dominated by Ebbinghaus, G. E. Müller, and Thorndike); intellectual functions and their assessment and measurement (as dominated especially by Binet); the impact of factorial concepts which began with Spearman; the parallel development of factorial concepts of personality based mainly on ratings (especially by the British School); and the beginnings of non-analytic personality testing (as represented, for example, in June Downey's will-temperament tests). A genuine psychology of personality, in the sense of German studies of character types and of the psychology of expression, still innocent of Freudian coloration, was taking shape in the early years of this century. And by 1920 there was a full-fledged American personality psychology, dominated by concepts from Pavlov and Bechterev, and especially J. B. Watson. Watson did, indeed, borrow a very considerable chunk from Freud in his discussion of dreams and of symbolic behavior; but there was likewise a very substantial personality psychology standing on objectivist or behaviorist legs. Kraepelin's clinical psychiatry was likewise well known.

Perhaps this survey will convince you that I am not just misremembering my own first days in psychology, when I tell you quite soberly that in those days at Yale in 1914 where I took psychology with Elliot Frost, Roswell Angier, and others, using experiments from Wundt, Ebbinghaus, and Titchener, tests taken from Whipple, and some serious experimental attempts in almost every division of psychology that then existed, we did definitely think hard about the psychology of personality. And there was one very exciting day in which Elliott Frost mentioned Freud's concept of dreams, against which he was in no way prejudiced. But that one day, a foreign body in the course, survived as a foreign body and had at first no particular effect on the rest.

But I have been describing general academic psychology. What about clinical psychology in those days? Was it likewise fairly innocent of Freud? Well, if by "those days" one happens to mean 1914, there were the new Binet tests which Goddard had translated; and both Yerkes and Terman were at work on new scales. Healy had ingeniously developed performance tests, and there were many tests of perceptual and motor functions. The concept of a personality test, I am quite sure, would not have been fully understood. The Woodworth Personal Data Sheet was a World War I product. At Columbia, when I began to teach there in the '20's, a clinical psychologist was a person in training in psychometrics who learned, of course, something about the work of a psychiatrist and a psychiatric social worker, and who fitted into the measurement role. When Beck offered a dissertation on the Rorschach at Columbia in 1930, the staff, including, of course, myself, were both ignorant and skeptical. We had passed our German examinations some time previously, I can assure you, but as to our keeping in touch with untranslated work, that was another matter.

If, therefore, you follow my attempt at a control method by *extrapolating* up to the present day, the system of viewpoints and methods already mentioned, *minus Freud,* you will have to imagine clinical psychology, as of 1956, as a fulfillment, refinement, and modern development of the Galtonian, Kraepelinian, and Watsonian conceptions of human individuality, but with heavy emphasis upon psychometric, perceptual, and motor measurement. You cannot even allow yourself to smuggle in sentence-completion and association tests to any great extent. For although these existed they seemed to offer no very great promise until somehow the work of Freud and Jung gave them a certain relevance for the study of unconscious conflict. It was indeed the psychoanalytic use of association tests, from the era before the split between Freud and Jung, that offered the most definite antithesis to the preoccupation with cognitive and motor measurements as such.

But have we done justice to the dynamic psychiatry that was already available? What about the French psychiatric giants, Charcot and Janet; the brilliant experimental work of Binet and Feré, dealing with hypnosis; the majestic medical psychology of Ribot; the Americanization of French psychiatry by Morton Prince? All I can say is that during my year at Harvard in 1916-1917, I saw psychology in action at the Boston Psychopathic Hospital, but later (1920) saw under F. L. Wells at MacLean the very great difference between this and the newly-flowering psychoanalytic orientation.

I have been attempting, you see, to meet squarely the question: Discounting Freud, was there not an equally dynamic approach from other quarters? Could one not have learned to view matters in terms of unconscious motivation and unconscious conflict? Could one not have developed a theory of the ego and of the relation between impulse control, reality testing, identification with the parents, and capacity for ordered social living? Could one not have learned to see the cognitive life as guided and molded in large measure by the unconscious life? Could one not have grasped the fundamental irreconcilabilities within the structure of human nature? All I can say is: I think not. It seems to me that if the question be phrased in this way, all we can do is to point to the fact that the massive impact began to be anticipated and greatly feared by many before it landed, and that a terrific rear guard action was maintained, so that when the impact once had to be faced the profoundness of its effects proved to be even greater than could have been foreseen.

Instead of the spread of this impact more or less evenly over a large surface, as would have been the case with a gentle plea for a new perspective in the manner of Locke or Spinoza, it was evident that the hammer blow had a shattering effect at certain specific points. The effect was evident at one point rather than at another, just as was true of Darwinism and was true of Marxism. It was where the blow was directed at an unprepared enemy that it had its crushing impact. Freud would have preferred to write a general psychology that could be systematically developed and wholeheartedly received, but he had no such good fortune. In point of fact, as I have tried to show, he left many areas of psychology unaffected. In many other fields, however, notably those having to do with problems of conflict and adjustment, he found the existing position of psychology weak, his blows effective, and a breakthrough inevitable.

4

It would be pleasanter to tell you that the Freudian epic, as an epic, as a work of art, has now settled down gradually about us as a thing to be reverenced, studied, reconsidered, and ultimately in some degree assimilated as part of our many-faceted view of human life on this planet. I must, on the contrary, give you my impression that the effect upon our conception of human nature has been a very one-sided one, being limited for the most part to our conception of the way in which the instinctual and ego forces are balanced. Many will urge, in rebuttal, that the influence of psychoanalysis is evident in an increased understanding of the cognitive functions, as in the case of the studies in perceptual defense, or in the studies of unconscious conflict as shaping the course of association. But to this the only honest reply is that factors of set and attitude, long recognized in the study of perception, in fact since the time of Helmholtz, have simply come to a somewhat richer fruition as a result of psychoanalytic doctrine, and that association psychology has gone on thriving, while borrowing a bit here and there from Freudian insights. What I have tried to do in my chart indicating influences graded as 1 or 2 is to indicate exactly this type of Freudian influences, whereas the main impact has come not in reference to specific specialized problems, but at the level of *acts of integration,* at which complex interacting impulsive factors and their control by still more complex control functions have been the theme of clinical investigation.

These points have perhaps some relevance with respect to the problem often called the "experimental testing of psychoanalytic hypotheses." The successful testing of certain psychoanalytic principles in the field of perception and memory has not yet greatly influenced these fields; while, on the other hand, those who work in complex clinical or interpersonal relations calling for Freudian insights are for the most part going along with Freud without any particularly telling experimental evidence that we ought to do so. To get experimental evidence which would get Division Three of the American Psychological

Association to set up a program on what can be learned from the study of Freud would be a task a little different from getting the Executive Committee of Division Twelve to ask for the kind of paper you are now getting.

I am saying, then, that although there were other forces moving more or less in Freud's direction, they were not really comparable in magnitude. Men of big caliber would have come along, and personality investigation would have been greatly enriched. Here is the difference, however, between a tall man and a giant.

But I think you would be right in objecting to the implied assumption that had there been no Freud, there would have been no similar psychology at all. Surely our control cases—persons who use the other great forces in modern psychology but do not use Freud—are in protected positions, as not being required to counsel or advise, or even understand the personality difficulties of others or indeed of themselves. Shall we say that without Freud the techniques of counseling could have been free to develop, without the burden of responsibility to the medical tradition, or, on the contrary, that the preoccupation of medicine with mental health, which became evident especially from the time of Clifford Beers before the First World War, must inevitably have pushed mental health services forward, whether administered by medical or by lay agencies? To all this I have no objection. My point rather is that the great insights regarding the unconscious were actively resisted; that the concept of sexuality, particularly infantile sexuality, had obviously occasioned horror in the hands of other therapists, as well as in Freud's own hands; that the conception of ego functions as needing constantly to keep a powerful control over instinctual tendencies was alien to the whole way of thinking which was associated with enlightened leaders like James, Dewey, and Cooley, who found a rational and organized ego a perfectly natural expression of evolutionary human development; and that the conception of conscience as derivative partly from dark forces of hostility of parents toward children and the fear of children for parents was patently one which the thoughtful and liberal world of the era rejected.

I can only say that reluctant acquiescence in at least the partial truth of such propositions as these is a tribute to the massive force of the Freudian system, and that those who have not begun to utilize such conceptions are those fortunate or unfortunate persons whose lives are cast in such lines as to make it unnecessary for them to deal with the tangled skein of personal maladjustment.

For those who, rejecting the prophetic tragedy implicit in Freud's system, can offer a prophetic belief at least as tremendous as his own disbelief—a belief, for example, such as that of the Catholic, the Marxist, the philosophical anarchist, the Quaker—those who have a rock-bottom confidence that they understand the essential moral and spiritual nature of man, it is not my task here to discuss who is right. It is, however, my task to insist that in issues as profound as this, man seeks the safety of such consistent and integral thinking as he can achieve and can share with his fellows, and that he tends to become more systematic than the data warrant. If he is a psychologist, he is pressed at this point into the Freudian position, unless for some reason some of these other faiths are even more powerful within him.

But it is not only in moments of anxiety that we need the safety of a system. Partly for the satisfactions of cognitive clarity and order—the beautiful solidity of a sound architectural plan—we need our observations articulated in systems in which each component has membership character with the rest. This inevitably means oversystematization, and a sort of paranoia.

But we go for it. I hope you will be patient with a little fantasy of mine on this point: In the acquisition of a systematic way of thinking, I should like to ask you to consider two modes of functioning: first, that of the apprentice or beginner in the world of science; second, that of the apprentice or beginner in the world of the arts. When one works as a student of science one learns the way in which observations can be ordered to give laws and principles; one learns that odd facts somehow fit in—they can be systematically conceptualized. If one makes a mistake in an atomic weight, there is the Mendeleev Table to indicate that we are wrong because we violated a systematic principle. If the experiment in chemistry goes wrong, the theory of the relations of valences was not properly grasped or applied. Treat the laboratory animal in a manner contrary to his nature, and he dies. There is inexorable logic imposed by the subject matter itself. Students of science acquire this through their teachers. The teacher is as much at the mercy of the laws and principles as is the beginner; he is merely prone to fewer errors because he has grasped the system more thoroughly.

The student of the arts, let us say the student of contemporary nonobjective painting, must in the same way deal with external realities, with other novices, and with masters. He goes forward as he achieves the skills of perspective, color relationships, brush stroke, to a discovery of what will work and will not work. He is applauded for some of his efforts, disapproved for others. He must to some degree learn to see it as others do; he must incorporate within himself a norm of judgment. This norm, however, is not given to the painter by the subject matter, in the direct way which was the case with the scientific materials. On the contrary, the student must find a logic in the material which arises from the concurrences of human observers with respect to problems of value. Often, the adherents of a new movement in the arts are even more sure of what is correct than are the adherents of a scientific viewpoint; and one suspects that they need to be so if they are to keep going. The artist's viewpoint is restrained somewhat more by social judgment than is the case with science.

Move on now to a third group—the adherents of a new religious movement—let us say the Hutterite movement of sixteenth century Germany, which produced a beautiful and stable religious system which flourished despite ruthless persecution. In this instance, objective demonstration of rightness is almost entirely different from that which attains in science; and indeed religious bodies, professing almost every conceivable type of faith and espousing almost every conceivable kind of practice, have been able somehow to maintain within themselves a sense of certainty with reference to reality, and to indoctrinate into their novices the sense of the sure step which leads to reality and salvation.

From the three examples which I have given, I suggest that we could, if we wished, construct a *continuum* of types of verification which may be found for systems of thinking, at the one end anchored by a verification which is imposed rather ruthlessly by a subject matter, regardless of human objections, and at the other end anchored to a large degree upon the group assent, to which each individual feels committed and which he characteristically regards as equivalent to an external reality.

I am sure that there is much autism and much blindness even in the best science, yet I think we can recognize the distinction implied. I have made this comparison in order to put before you the following question: Where, on such a continuum as this, does psychoanalysis lie? If you say that it depends upon what part of psychoanalysis we are considering, then you have granted my point, namely that we can and must judge it by its parts, not by the heroic faith of those who are complete adherents to its doctrine. It is my suggestion that the capacity to observe with open eyes and to test empirically had been part of Freud's approach from the beginning, and that despite many premature conclusions the entire system can be pushed gently in the direction of science as I have described it. While I think the experimental testing of psychoanalytic hypotheses will have *some* value, it has become evident by now that the experimental is only one of several and by no means necessarily the most suitable method to be used in the development of such a science. Often, in biological phenomena, the genetic and comparative methods take precedence over the experimental, or, more commonly still, combine with them. When large time-spans are involved, as would certainly be true in the case of the human life pattern and still more so in the case of cultural phenomena, the complex morphological, functional, and statistical testing of such hypotheses may be required by a carefully-planned design, rather than locally-improvised experiments. Objective checking is certainly required, and it will certainly have to come through the vision of those who are, themselves, fully familiar with analytic theory and practice but at the same time eager to learn from those who stand just outside the window of deepest commitment to the system.

Ultimately, of course, in the same sense in which the evolutionary theory has outgrown Darwin, the psychoanalytic system must outgrow Freud. For the very reason that Freud's observations on the nature of identification with the father seem so brilliantly correct, I fear there can be no safety in that assent which comes from filial reverence to the august father figure as a guarantee of truth. The attitudes, even today, of many orthodox Freudians to those who once were Freudian but have deviated from the correct line, suggest the prevalence everywhere of that family psychology, that psychology of siblings and their parents, to which Freud repeatedly gave his deepest thought. Perhaps this kind of emancipation from family psychology will be one of the essential steps in the achievement of a broadly human psychology, with anchorage upon criteria universally useful in the study of human beings, allowing for a pantheon of men of vision but allowing no single absolute power. There must always be a Prometheus ready to defy the Divine Father, steal the fire, and suffer the consequences.

As a matter of fact, there are members of even the most orthodox analytic groups, who today offer important innovations. It seems to me, for example, that the attention given by Erikson to the theory of the self and of identity, attention given by Hartmann and others to cognitive functions free of the distorting effect of unconscious conflict, are movements of great significance for the integration of Freudian psychology with psychology of other origins, and instances in which those of us who are not ourselves committed to the Freudian system as a system may well take note of the possibilities of genuine collaborative and integrative thinking. David Rapaport's studies indicate many points of articulation between Gestalt psychology, association psychology, and psychoanalytic principles. Again association psychology, Pavlovian psychology, and psychoanalysis have been brought into vivid articulation in the work of Razran. The refinement and integration of concepts from many sources waits only upon the willingness of each of us to try to see the reality to which someone else might have been pointing, though using different spectacles and a different language from our own.

5

After taking so much of your time, where do I come out? Thirty-three years ago at the Annual Meeting of the American Psychological Association, L. L. Thurstone, in a symposium entitled *The Influence of Freudism upon Psychology,* noted an issue which I believe is still *the* central issue for us as we try to take stock today of the impact of Freud. Thurstone was discussing the stimulous-response relationship. He noted the importance of defining, systematically and scientifically, the relation between the situation in which the organism is placed and the response which it makes. He then noted, however, that the stimulus-response relationship is a superficial relationship, one which must be considered in the course of the life-long struggle of the organism to cope with the problem of its own needs. Basically what the organism has to do is to meet its life-preserving and species-preserving needs. Instead of waiting to be stimulated, the organism experiments with the environment, selects from it, yields to it, escapes from it, returns to new aspects of it. The stimulus-response psychology, said Thurstone, is a real but secondary aspect of the more fundamental psychology of need fulfillment. It was Thurstone's tribute to Freud in 1923 to point out, in the heydey of American stimulus-response psychology, that a more comprehensive psychology had been attempted. I think Thurstone hit the nail on the head with such absolute accuracy that it remains only for us to reiterate the point a third of a century later.

The chief reason why we cannot integrate a stimulus-response psychology with a drive-centered psychology, or, as Tolman says, with a "stimulus-expectancy need-cathexis psychology," is that we have not mastered the complex materials derived from the various systems of observations. I think I notice a recurrence in modern psychology to Sherrington's conception of the enormous importance of proprioceptive functions in perception, and the belief that the organism, while responding to its environment, is always at the same time responding to itself—its task being to make an integral response to self and other at the same time. This inclusive Sherringtonian concept—this Freudian concept—this Thurstonian concept—this Tolmanian concept is perhaps the most promising of those which we might today fashion into the flexible system of an integral psychology.

We may then work back from the areas in which Freud has helped us most to other areas in which he could be more helpful if we could attempt a tentative but generous utilization of Freud as a systematist. If we find him indispensable in our study of conflict, we may next become Freudian in our theory of perception or memory or judgment. Being human and hero-worshippers, we like to identify with our great leader, our great father; and those who have other heroes, other fathers, will deride us for an uncritical swallowing, as Harry Murray says, of the whole indigestible bolus. They will be right. I pleaded a minute ago for the recognition of the integrity of a whole epic-view of man. I asked, however, that it be considered as an epic, not as a solemn revelation of truth. When it comes to our work as psychologists applying our science, woe be to us if we allow either hero-worship or epic-worship to falsify our observations or our reasonings from our observations. But let us attempt his dynamic view, test it, and work with it till we have gauged its full value in every area of research.

If you saw those extraordinary photographs of Freud, almost from the cradle to the grave, which were exhibited at the time of the Centennial Exhibition of the American Psychoanalytic Association, you will have noticed with especial poignancy the amazing photographs from his 50th year—that piercing, harried look of a man who is peering as hard as he can into an almost lightless jungle. In the "prologue in heaven" in which he sits at table with all the great, he will not forgive you if you enter as his abject disciple. Only those who dare to speak up when they disagree can be admitted to sit beside him.

PART IV: *Society and Politics*

NINE

FREUD, MARX, AND KIERKEGAARD
FREDERICK J. HACKER

The attempt to find the common denominator of great thinkers is often neither rewarding nor enlightening. One can, of course, by resorting to the trivially obvious or the fancifully arbitrary, discover innumerable similarities and dissimilarities between ideas and men; but comparisons are really meaningful only if they lead to new insights, which would not have been gained except by such confrontation.

Comparisons between Marx and Freud seem almost inevitable. Both discovered and described systematically the powerful motivating forces of the individual and of mankind, which lay within the submerged "five sixths of the iceberg," in what is under and beneath the surface; and viewed the surface as not only revealing but also as covering up and concealing reality. Both thinkers also seem to have had a common enemy, or at least a very similar one: Marx, the economic structure of bourgeois society; Freud, the sexual code of this same society. Moreover, in his writings Freud not infrequently mentioned Marx by name and made reference to his concepts. In many contexts, Freud was deeply dependent upon him; in others, firmly against him. A study of these various contexts leads one directly to a clearer recognition of the sociological conditioning of Freud and the sociological elements in his thought.

Freud's intensive concern with Marx was powerfully reinforced by his great interest in the Russian revolution, which, inspired by Marx, had become the burning topic for all Western intellectuals. On the other hand, Freud's concepts were becoming well known in Russia: in 1911, a Society for Psychoanalysis was founded there, and two years earlier the periodical *Psychotherapia* had published many articles about Freud. After 1917 the popularity of psychoanalysis increased by leaps and bounds, until several years later the intuitively-felt kinship of a similar revolutionary pathos changed into a conflict of different methods and goals; and psychoanalysis became no longer a respected scientific ally but the despised anathema of the "only true" revolution.

But while comparisons of Freud and Marx are easy and natural, the connections between Freud and Kierkegaard at first glance appear forced and of questionable value; it would seem as if it were a completely hopeless undertaking to establish any parallel between Freud's cautious hypotheses about anxiety and Kierkegaard's passionate meditations.[1] Here two entirely incomparable efforts seem to be fortuitously brought together.

The founder of modern religious existentialism and the founder of psychoanalysis could not have known one another. Kierkegaard died one half year before the birth of Freud, and it is very unlikely that Freud ever read any of Kierkegaard's works. Yet the two have much more in common than their lifelong preoccupation with the phenomenon of anxiety. The elucidation and treatment of the problem of anxiety in the works of both thinkers—who knew nothing of each other's work—leads to most surprising results. They confirm each other in their conclusions; they criticize each other in their limitations; and they match each other perfectly. Those aspects omitted by the one are brilliantly treated by the other, and rarely in the history of thought have two thinkers explored a common problem so thoroughly in entirely different manners, so that the efforts of both represent a grandiose whole.

FREUD AND MARX

Behind the skirmishes between Marxism and psychoanalysis lies the essential accord between Marx and Freud as well as their essential conflict. Freud once said, "Communism and psychoanalysis mix very poorly," which indeed seems to have been a prophetic remark in the light of further developments. But his relationship to Marx is not as simple as this brief statement seems to imply.

In the first place, Freud's conception of dynamic development, his elaborate description of progressive stages in the history of the individual, is, of course, more than superficially similar to basic Marxian views of the development of societies. Freud visualized the course of human life as a regular, lawful succession of biological stages, of which—in true Hegelian fashion—every successive stage preserves, supersedes, and "lifts" the former.[2] This developmental scheme implies the significance of the specific historical moment, so that not only *what* happens in an individual's life but *when* it happens becomes of crucial importance. Only the coincidence of an external event with a specific internal developmental phase can mark the external event as trauma, producing neurosis. Individual history thus becomes more than mere chronology; and a particular historical setting of an event assumes as much importance as any qualitative or quantitative feature of this event itself. Some crucial episodes in the phylogenetic development of mankind are repeated in the individual growth process, which, from the beginning, occurs in a social setting. Even the very first "biological"—that is, drive-determined—conflicts take place between the infant and his early objects, his parents, as existing in reality or introjected and incorporated as images into the system of the individual, who is in constant dynamic change. This change-pattern, confusingly colorful in its individual variety, follows certain general laws that are not metaphysically preconceived or normatively given from a source outside the psychological universe, but are the inevitable consequences of the bio-psychological processes that push toward the ideal stage of maturity, which is rarely reached because of all sorts of deviations, blocks, and frustrations. Marx's ideas about the lawful succession of various forms of social organization—all leading to the allegedly inherent goal of the classless society—express the same underlying notion.

Both Freud and Marx were adamant in their assertion of a nonmetaphysical bias. They may have used Hegelian phraseology, but they insisted that their theories were scientific, observable, and verifiable. Expressed as they are in the language of positive science, their concepts have been attacked and rejected as shallow and materialistic, although they are no more so than any other attempt to account for the historical process by means at the command of empirical science. Both psychoanalysis and Marxism represent, despite all their acknowledged predecessors, fundamentally novel and original viewpoints. Intellectually seductive and appealing in their consistency and ability to pierce through the random irregularities of the surface to the depth of the grandiose logic of the hidden, they share a radical distrust of appearance, which displays as well as conceals the deeper reality, and a radical dissatisfaction with the merely existent. By penetrating to that which is hidden behind the "façade," they have a tendency to debunk the significance of what can be easily perceived, and to stress the underlying fundamental uniformities of existence.

This insistent tendency toward debunking may deteriorate into reductionism, the attempt to explain and reduce the colorful variety of life to the arid, if lawful, simplicity of a few dogmatic notions. But nothing is more unjust than to confuse Marxism and psychoanalysis with the reductionist fallacy which asserts that Freud sees the individual as "nothing more than a bundle of instincts that press blindly toward gratification"; or that Marx's economic interpretation of history means that man, being "nothing more" than consumer or worker, is consciously or unconsciously actuated only by economic motives. Neither Freud nor Marx believed that faith, religion, metaphysics, schools of art, ethical ideas, and political systems can be reduced either to psychological or economic motives, respectively, or be considered of no importance. They merely tried to discover and exhibit the psychological and economic conditions that determine and influence them—a most important qualification, which has proved equally obnoxious to their blind detractors and to those of their adherents who, in the guise of modern science, use psychoanalysis or Marxism as pseudo-religions or magic wands to "solve" any and all psychological or sociological problems.

The foremost enemies of both Freud and Marx are those who do not believe that such earthly evils as sickness in the individual or in society are primarily psychological or political (thereby removing them from the realm of theology and metaphysics) and who oppose efforts to correct them as such. Both saw the beginning of evil as a definite, historical event: Marx, in the separation between masters and slaves, a conflict which had assumed various forms through the centuries; Freud, in the bio-sociological fate of every individual, his ambivalent relationship to father and leader, a conflict which similarly had assumed various forms through the centuries. They were more concerned with the effect of this evil upon the patient, the sick human being and the sick society, than with Lucifer or original sin. Both saw the individual as crippled, and sought to restore him to his full stature as a healthy human being. Much as they were at odds in their image of man and his future, they were often united in their will to alter things in the direction of man's legitimate needs and wishes. A scientific clarification of the past and present was to furnish them with implements for the molding of a better future. This idealistic devotion to a future not beset by the struggles of the past and present gives both theories a humanitarian, didactic, and progressive tinge, and characterizes Freud and Marx as founders of schools, teachers, and prophets, as well as the scientists which they wished to be considered. In the tradition of Humanism, they both investigated the world in order to improve it.

But their greatest inner similarity lies in their inability to hold on to the illusions which their contemporaries still cherished. The militant Freud wrote that the world is not a child's playroom; like Marx, he had little patience with the gentle babblings of infantile adults who could not bear to be grown-up and had to deceive themselves with childish fairytales. They were not content, oratorically, to praise humanist hopes and relegate them to the role of ever-unfulfilled wishes, so that they could serve as mankind's eternal dream-content. They considered man's longing for a better life as their greatest obligation; and they saw in this longing the fundamental incentive to all worthwhile human action, which has to be based firmly and realistically on a maximum of knowledge. For both Freud and Marx, knowledge is decidedly not an end in itself, but a necessary condition for action. In order that action may achieve optimal results, it must be preceded by an analysis of all premises and biases. For action to be rational, knowledge has to include full awareness, even of the irrational.

In the individual, the irrational is mostly, though not exclusively, disclosed in unconscious processes; and the whole grandeur of the psychoanalytic method proves itself in its ingenious investigation of the numerous devices, maneuvers, and mechanisms of unconscious repression, concealment, disguise, and subtle symbolization. Primitive and infantile man (and every man is in some way primitive and infantile) cannot stand much truth, and yet he has to believe that his very self-deception is truth. This he accomplishes by rationalization, giving himself good reasons instead of true ones—a deceptively successful accomplishment, which, just because it works for the moment, will destroy him in the long run. And in Marxism, ideology for a group or class is exactly the same as the Freudian concept of rationalization. Ideology is the collective rationalization of a group, while rationalization is the private ideology of an individual.

Originally, perhaps, rationalization and ideology were not necessarily distortions, but merely denotations of the situational, historical, existential conditions and their inherent limitations, bound up with the concrete position of the individual or the group in the psychological or social milieu. Yet when rationalizations and ideologies are not thus analyzed and recognized, but are taken at the face value of truth—which they conceal as much as they reveal—they become the great deceivers, producing the "false consciousness," which distorts everything that comes within its purview. The consequences are fearful: the price of ideology is exploitation; the price of rationalization, neurosis. Both Freud and Marx were true products of the Enlightenment, obsessed with the search for truth, ruthless in tearing off the mask of soothing illusions, because they saw that man can become happier only if he knows more about the environment that has created him and that he has created, and particularly about himself—including his tendency to soothe himself with deceptive beliefs.

Even in very concrete practical matters, Freud seems to display sympathetic bonds of kinship to Marxism. He fully realized that our civilization is primarily a middle-class civilization, and he concluded that such a civilization has little likelihood of surviving, and in fact probably does not deserve to survive. Marx himself never put it more strongly. Moreover, the cautious, skeptical, only unwillingly partisan Freud nevertheless came out with the programmatic proclamation, although hedged with qualifications, that a real change in man's relation to property would undoubtedly be more beneficial than any ethical commandment.

Thus, Freud did not part company with Marx at the crossroad where materialism begins. He did not underestimate the strength of the economic and political motives at the root of all the creations of the soul; on the contrary, he admired Marx because the latter had seen this connection so clearly. Freud himself explained the rise of monotheism in Egypt as a side effect of imperialism and wrote, quite in the spirit of his most vigorous opponent, that with the abolition of private property, human lust for aggression would be deprived of a vital weapon.

Freud did not reject Marx's materialism, but rather his philosophical idealism, his theoretical and practical metaphysics, and his chiliasm. He rejected Marx the Hegelian, the secularized theologian. The Marxist philosophy of history was for him no less an illusion than the one he had exposed in his book *The Future of an Illusion* (1927). Against the so-called socialists, he wrote that their insights are clouded anew by an idealistic and impractical misconstruction of human nature. He used the word "anew," for he did recognize that they had shattered many old illusions in a splendid fashion; but he found the Marxist illusion in the dogma that all aggression stems from a capitalist society. Freud knew that all aggression is not created by private property and will not perish with it. Although he emphatically refused to criticize the economic system of communism, declaring that he did not feel competent to decide— as any schoolboy would today—whether the abolition of private property would serve a useful purpose or not, he did, however, feel competent to assert that the aggressive instincts, after the abolition of private property, would find still other forms of expression. He saw that a classless society had essentially the same characteristics as class society, and he could not be convinced that a society without any compulsion was possible.

Psychoanalysis cannot share the Marxist belief in the exclusively liberating effect of social and economic changes. It holds fundamentally differing views about the origin of aggression, war, and human conflicts, and it sees the desired future of mankind and the best means of achieving it in a very different manner from Marxism, socialism or communism. On the other hand, Marxism regards psychoanalysis as an enemy, as bourgeois softness which deflects revolutionary energy into selfish, asocial contemplation; and wherever Marxism is in power, intellectual disapproval is swiftly translated into prohibition of all forms of psychoanalytic theory and practice.

Freud also recognized, without saying so explicitly, that Marx had corrected a false picture of man by substituting another image, which, in its reversed enthusiasm, was just as false. He once said that, strictly speaking, there are only two sciences—psychology, pure and applied, and natural science; and he classified sociology as applied psychology. But it can be said epigrammatically that Marx does not seem to acknowledge the natural man at all. In a somewhat primitive manner, Marx had turned the tables: whereas everything had previously been called natural—even that which was the product of society—in a sort of over-correction, Marx termed everything society.

But Freud did more than criticize Marx, the scholar, merely because of theoretical disagreements. He wrote against Marx particularly because he saw in him the great instigator of disaster. He recognized that in Marxism a philosophic and idealistic illusion concerning the nature of man is tied to the terrible generosity of sacrificing millions of human beings to this fantasy. It was neither as stubborn psychologist nor as reactionary that Freud protested and rebelled, but as a humanitarian, who regarded the Marxist illusion to be just as dangerous as the bloodiest crusades of earlier times.

When Freud was informed that Lenin had said Europe would go through a period of crisis much worse than Russia's civil war and famine, but that then eternal peace would prevail, Freud replied that he was ready, at any rate, to believe the first half of Lenin's statement. In his writings regarding Marxism, he was coolly reserved. He did not belong to those enthusiasts who celebrated the supposed realization of the ideals of 1789, but neither was he an enraged and indignant enemy. Interested, polite, and at times not without warmth, he spoke of the great social and cultural experiment which was being put into practice in the gigantic country between Europe and Asia. But at the end of his life, he found to his surprise that the vanguard of progress had entered into a compact with the rearguard of barbarism. Even then, he did not forget the accomplishments of the revolution—for instance, the uncovering of the role of the clergy and the more liberal legislation with regard to sexual matters; but he did direct the attention of his readers to its cruel oppression and its destruction of freedom of thought—adding, since he was no simplistic anticommunist, other contemporaneous, non-Russian forms of slavery as well.

From Freud's scattered writings on the subject, it would not be difficult to construct a psychology of social utopias in general and of the Bolshevist utopia in particular. Among the many sources of human suffering, the pain inflicted on man by man holds a special rank because it is not generally regarded as inevitable and natural. But Freud did not share the optimism that therefore it could be easily avoided. He saw in the unhappiness which is produced by society "a piece of unconquerable nature." One should not forget to add, however, that it is also a piece of conquerable society.

Precisely because of his sympathy for the great thinker Karl Marx, Freud was one of his strongest opponents. He understood Marxism well and felt fraternally linked with some aspects of it. Hence, he could so effectively indicate the inherent menace of Marxism, which enslaves man in the guise of liberating him.

Has their conflict been resolved by historical reality? The economic message has had much stronger repercussions than the analytic. Marx was very concrete and very sure. Freud was, in his philosophy of life, very vague and full of doubts. Marx's solution has an unforgettable outline—the destruction of a system which permits the means of production to remain in the hands of privileged individuals of a privileged group; once this system is destroyed, presumably the darkness, which has reigned as far back as we can look into history, will vanish. Freud's scheme is not so clearly discernible, and offers besides only a moderate hope. With only a little hope, however, one cannot lure the masses.

Both captured the imagination of mankind—Marx, by the impressive dialectic story of man's exploitation of man; Freud, by the equally powerful tale of man's unconscious infliction of damage upon himself. Somewhat puritanical and disciplined, Marxism holds out the optimistic hope of an imminent terrestrial paradise. Freud believed in the ultimate triumph of reason in the individual and in mankind; but this is a triumph in the far-distant future, and a limited one at that, since Eros and Thanatos can only be tamed, not eradicated by reason.

FREUD AND KIERKEGAARD

In his early writings, Freud described anxiety as a symptom, a manifestation of disturbance. He found it consistently associated with disturbances of sexual function and hence concluded that anxiety must be the result of sexual repression and could be cured by recognizing and eliminating the reasons for the repression.

Searching further, however, Freud was forced to admit that anxiety is at times justified by actual realistic danger—that at times man has every rational reason to be afraid; and he discovered that although repression creates anxiety, originally it was anxiety that begot repression. Danger and anxiety thus become inextricably bound together in ever-novel nuances and complications. Anxiety is the signal of the ego, warning the organism of existing danger originating either in his physical or social environment, or particularly within himself. This danger signal, alerting or overwhelming the individual, is perceived in the same way regardless of whether the danger is real or unreal, factual or imaginary, justified or neurotic. The human being, constantly beset by external and internal danger, is therefore always exposed to anxiety, which may appear in as many different forms as the dangers to which it responds. And, even more complex, anxiety is often found *before* the danger which it presumably signifies, and some dangers are created in order to justify, to rationalize, anxiety. The history of every individual at any time thus becomes a history of his anxiety.

Freud always refused to proclaim dogmatically that any specific form of anxiety is the archetype of all anxieties. He argued against his follower Rank, who declared that all anxieties are caused and patterned by the original anxiety of the birth process. For Freud, no single event is the creator, nor any single form of anxiety—separation or castration or death—characteristic of anxiety as such. Freud demonstrated his concept of anxiety by describing a sequence of bio-physiological situations—in coordination with their dominant danger, which creates, or is created by, typical anxieties. He would have agreed with Heidegger (who wrote that "physiological manifestations of anxiety are possible only because existence, at the basis of its being, is afraid") and with all the spokesmen of the age and the century of anxiety, who discovered existential anxiety as a constitutive element of human life. Freud went even further than that. In clinical detail, he showed the specific scenes and guises in which anxiety appears in the life of the individual. He proved that the unique experience of the human being—his prolonged period of biological, infantile dependency—deeply imprints the feeling of impotent helplessness within him. It was probably Freud's limitation that he did not elaborate on the collective forms of expression of anxiety. In the world-history of anxiety, he had no interest; otherwise, he would probably have described the discontents of civilization as collective representations of the eternal human helplessness which soothes its anxiety by ever-new compromise solutions and, with the collapse of these compromises, suffers ever-new anxiety.

No greater external contrast is possible than that between the eternally burning, offensively maladjusted Kierkegaard—steeped in Christian theology and idealistic metaphysics; reared by Hegel and a melancholic father, whose obsessive preoccupation with Christianity had its roots in traditional piety—and the detached, respectable Freud, descendant of the Enlightenment, whose objectivity was nourished and trained primarily by the strict rules of natural science (physics, chemistry, biology) and secondarily by the only slightly less strict methodology of psychology and sociology. When Freud spoke of anxiety, he thought primarily of case histories, and, as healer and physician, tried to discover how anxiety can be diminished or eliminated. When Kierkegaard speculated about anxiety, he suffered again through the many agonizing crises of his own life, which was replete with catastrophe, and struggled to determine what terrible sin in the human being had created anxiety.

But sometimes their roles are strangely reversed. Kierkegaard often appears more enlightened than the enlightened Freud; paradoxically, the "atheist" was closer to the myth of the sinful fall of man than was the "Christian." Freud—in biblical fashion—described the fall of man as an historical event—the first patricide—and thus gave sin and anxiety a definite historical origin. For Kierkegaard, the essential determinations of the human being have not developed but have always existed. With tremendous acuity, he labored on the theme Adam and Eve to convince the reader that everybody loses his paradise anew. He would have ridiculed Freud's myth of the father murder; and had he lived after Darwin, he would undoubtedly have cast the venom of his derision upon the dogmatic element in the history of evolution. In this respect, he was more perceptive than the alert and hyper-objective Freud, who nevertheless indulged in the consoling superstition that the problem of original guilt can be clarified by tracing it to the painful experience of a son, who, in the beginning of time, had killed an ambivalently loved and hated father. Although Kierkegaard—uninterested as he was in development and the process of becoming—neglected innumerable phenomena which Freud elucidated, his criticism of the limitation of psychology is still valid. The topic of psychology is *how* sin (or anxiety) originates, not *that* it originates. It is exactly at this point, where Freud stopped and had to stop, that Kierkegaard's main contribution lies—in his reflections about anxiety not as personal pathology but as the general human phenomenon.

For Kierkegaard, anxiety is central, at the very core of the human being. It is the awareness of radical freedom that is the source of all great human accomplishments; the inevitable, ineluctable condition and nobility of suffering, which gives rise to intellectual and artistic creation and everything valuable in human life. The object and cause of anxiety is "the nothing." Hence, Kierkegaard's freedom is entirely different from mere liberation or liberty. From time immemorial, it has been a rationalizing human habit to call dependencies—for instance, obedience to God or obedience to the demands of strict reason —by the glorious name of freedom, so that Catholics, Protestants, and Idealists alike have often extolled a particular dependency as freedom. Kierkegaard left all such self-deceptions and substitutes far behind and arrived at the only real freedom —that which does not support at all and merely permits the fall into nothingness. Kierkegaard's freedom is more than just another cherished dependency; that is why freedom creates anxiety—in fact, is anxiety.

Kierkegaard did away with the philosophical enthusiasm for the value of necessity. He unmasked the cult of necessity as merely another form of protection against the unprotected nakedness of freedom. He saw the cultural history of man, including the "Enlightenment," as consisting in the constant creation of dependencies and institutions on which one can lean and under which one can seek shelter. Thus, history is not only progress toward ever-greater freedom and knowledge, but a constantly renewed attempt to escape this freedom by political, religious, metaphysical, or utopian dependencies. He knew that we cannot depend on anything, since we continue to "know" more and more and yet fall back into ever-growing uncertainty. The Romantics had prophesied this catastrophe, but Kierkegaard, torn by doubts and scruples, overwhelmed by his feelings of desperation and fright occasioned by his doubts and uncertainties, experienced anxiety (or freedom) so impressively in his life and in his work that this experience has become crucial for our century. Freud, with all his clinical knowledge, never arrived at this stratum of feeling, insight, and personal experience.

So, for Kierkegaard, anxiety was not just an inevitable fate to be suffered. To be and to remain afraid became a command, a *desideratum,* an imperative: You *should* have anxiety; you should develop into an individual with absolute freedom; you should not swim in any stream and hide from the anxiety which accompanies the free, unprotected decision. The atheist Freud was still protected from the last dizziness by his attenuated faith in Science. The Christian Kierkegaard was without such comfort. In Kierkegaard, anxiety is not so carefully described in all its differentiations as in Freud; but the Danish theologian, in his monotonous, monomanic preoccupation with anxiety, penetrated to a depth of perception which nobody before or after him possessed.

Pascal had asked, "why are people not more afraid than they are?" The answer is that they escape—they look away and "act away" in as many overt and covert forms as are manifest by the various kinds of anxiety. And here again Freud and Kierkegaard meet: the one considered this escape damaging and unhealthy; the other, unworthy and degrading. But how can one survive in the face of anxiety? Kierkegaard's and Freud's answers are equally uncompromising in their rejection of the ways of escape. Kierkegaard's emphasis on Christian thinking and opposition to rationalizing theology has accents similar to Freud's insistence on full consciousness and opposition to rationalizing private or collective illusions. But while Freud believed that gradually and slowly reason and knowledge would make life and its anxiety tolerable (though not much more than that), Kierkegaard perceived salvation only in the leap of faith of the solitary, concerned individual. He fervently asserted that salvation is to be found in the belief that God's son, standing as absolute, outside of and above history, had come to earth in history to save the other children of God. He was deadly serious about the facts of faith; he did not permit himself to play around metaphorically with this a-historical event, and he upbraided all those who wanted to modify or dissolve this fact into a metaphor or a symbol.

But he himself could not believe in it. He consecrated a mountain of books to this one problem—how and what one believes, if one believes—because it was denied him to believe. He was not a Christian, according to his own definition, only unhappily and passionately in love with Christianity. He knew what Christianity was not—namely, everything he saw around himself that declared itself to be Christian, particularly the Church which he violently attacked. And yet he could not accomplish what alone would have conquered anxiety—the life in Christ. He could honestly believe only in freedom, which he equated with the good; in human possibilities; and in ineradicable anxiety. As consolation, he described over and over again the blissful state of the individual who, by faith, has overcome freedom and his possibilities and his anxieties. But he never deceived himself that he could possibly let go of his terrifying freedom, of which he wished to be rid, but which he could not surrender. Though he too said that the Christian church was an abomination and perversion of Christianity, he was no reformer like Savonarola or Luther. He tore away the illusion of any protection, even by a reform of religion: "Luther had ninety-five theses. I have only one: Christianity does not exist."

Kierkegaard saw the solution and salvation in an act of faith, of which he was not capable. He visualized the promised land in glowing poetic prose of passion, without ever reaching it. Since he could not make the decisive leap, he attenuated his anxiety to melancholy, which occurs "when freedom has passed through the imperfect forms of its history." Melancholy is clarified and accepted anxiety. How obviously similar is this solution—or rather its absence—of the fervent would-be believer and theologian turned radical atheist, to the sober answer of the cautious scientist who permitted himself just a bit more unexamined faith. Freud—forever clinical and skeptical of radical solutions, and so firmly conservative in his steady humanism that he mistrusted all major changes, be they of the Marxian or Kierkegaardian variety—was never even concerned with Kierkegaard's aspect of the problem of anxiety. He confined himself, in the poetic prose of sobriety, to demonstrating that people become ill when they try to evade anxiety through unconscious mechanisms. He tried to develop techniques and show the way to the reliable establishment of better health by the higher truthfulness of increased consciousness. But he was always aware that this solution did not reach too far and was forever incomplete, unfinished, painfully slow and, even at best, painfully inadequate; therefore, he was not crushed, just moderately disappointed, when it turned out to be just that— only maybe a little more so than he had expected.

But small as this gain may be in comparison with the idealistic hopes of man, it is immensely worthwhile to eliminate at least some unnecessary suffering; and so Freud's moderate enthusiasm for the small solutions could remain unshaken from beginning to end. Some suffering can, for a limited number of people, be cured by sublimation, with the help of man's intellect and his creative possibilities. For the rest, man has to learn to deny himself ultimate gratification; he has to resign rather than to repress. This is only a slightly more optimistic form of Kierkegaard's melancholy.

For very different reasons indeed have these three thinkers— the cautiously scientific psychiatrist, the didactic social reformer, and the solitary passionate theologian—influenced the climate of our opinion, our conscious awareness and, even more, our unconscious fears and expectations. Their personalities and backgrounds, their stated aims and purposes, the molds in which they cast their questions and gave their answers, their style and their approach were as different as can be; and yet they share a common concern for the great topics and meaningful issues of our time and perhaps of all time: truth, anxiety, and the possibilities of survival. How much truth can man face without being blinded by its brilliance? What does he do if he cannot and will not tolerate his glorious burden? How much and what kind of anxiety does he need or can he take? What are the various forms of deception and manipulation that he uses to console himself and to escape? What are the conditions of truth and freedom? How does man survive with them or live without them? These are the great ever-recurring themes, appearing in the main motifs of true and false consciousness, faith and reason, historical relativism and absolute certainty, the paradise lost and the paradise to be attained.

Freud, Marx, and Kierkegaard, all of them, had the nerve of failure; none of them, the temperament of conformity. They philosophized with the hammer, and first and foremost they were critics, turning the incandescent light of their search on the institutions surrounding them and the forces within them. It was not given to them to be satisfied with reality just because it existed; they did not permit themselves to set up the chance order of the historical moment as absolute, and thereby to minimize the hazardousness of life and the adventure of thought. This radical dissatisfaction with the merely given and existing made them the merciless antagonists of smugness and complacency.

Kierkegaard, who saw knowledge and faith as polar opposites to be overcome only by the famous leap of faith, was himself never able actually to perform this act which he so fervently desired. He was honest and uncompromising enough to admit that he had failed. He could not qualify himself as a Christian, but he was too proud to accept the counterfeit of compromise for the genuine solution he could not attain.

Marx—who, in his study of the inherent contradiction of capitalism, discovered and systematically explored historical relativism and the situational determination of all thinking—surrendered his precious insight in favor of the grand solution.

This made him an omnipotent leader to his followers, who believed he had found the panacea for all human ills, and created a powerful political movement which has changed the face of the earth. But this new solution is really the same old assurance of irrational belief in the new guise of modern science. The only genuinely new feature of this mundane religion is, ironically enough, that in the name of the most ingenious discoverer and chronicler of exploitation, novel and unheard-of forms of exploitation are practiced.

Freud was too skeptical even to try any sort of dramatic leap and too wise to believe in the revolutionary inner effect of no matter how sweeping an outer change. No less inspired and courageous than the others, he discovered the tenaciously defended secrets of the inner man and slowly, painstakingly, and patiently hewed a path into the uncharted land of the soul. His procedures are prosaic and unglamorous; they lack the ardent appeal of the sweeping solution, which is dramatically spectacular even in its failure. Nevertheless, he may have forged the most powerful weapons of all in the fight against external exploitation and internal slavery—against the intolerability of anxiety and the even more intolerable perversion of man's self-deception.

TEN

FREUD, THE REVISIONISTS, AND SOCIAL REALITY

WILL HERBERG

Although psychoanalysis emerged first as a therapy and then as psychological research into the anomalous and pathological in human behavior, its impact on social thought was immense from the very beginning. I have reference not so much to the early ventures of Freud and the Freudians into anthropology and the cultural disciplines; these were usually too rash and ungrounded to be more than suggestive. What I have in mind rather are the profound changes that Freud and the psychoanalytic movement effected in the very outlook and methods of the social sciences, to the point indeed where these sciences may almost be dated as pre- or post-Freud. It is not for nothing that two eminent American sociologists, acknowledging their debt to the "work of the great founders of modern social science," name Freud along with Durkheim and Max Weber.[1] If Talcott Parsons and Edward A. Shils can hail Freud as one of the Founding Fathers of modern social science, it is surely appropriate in this colloquium marking the centenary of his birth to try to assess, if not the full scope of his influence—that would obviously be impossible on this occasion—at least some of its major aspects. In a rough sort of way, I think, we can describe the varied impact of Freud and his thinking on the social sciences along the following lines:

1. It has transformed the social sciences—as it has psychiatry —into disciplines concerned with dynamics rather than with statics. It would not be entirely true to say that before Freud the social sciences were exclusively devoted to classifying, formulating, and methodologizing, but neither would it be entirely false. Official sociology was largely preoccupied with conceptualized description of social phenomena and with interminable debates as to the nature of sociology and its methods. The academic psychology of the time was almost useless for an understanding of any but the very simplest forms of human behavior, and was therefore of little help to the sociologists, even if the sociologists had been inclined to avail themselves of it. With Freud, the picture changed drastically; human behavior could now be studied in its dynamic complexity, and a new depth-psychology of man emerged. Directly and indirectly, this new psychology made a deep impress on the social sciences, above all by showing the real possibility of a dynamic approach to an understanding of man in society.

2. Psychoanalysis has given substance to this dynamic approach by discovering, isolating, and defining certain basic mechanisms of human behavior. So familiar have these become to us that we rarely bethink ourselves of their source and origin. We speak of frustration and aggression, of guilt, insecurity, and anxiety, of projection and displacement, of repression, reaction formation and transference, of unconscious impulses, wish fulfillments, and defence mechanisms, without always realizing that most of these, at least in the sense in which we use them today, are the coinage of the Freudian mint, usually the work of the master himself.

3. Very much the same is true of the motivational factors with which we work in the social sciences and cultural disciplines today. They largely stem from the psychoanalytic researches that began with Freud. The central place given nowadays to such motivational forces as sex and aggression, with all their derivatives, is evidence of the new outlook, which has

become virtually universal despite differences as to evaluation and interpretation.

4. The Freudian influence has tended to add a new dimension to our social thinking—a time-dimension, it might almost be said, though not in the historical sense. Freud's own early ventures into anthropology—or rather into pseudo-anthropology—helped open the way. The psychoanalytic penchant for finding the same basic mechanisms and motivations operating in primitive cultures as in contemporary societies has been subjected to all sorts of criticism, much of it not altogether unjust. It has had this consequence, however: it has encouraged us to look upon our own culture in the same anthropological spirit as we have become accustomed to employing in dealing with so-called primitive societies. We do not always realize how essentially new such an approach is in the social sciences. If today we have anthropologists and sociologists studying a New England community, the medical profession, or the Hollywood movie industry in much the same way as they would study the cultural system of a primitive tribe, this too we owe in large part to Freud, who was always striving to discern the contemporary in the archaic and the archaic in the contemporary.

5. Least enduring, perhaps, of all Freud's contributions have been his own particular ventures into sociological and anthropological speculation. There is no need in this day to repeat the severe strictures that have been levelled at the bold and arbitrary constructions to which Freud was so prone. No doubt these strictures have been well deserved; I should not care to defend Freud's visions of the primal horde, the primordial murder of the father by the band of brothers, the emergence of totem and taboo, religion and conscience, out of this ancient crime, and its endless repercussions through the ages. We may well admit that these visions have little or no relation to sober anthropological fact, and never can be taken seriously as science. And yet even the most unfounded of Freud's anthropological speculations have not been void of a certain significance, even in some cases of a certain truth. The seventeenth

and eighteenth century notions of the "state of nature" and the "social compact" initiating society were every bit as unfounded and scientifically untenable as Freud's primal horde and band of brothers; yet these anthropological myths not only influenced social philosophy very deeply, but also revealed aspects of contemporary social reality that had not hitherto been seen or appreciated. To some extent, at least, the same may be said of Freud's anthropological speculations. When we are dealing with genius, even the errors, even the extravagant errors, may prove illuminating.

In all of these ways, and no doubt many others, Freud's impact on the social and cultural sciences has been immense. In recent years, however, there have arisen in psychoanalytic and related circles various movements and tendencies challenging not merely this or that theory or teaching of Freud's, but his very presuppositions and postulates. These revisionist tendencies have generally claimed support and substantiation from the social sciences, or at least have insisted that their approach was more in accord with the spirit of modern social science than Freud's own outlook. In view of this challenge, it would appear to me that a fruitful way of assessing the significance—the strength and the weaknesses—of Freud's thinking in the field with which we are now concerned might be to examine Freud's views on the basic issues of social life, and compare what he has to say with revisionist thinking on the same issues. For this purpose, I have chosen the problem of culture, which, as Freud treats it, means the problem of the foundations of society and the individual's place in it.

All of Freud's thinking in the field of human relations hinges on a twofold dualism—the dualism of ego and id within the psyche, and the dualism of individual and society within the culture. The two dualisms are not unrelated.

In his mature account of the structure and "topography" of the psyche, Freud repeatedly emphasizes that it is the id, the repository of the deep instinctual drives, which is the dynamic part of the self. It is the "oldest of mental provinces or agencies"; it is wholly unconscious, and supplies the psychic energy for the functioning of the entire organism.[2] Its law is to press for immediate gratification: "instinctual cathexes seeking discharge—that is all that the id contains." [3] The id knows only the pleasure principle, which it obeys "inexorably." [4] Such gratification of instinct is "happiness"; indeed, Freud often speaks as though it were the very purpose of life. [5] At any rate, it is the primordial law of the organism.

But the immediate satisfaction for which these instincts in the id press might well imperil the entire organism by bringing it into conflict with its environment, natural and social. Of this, the id knows and cares nothing, since it is governed entirely by the pleasure principle. The survival of the organism requires the functioning of another agency that will restrain and control the unregulated activity of the id. This agency is the ego, described by Freud as "a special organization which henceforward acts as an intermediary between the id and the external world." [6] The ego is concerned with "keeping down the instinctual claims of the id," but also with "discovering the most favorable and least perilous method of obtaining satisfaction, taking the external world into account." [7] It is the ego's task, in short, "to mediate between the pretensions of the id and the preventions of the outer world." [8] To achieve this purpose, the mature ego operates with the reality principle; it is the rational element of the self. [9] In a word, "the ego stands for reason and circumspection, while the id stands for the untamed passions." [10]

The deep tension, and frequently open conflict, that prevails between these two agencies of the psyche is thus grounded in their diverse natures and principles of operation. The picture becomes even more complicated as we recognize a third agency in the psychic life, the superego, the internalized "successor and representative of the parents and educators," which stands over the ego, out of which it has emerged, as an inward monitor, exercising the powers of "observation, criticism, and prohibition." [11] Assailed by the id, which demands instinctual gratification, and harassed by the superego, which keeps watch and threatens lest its rigid standards be violated, the poor ego must try to promote "reason and sanity" [12] as best it can in order to preserve the organism and see that instinctual gratification takes place in a manner and form that is not self-destructive.

The conflict between the ego and the id takes place within the depths of the psyche, but it is a conflict writ large in the life of society. The ego, let us remember, is described by Freud as an "intermediary between the id and the external world," while the superego, in whose shadow the ego operates, is characterized as the outcome of a process by which "part of the inhibiting forces of the outer world become internalized." [13] The inner tension between the ego and the id is thus reflected in the tension between the self and the outer world.

The immanent purpose of life, as Freud sees it, is happiness—that is, the gratification of instinctual desires.[14] But, as we have noted, the unregulated gratification of instinctual drives would not only disrupt the psyche; it would make the coexistence of man with man in society impossible. Something of the same functions of the ego and the superego must now be exercised in the larger context of social life.

For Freud, the very possibility of social coherence constitutes a grave problem. He sees community emerging under the influence of the two great forces Eros and Ananke, love and necessity—the former by giving the male a "motive for keeping the female, or rather, his sexual objects, with him"; the latter by bringing about some sort of cooperation for work.[15] But these forces, Freud feels, would hardly of themselves avail to sustain society and "domesticate" man, who is basically so anti-social. Something more is necessary if men are to survive. That something is supplied with the emergence of culture or civilization.

Freud has many wise and penetrating things to say about culture scattered through his writings, to which I cannot possibly do justice in this essay. But essentially what Freud means by culture in this connection is the vast and intricate complex of psychological and institutional devices by which society is held together and man converted into a social being. The superstructure of culture is vast and far-reaching, and no one admires the fine flowers of cultural creativity more than Freud; but no one can be more pragmatic, more realistic—more crude, some would say—than he in interpreting its social function.

Culture demands increasing amounts of instinctual renunciation, Freud insists. This is so because, as we have seen, unrestricted and unregulated instinctual expression would make social life impossible; it is so for the even more important reason that cultural creativity requires a considerable amount of psychic energy, which can only be obtained by diverting it from its primary instinctual aims and using it for cultural purposes. This applies to both sex and aggression, the two great drives with which Freud is concerned.

Culture requires extensive "restrictions on the sexual life," [16] for sexual activity must be carefully regulated if any society at all is to be possible. Moreover, "culture obeys the laws of psychological economic necessity in making the restrictions, for it obtains a great part of the mental energy it needs by subtracting it from sexuality." [17] A good deal of the sexual energy is sublimated, and a good deal is transformed into what Freud calls "aim-inhibited libido," which helps "strengthen communities by bonds of friendship." [18] Freud is fascinated by the "law of love," the injunction to love one's neighbor as oneself. This "law" is absurd on all "rational" grounds, he feels; yet necessary for civilization. "Culture has to call up every possible reinforcement," he says. "Hence its system of methods by which mankind is to be driven to identifications and aim-inhibited love relationships; hence the restrictions on sexual life; and hence too, its ideal command to love one's neighbor as oneself, which is really justified by the fact that nothing is so completely at variance with original human nature as this." [19] Unfortunately, however, Freud acknowledges, such extremities of "aim-inhibited friendliness" as are required by the "law of love" are possible only for a very few. St. Francis is Freud's favorite example.

For, after all, it is man's aggressiveness that is the "most powerful obstacle to culture" [20] and social cooperation. What means does civilization employ to control this self-destructive aggressiveness of man? As with sex, aggression has to be sharply restricted by repression and by other devices. As with sex, too, there are carefully regulated and socially sanctioned forms of expression. As Zilboorg points out, "direct violence in a social setting becomes temporarily an ally of both the ego and the superego; the individual participating in an act of violence of a social nature—whether he is a striker, a revolutionist, a soldier, or a policeman—rarely if ever feels guilty about it . . . The super-ego lends its full support to the ego in that it justifies the violence on grounds of ethical social principles." [21] In this way, a certain amount of aggression can be gratified not only without endangering the position of the ego and social control, but even in a manner that strengthens it.

But the most subtle device by which society protects itself against the disruptive forces of human aggression is the introjection of the latter into the superego. The aggressiveness is turned inward and supplies the stern superego with its power to keep the ego, and through the ego the id, in line. "Civilization," Freud points out with telling effect, "thus obtains mastery over the dangerous love of aggression in individuals by enfeebling and disarming it, and setting up an institution within their minds to keep watch over it, like a garrison in a conquered city." [22] The supreme irony of the situation is, of course, that the power by which aggressiveness is controlled is derived from the very aggressiveness itself.

Freud goes even further, and in his studies of group psychology suggests that an essential factor in the cohesion of the group, and in group relations generally, is to be found in the projection by all members of the group of their superego on to a single figure, the leader.[23] Where no leader figure emerges as a sort of corporate superego, the culture is enfeebled and confused, Freud feels. This was his criticism of American civilization in the 1920's, where (according to him) "leading personalities failed to acquire the significance that should fall to them in the process of group formation." [24]

Such are the complex, hidden ways in which the culture of a society, according to Freud, operates to tame, divert, and make use of man's instinctual drives to preserve the social life that these very instinctual drives threaten to destroy. Culture accomplishes an amazing work, but can it do more than establish a precarious balance always threatened from below? Freud points to "the difficulties inherent in the very nature of culture, which," according to him, "will not yield to any efforts at reform." [25] "Every culture," he repeats, "is based on coercion and instinctual renunciation." [26] He therefore warns against the panacea-mongers with their patented schemes of achieving a perfect adjustment of man and society. "A great part of the struggles of mankind," he says, "center around the single task of finding some expedient . . . solution between . . . individual claims and those of the civilized community; it is one of the problems of man's fate whether this solution can be arrived at in some particular form of culture, or whether the conflict will prove irreconcilable . . . The fateful question of the human species seems to me to be whether and to what extent the cultural process developed in it will succeed in mastering the derangements of communal life caused by the human instinct of aggression and self-destruction." [27] On this ominous note, Freud ends his remarkable tract, *Civilization and Its Discontents,* upon which I have mainly drawn for this exposition.

When we turn to Erich Fromm, the most influential of the neo-Freudian revisionists, we enter, as it were, a new world. Where Freud is dualistic, Fromm is harmonistic; where Freud is somber, even pessimistic, Fromm exhibits an amazing confidence in the possibilities of human progress; where Freud assumes the posture of a disillusioned observer, Fromm is always the reformer.

To Fromm, man is not divided against himself in the very structure of the psyche, but is essentially unified, intact, perfect. The imperfections and distortions of human nature Fromm traces to the corrupting effects of the culture.

It is not easy to get a clear picture of man from Fromm's writings because he still wavers between his earlier conception that it is "the social process which creates man" and his more recent view that there is a normative human nature which "is the same for man in all ages and all cultures." [28] But, however man is understood, he is seen as essentially good and rational; there is practically no vestige in Fromm of the dark Freudian picture of the primordial struggle between ego, superego, and id in the depths of the self. All man really wants, according to Fromm, is to "relate himself to the world lovingly . . . [to] use his reason to grasp reality objectively, [to] experience himself as a unique individual entity, and at the same time one with his fellow man, [to be] one who is not subject to irrational authority, [but who] accepts willingly the authority of conscience and reason. . . ." [29] That is all man wants to be, but society will not let him, at least society hitherto has not let him. The locus of evil and irrationality is thus not in man, but in the society. The real conflict, in other words, is between the good, healthy human nature, on the one side, and a "sick" society, on the other. It is the evil society that corrupts the perfection of "normative" man.

Viewing man and society from this angle, Fromm sees the real problem not as the taming of the innate destructive drives in man through the devices and institutions of civilization—which is Freud's view—but as the reconstruction of society to fit normative human nature. Once such reconstruction is achieved—and to Fromm it is well within the realm of human achievement—once society is restored to "sanity," the essential goodness and rationality of human nature will have the opportunity of expressing itself in social life. Sane men in a sane society might be described as Fromm's vision, and men become sane when they have a sane society to live in, a society that will not distort or corrupt their personalities. "Fromm promises the advent of loving, creative, and reasonable man"—Paul Kecskemeti thus acutely summarizes the argument of *The Sane Society*—"on condition that society recognizes the sovereignty of the individual. Society can become perfect because human nature already is: the only thing needed is that society no longer dim the light of natural perfection." [30] "It is our first task," Fromm himself writes, "to ascertain what is the nature of man, and what are the needs which stem from this nature. We then must proceed to examine the role of society in the evolution of man and to study its furthering role for the development of man as well as the recurrent conflicts between human nature and society, and the consequences of these conflicts, particularly as far as modern society is concerned." [31]

It is possible to pay tribute to the brilliance, even profundity, of much of Fromm's criticism of contemporary culture without overlooking the incredible *naiveté* of the panacea he offers for our ills, for it is a panacea that he offers. "The only alternative to the danger of robotism," he says, "is humanistic communitarianism" [32]—by which he means the restructuring of society into small and decentralized communal entities, in which the functions of worker and manager will somehow be combined. How, in the face of all experience, Fromm can believe such combination to be really possible, or why he should assume that were it achieved there would be nothing in life but love, rationality, and creativeness is very far from clear. But sufficiently clear is Fromm's basic understanding of man and society that emerges from it. And it is so different from Freud's that one might not know that it is the same man and same society that they are talking about.

Both Freud and Fromm see a conflict between man and society. But Freud sees the conflict as one between man's "biological self," with its destructive instinctual drives, and society, with its apparatus of coercion and enforced renunciation. Freud's view, in short, is Hobbesian both in its conception of man and in its notion of the function of society. "There are present in all men," Freud says, "destructive and therefore anti-social and anti-cultural tendencies." [33] "Civilized man has exchanged some part of his chances of [instinctual] happiness for a measure of security." [34] Fromm, on the other hand, is a most manifest Rousseauean, for to him natural man is born free and good, only to be enslaved and corrupted by an evil society. Freud finds the evil drive in man's biologic nature ("The tendency to aggression is an innate independent and instinctual disposition in man" [35]), whereas Fromm sees man's aggressive anti-social tendencies to be the result of social pressures, particularly social frustration and insecurity. As a natural consequence, Freud refuses to reassure us by holding out the possibility of a cure for the "discontents" of civilization; Fromm has his program all ready.

Freud and Fromm are both essentially rationalists, but of very different kinds. It may seem strange to call Freud a rationalist, but David Riesman not only calls him that, but goes on to say that "it would be difficult to find anyone in the Enlightenment who was more so." [36] And Riesman is right, though perhaps his statement is somewhat extreme. For reason is Freud's god, and truth—which he identifies with scientific truth—the only epiphany he recognizes. He is even a little Platonic in his rationalism. "One might," he says with a gesture at Plato's celebrated figure of the rider and the chariot, "one might compare the relation of the ego to the id with that between a rider and his horse," "the ego standing for reason . . . [and] the id standing for the untamed passions." [37] His whole conception of the psychoanalytic cure is rationalistic, for (as Fromm correctly points out) Freud's "psychoanalysis is the attempt to uncover the truth about oneself . . . The aim of the cure is the restoring of health, and the remedies are truth and reason." [38]

Freud's rationalism is reflected in the way he envisages the conflict within the self. To him it is essentially a division between the ego and the id, between the reason and the passions, with the superego hovering above as a stern internalized monitor. He does not see that the conflict in the self is not merely the assault of the ego by the id and its harrassment by the superego, but is actually the self divided against itself at all levels—the cleft runs *through* the ego, superego, and id alike, and not merely between them. Because he does not see this, his picture of the ego strikes one as altogether too simple. The ego can hardly be as rational as Freud makes it out to be.

Even in his view of society, Freud permits a strong element of rationalism to creep in, particularly when he deals with religion. To Freud, religion is, of course, an "illusion," but it is an illusion that somehow does not meet with the same kind of tolerant understanding that he extends to most other forms of human self-deception. Now suddenly he discovers that "the time has probably come to replace the consequences of repression by rational mental effort," and so he makes a plea, in just so many words, for "a purely rational basis for cultural laws." [39] This from Freud, who more than anyone else has convinced us that society and culture cannot have any "purely rational basis"! So Freud's rationalism penetrates even his social thinking. Yet, on the whole, it is a secondary and muted influence in this area, at least so long as he keeps away from religion.

Fromm is somewhat less rationalistic in his view of the self, for his picture of human normativeness is complex and many-sided. But he makes up for that by his extreme social and political rationalism, which expresses itself in an embarrassingly simple-minded utopianism with its optimistic faith in schemes of social reconstruction and their power to achieve perfection. Freud is, in a sense, a Voltairean: reason should rule society through a rational scientific-minded elite, taking account of, perhaps even manipulating, the illusions and self-deceptions of mankind. Fromm, I emphasize again, is essentially a Rousseauean, who envisages man in his perfection and looks to the perfect—that is to say, the rational—society to release this perfection in man.

Both Freud and Fromm are naturalists—Freud a biologistic naturalist and Fromm largely of the culturistic variety. Freud's biologism may be interpreted as a reflection of the late nineteenth-century scientific outlook which pervades all his thinking, for this outlook was biological, evolutionary, and materialistic to the very core. Fromm's culturism may, in much the same way, be understood as a reflection of the current scientific mind, with its sociological bias and its uneasy hesitation between a sociological relativism and the effort to find some fixed point in a "pan-human" normative type. But while all this is no doubt true, it is important not to overlook that Freud's biologism and Fromm's culturism both have deeper significance. Insistence on the "biological self" is so necessary for Freud because, as Lionel Trilling has pointed out, for Freud this "biological self" represents the "hard, irreducible stubborn core from which the culture may be judged." Freud "needed to believe that there was some point at which it was possible to stand beyond the reach of culture," and that point he found in the inviolable "biological self." [40] Fromm, on the other hand, no doubt finds culturism so appealing because he is so passionately concerned with believing that the perfect society (which he imagines to be achievable in history) will provide the necessary and sufficient condition for the emergence of the perfect man. The type of naturalism each espouses is thus seen to be closely related to his underlying interest and concern.

Both—each from his own standpoint—very largely misunderstand the inner relation of the self and society. To Freud, the self is essentially individualistic, a self-contained entity prior to society and requiring community for external reasons. Society is, at bottom, no more than an aggregation of individual selves held together by derivative psychological bonds. Freud does not see what the Jewish-Christian tradition has always stressed, and what modern existentialists such as Buber, Jaspers, and Marcel are reemphasizing, that the human self emerges only in community and has no real existence apart from it, in isolation. The self is not prior to society, but in fact coeval with it. On the other hand, Fromm sometimes tends to lose the self by identifying the community which the self needs for its being with the "right" social order, according to his blueprint, never realizing that even the best social order necessarily institutionalizes—and therefore corrupts as well as implements—the I-Thou community which is the self's true context of being. In neither system does the self really come into its own.

Nor can either system do full justice to the self in its "dramas of history." Freud's interest in history is primarily to find invariant patterns biologically grounded amidst the multifarious diversity of the historical process. Fromm's interest in history, like Rousseau's, is to lay bare the many ways in which evil institutions have corrupted man in the past, and to draw appropriate lessons from the story. Neither understands the full historicity of man, or what this implies for human existence, because neither has a proper sense of human transcendence, of the capacity of the self to transcend all the coherences, social as well as biological, through which it is provisionally defined and in which it is provisionally enclosed. Freud tries to guarantee the integrity of the human self by making it biological, Fromm by grounding it in a normative human nature "the same for man in all ages and all cultures." [41] Neither sees it where Christian thinkers like Reinhold Niebuhr have placed it, in the dimension of being where the "self is enabled to stand as it were above the structures and coherences of the world" [42] facing the eternal.

In such an ultimate perspective, Freud's biologism must be judged inadequate and misleading. Yet it does contain a profound insight which idealistic and spiritually-minded people often tend to forget: man's inescapable biological grounding. If it is true, as Paul Tillich insists, that "in man nothing is 'merely biological,'" it is also true, as Tillich goes on to say, that "in man . . . nothing is 'merely spiritual.'" "Every cell of [man's] body participates in his freedom," but "every act of his spiritual creativity is nourished by his vital dynamics." [43] We have Freud to thank for emphasizing one half, and an important half, of this truth. In a way, Fromm stresses the other half, for he does constantly emphasize that man's nature is more than biological. Yet, because he remains a prisoner of his naturalistic presuppositions, he cannot really say what this "beyond-the-biological" is and how it manifests itself in man.

Freud's biologism serves him well in fostering his stubborn insistence that the trouble lies deep in man, and is not simply the result of adverse social conditions. Freud's view is, as Robert Merton has suggested, a "variety of the 'original sin' doctrine," [44] a biologistic variety. Despite its obvious shortcomings, it preserves him from the pitfalls of social utopianism and perfectionism. It brings him to the Niebuhrian insight, although reached on vastly different grounds, that history remains ambiguous to the very end.

Fromm's Rousseauism very largely blinds him to this hard wisdom. For him, "sin" is socially derived, and history is ultimately redeemable through human effort. Yet Fromm is surely right in feeling that human aggression and destructiveness are not merely biological, but are somehow emergent out of the human situation, which, however, Fromm wrongly takes to be identical with the social situation. What both Freud and Fromm need, it seems to me, is some of the insight that has come down to us in the biblical tradition and that has recently been restated by some of the existentialists. It is not the biological constitution of man that can be held responsible for the human evil we know in history, nor is it the social order, although both the biological constitution and the social order are involved. It is out of man's existential situation—out of the tension between his self-transcending freedom and the inherent limitations of his creatureliness—that is engendered the basic insecurity and anxiety that prompt him to "pride" (in the theological sense) and self-aggrandizement. This "pride" and self-aggrandizement enlists all suitable biological impulses in its service and exploits all serviceable social institutions, but it is not itself the product of either. It emerges out of the depths of the self in its existential situation. Freud and Fromm each sees an aspect of this truth, but Freud, I feel, somehow comes closer.

If we were to permit ourselves a theological vocabulary in this discussion, we might, I think, without going too far afield, say that Freud tends to a Manicheanism of a biologistic kind, while Fromm tends to an extreme Pelagianism, which glorifies human autonomy and holds man to be sufficient unto himself for salvation. Freud does not see that the tragic dualism pervading human life, however real and beyond the reach of idealistic conjurations, can be neither the first nor the last word of human destiny. Fromm, on the other hand, does not seem able to understand that man's desperate plight today, which he describes with such feeling, is, in great part at least, the direct consequence of the unbridled pretensions to autonomy that have characterized modern culture from the Renaissance to our own time. Freud sees man desperately caught between the upper and nether millstones of his instincts and his culture; Fromm exalts the "all-powerful 'I'." Neither really understands man's plight or man's hope.

Zilboorg is right in pointing out that what Freud devoted his life to studying was the "psychological reactions of man *in the state of sin*";[45] but Freud was not fully aware of what he was doing. He took the "fallen," the sinful condition of man, the condition of man with which he was empirically acquainted—man at war with himself and his fellow men—as man's original, and so to speak, normative condition. His attitude was therefore deeply pessimistic, though his pessimism was inconsistently relieved here and there by a dim hope engendered out of an irrational faith in reason. Fromm, on the other hand, like all idealists, simply ignores the "fall," brushes aside the insistent lessons of experience, and deals with man as though he were still in his "original rightness." No wonder the glorious creature he describes—glorious when uncorrupted by an evil society—bears little resemblance to Freud's aggressive, libidinal being whom civilization has to beguile and restrain. Fromm's man is essentially untouched by the dreadful disorder of human sinfulness; Freud's man is an imperfectly tamed beast desperately trying to domesticate himself. Neither Freud nor Fromm sees man in his full complexity and his many dimensions, in both his "grandeur" and his "misery," *at once* in the perfection of his original creation and in the radical imperfection of his actual existence. It was to them both that Pascal was speaking, when he described his purpose and vocation:

> If anyone exalts man, I humble him; if he humbles man, I exalt him; and I always contradict him until he understands what an incomprehensible monster man is.

We could go on drawing these comparisons indefinitely, displaying the relative strength and weaknesses of Freud and the revisionists. We cannot accept either completely, and we can certainly learn from both. *Is there no way we can judge between them, and in the end prefer one to the other?* I think we can, though of course our judgment will depend on our fundamental philosophical and theological outlook. For myself, I think that it is Freud who speaks with greater power and out of a deeper reality than do any of the revisionists. Let me say why.

It seems to me that the first thing modern man needs to know is that his multitude of troubles have their source and origin in something radically wrong within himself which requires an equally radical cure. He must come to see the evil and irrationality infecting his existence from within and reaching out to all the enterprises in which he is engaged before he can possibly open himself to the grace of God and receive the courage and insight to deal with life in creative fashion. Freud is always telling us the first part of this truth, and he tells it with deep earnestness and conviction. What he tells us about ourselves is not always pleasant to hear, but it is of vital importance since it challenges our many devices of self-exculpation. Freud will not permit us to see ourselves as blameless innocents victimized by history, society, or culture. But that is precisely what Fromm's social philosophy encourages. Fromm's picture of normative man, with which every one of us naturally identifies himself, is quite flattering: flattering too is Fromm's thesis that our troubles come to us from the outside, from the evil society into which we are cast: it is not our fault, it is society's. Freud's teaching reinforces the Jewish-Christian conviction of the dubiousness of all human virtue and the ambiguity of all human achievements; Fromm repeats the Enlightenment themes of the essential innocence of man, the wickedness of existing society, and man's unlimited power to establish the Kingdom of God on earth—without God. Freud too left God out of his calculations, but at least he did not pretend to do God's work for him. For that much, and it is no little, we may well be grateful.

Grateful, too, we may be for Freud's stubborn integrity, his refusal to conciliate, his indignant rejection of sham. Consider his views on religion. It is surely unnecessary at this time to repeat once again that Freud's philosophical outlook was crude and confused, his understanding of religion embarrassingly superficial, and his venture into the critique of religion (*The Future of an Illusion* as well as the first part of *Civilization and Its Discontents*) a lamentable error. But there is another side to the story. It is true that Freud declares religion to be an "illusion," the "universal obsessional neurosis of humanity," [46] and he is very impatient with it. Many of Freud's admirers and disciples have been embarrassed by what they have felt to be his unnecessary intransigeance in this matter, and they have attempted to correct the impression by showing that psychoanalysis, even Freudian psychoanalysis, is not hostile to religion at all. Let us pause to examine one such attempt and see what it can teach us about Freud and his outlook. In its November 1953 issue, the *American Journal of Psychiatry* ran an article by Jules H. Masserman, the distinguished teacher and writer on psychoanalysis. It is entitled—very significantly —"Faith and Delusion in Psychotherapy: The Ur-Defenses of Man." What does Dr. Masserman say in this article?

Dr. Masserman begins with a sensational reversal of Freud. Freud considered religion to be an illusion, and good rationalist that he was—at least in this sphere—he felt it his duty to try to dissipate the illusion. Psychic disturbances he regarded as at bottom disturbance of the patient's sense of reality; the underlying aim of psychotherapy, as I have pointed out, he held to be the restoration of that sense, with the consequent strengthening of the ego (that is, the reason) over against the id and the superego. Masserman, in his very opening paragraphs, breathtakingly invites the reader to turn Freud upside down. Is it not possible, he asks, that "psychotherapy actually consists in the reestablishment of certain delusions necessary to mankind?" One such delusion "necessary to mankind" he finds in religion, and he proceeds to show how religion actually consists of certain "curiously unrealistic, paradoxical, but ubiquitous Ur-defenses of man," as "essential to man's 'psychic' economy as [physiological processes] are necessary to the maintenance of his bodily integrity." What are these "Ur-defenses of Man"? Masserman mentions three: (1) "the delusion of invulnerability and immortality"; (2) "the delusion of the omnipotent [divine] servant," God always at the command of man; and (3) the delusion of "man's kindness to man," that "in time of need one can seek and actually obtain succor from one's fellowmen." Masserman brilliantly describes these "Ur-defenses" and relates each to some phase of infantile experience. So far from condemning these illusory beliefs "men cherish and live by," Masserman even raises the question of whether it would not be better to drop the word "delusion" in dealing with them, though of course they are "unrealistic." "As to therapy," he goes on, "we dare not disregard the evidence that delusions, in a deeply humanitarian sense, are indeed sacred, and that we tamper with them at our patient's—and our own—peril."

There we have it. What Freud regards with such distaste as irrational delusion, Masserman holds to be "essential convictions . . . sacred . . . necessary to man's very existence." What Freud, in his rationalist zeal, is so intent upon dissipating, Masserman urges us to cherish and not tamper with. On a psychoanalytic basis, mind you, Masserman, the Freudian, reverses Freud and vindicates religion.

Is that all to the good? What kind of religion does he vindicate? Any one at all acquainted with the Bible and the structure of biblical faith will be struck by the strange fact that the very beliefs Dr. Masserman strives to vindicate as the essentials of religion because they are the Ur-defenses of man, are the beliefs that biblical faith is especially concerned to question and reject. Surely it is obvious that in biblical faith man is *not* immortal and invulnerable; he is as the grass that withereth, here today and gone tomorrow, and whatever "eternal life" he may look forward to, or hope for, comes to him not by virtue of his nature but as the promise and grace of God. As for the second article in Dr. Masserman's creed, the belief in God as "omnipotent servant," merely to state this belief is to indicate how abhorrent it is to biblical faith, in which it is God who is sovereign lord and man his servant or slave. Nor does the third Ur-defense fare any better. The Bible warns repeatedly against illusions about man's goodwill: "The heart [of man] is deceitful above all things, and desperately wicked; who can understand it?" (Jer. 17:9).

No; the Bible denies most emphatically the beliefs that Dr. Masserman is concerned with vindicating as the essence of religion; it denies them because they are false and idolatrous. Whatever else he may be vindicating, it is not the biblical faith of Judaism and Christianity.

Dr. Masserman's Freudian vindication of religion against Freud is something that the man of biblical faith cannot easily accept. Incredible as it may seem, Freud, with his *rejection* of religion, was closer to, or at least less distant from, the biblical position than Dr. Masserman with his *vindication* of it. For Freud regarded the religious beliefs that Dr. Masserman calls the "Ur-defenses of man" as essentially delusions, and here biblical faith agrees with him; they are delusions. Freud's own Ur-defense was his faith in science; this, too, biblical faith strips away as idolatrous and delusive. It is, therefore, even more radical than Freud, but it cannot help recognizing, it seems to me, that in Freud's iconoclasm there is an aspect of God's truth almost completely lost in the "pro-religionism" of our time.

Freud was hostile to religion, but much of what he took for religion was sham and deserved his hostility. Above all, he hated sham. He had nothing but contempt for those who were trying to win favor for religion by presenting it under false colors so as to deprive it of its "scandal" and challenge. In the midst of one of his diatribes against religion, he breaks out with these impassioned words: "One would like to count oneself among the believers so as to admonish the philosophers who try to preserve the God of religion by substituting for him an impersonal, shadowy, abstract principle, and say [to them], 'Thou shalt not take the name of the Lord thy God in vain.' " 47

It is in such outbursts, reflecting a spirit that runs right through his writings, that we, who espouse a faith he rejected and reject the faith he espoused, can nevertheless see in Sigmund Freud, despite himself, a witness to the God of Truth we serve.

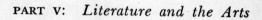

PART V: *Literature and the Arts*

ELEVEN

PSYCHOANALYSIS AND THE CLIMATE OF TRAGEDY

STANLEY EDGAR HYMAN

Psychoanalysis and tragedy are not easy matters to discuss from a mere reading knowledge, with no experience either behind the footlights or on the couch. Yet if we take tragedy not as a subdivision of drama but as a larger complex of attitudes and actions found in many literary forms, and psychoanalysis as a cultural rather than a medical phenomenon, specialists have written little enough to our purpose, and the overlap between the two areas has been so inadequately discussed that a critic of literature may perhaps be pardoned for stepping in brashly where theater people and analysts hesitate to tread.

Tragedy as we know it had its first and greatest flowering in fifth century Athens, in the plays of Aeschylus, Sophocles, and Euripides, and its fullest theoretical formulation in the *Poetics* of Aristotle. The forms of Attic tragedy, as Aristotle half knew from tradition, derived from the sacrificial rites of Dionysus, in which the god in bull or goat form was annually slain, dismembered and resurrected. The plots of Attic tragedy came principally from Homer, and the bloody stories of incest and murder fit the ritual forms so well because the Homeric tales themselves, as Rhys Carpenter has shown most fully in *Folk*

167

Tale, Fiction and Saga in the Homeric Epics, derive from similar rites far from Mount Olympus. Out of the *agon* or dramatic conflict between the god in human form and his antagonists, evolved the ethical concepts of *hamartia* or shortcoming, the tragic flaw, and of *hybris* or pride, the imperfect insight into man's true stature in relation to destiny and the gods. These defects motivated the action, and for the spectators, in Aristotle's formulation, the tragic action aroused pity and terror and symbolically purged them through catharsis. The moral ingredients of tragedy are thus: the flawed protagonist swollen with pride; *peripeteia,* the sudden pitiable and terrifying change in his fortunes; and a cathartic climax that Herbert Weisinger in *Tragedy and the Paradox of the Fortunate Fall,* borrowing the phrase from Isaiah, has called the "small moment," that desperate awaiting of the fateful outcome when all seems in doubt.

Buried in the Old Testament there are tragic dramas, particularly the very Greek story of Saul and his "bloody house" in the books of Samuel, but the later priestly theology has imposed its institutional conception of the sacrificial animal without blemish on the earlier *hybris* stories, and revised such obvious tragedies as Jonah and Job, the former into a curious redemptive comedy that concludes on the parable of the gourd, the latter with an ending that begs all its questions and blandly returns all Job's earthly property twofold. On the basis of a theology where the only sins are disobeying God or worshiping rival gods, and the consequences of those are never in doubt, no agonistic form is possible, and the Judaic tradition has produced nothing like a tragic or dramatic literature.

Building on this tradition, Christianity too seems incompatible with a tragic literature, as Weisinger among others has shown. The great Christian drama of the Passion cannot be tragic because the perfection of Jesus eliminates *hybris* or any shortcoming, neither pity nor terror in Aristotle's sense is possible because of our inability to identify our own flawed human nature with the image of perfect goodness suffering absolute injustice, and the final victory is always certain. Drama with a human protagonist, insofar as it is Christian, cannot be tragic, since the issue has been settled once and for all by the victory of Jesus in His Incarnation, and His Atonement makes all subsequent private atonement unnecessary for the Christian, who needs only some combination of Faith and Grace to participate in the antecedent act. Dante properly recognized this in identifying his great poetic drama as a divine comedy. Where tragic possibility is reintroduced in Christian history it is invariably repudiated as heresy, the Manichaean belief that the issue has not yet been finally settled, denying Incarnation its victory, or the Pelagian repudiation of Original Sin, obviating divine Atonement.

Nor have the great Oriental faiths produced anything we could properly call tragedy. Since their common sacrificial figure, as William Empson has pointed out in *Some Versions of Pastoral*, is not the Western Dying God, typified by Jesus on the Cross, but an antithetical image of The Sincere Man at One with Nature, typified by the Buddha under the Bo tree, no Passion is possible, and there can be neither struggle nor victory. Lacking our characteristic Western philosophy of change, the great Oriental faiths seem to lock man in a permanent dualism, which does not become resolved in time, but has always been transcended in a higher unity pre-existent in the blinding moment of eternity.

I would submit that the great tragic literature of the modern world has escaped divine comedy by being only nominally Christian, and in fact deeply heretic at key points. Shakespeare may be Christian in *Measure for Measure* and *The Tempest*, but *Lear* and *Macbeth*, *Othello* and *Hamlet*, are Christian only in their insistence on the radical imperfectibility of man. They exist in a Manichaean and Pelagian universe where the Incarnation has never happened and the Atonement consequently did not come off. In this universe proud man is locked in mortal struggle with the inner forces of evil, and must win through to some private redemption and true-seeing by means of his own suffering, with no otherworldly allies. The great tragic novels like *Karamazov* and *Moby-Dick* are similarly Manichaean and Pelagian, with Jesus appearing in person in the first to hear from the Grand Inquisitor the failure of his

Incarnation, and Ahab in the second striking through the mask of the Christian Atonement, and finding his own sacrificial atonement, a Pelagian mangod, in the consubstantial mystery of immolation with the great whale.

The rise of rationalism, whether in its characteristic eighteenth-century form as mechanical determinism or its characteristic nineteenth-century form as optimistic perfectibility, killed the tragic possibility that had coexisted with Christianity as pagan survival and Christian heresy. Francis Fergusson has defined the tragic rhythm of action in *The Idea of a Theater* as the movement from "Purpose" through "Passion" to "Perception" (acknowledging his debt to Kenneth Burke's *"poiema,"* *"pathema,"* *"mathema"*). Taking, as Aristotle did, Sophocles' *Oedipus Tyrannus* as the archetypal tragedy, Fergusson has discussed later dramatic literature as the hypertrophy of one or another phase of the larger cycle. In his terms, the rationalist world of mechanical determinism would permit no Purpose because we can have no free will or choice, no Passion because suffering becomes meaningless where we "understand" all and forgive all, and no Perception because no increase of self-knowledge could come from the discovery that everything has been externally caused. In the Victorian world of optimistic perfectibility, to return to our earlier terms, *hybris* can be dissipated by a bracing daily cold bath, *peripeteia* waits only on improvements in the social machinery, and what small moment of terror, doubt or despair could survive the splendid teleological faith that the Heavenly City is at this moment having its building plots laid out on earth?

It is my belief that the writings of Sigmund Freud once again make a tragic view possible for the modern mind. Insofar as psychoanalysis is a branch of clinical psychology aimed at therapy, it is optimistic and meliorative (although Freud, in such statements as "Analysis Terminable and Interminable," was far more pessimistic about the difficulties and ultimate limits of cure in biological "rock-bottom" than the majority of his followers). Insofar as it is a philosophic view of man and a body of speculative insights that can be turned on every area of culture (that is, what Freud called "applied" psychoanalysis), it is gloomy, stoic, and essentially tragic. Its basic recognition is the radical imperfectibility of man, a concept it derives not from the Christian Fall, but from the Darwinian Descent. Freudian man is an imperfectible animal, and, as the biological punishment for having risen in the scale beyond the micro-organism, a dying animal. The first protoplasm "had death within easy reach," Freud observes in *Beyond the Pleasure Principle*. For Freud, the aim of human existence is the reclamation of some cropland of ego from the "Zuyder Zee" of id, and the limited victory in this bitter struggle is achieved primarily through the traditional philosophic means of self-knowledge. Man's animal nature is to be controlled and channeled in the least harmful direction possible, not changed or abolished, and cure lies not in extirpating animality but in facing it and living with it.

Human life "is hard to endure," Freud says in *The Future of an Illusion,* but we must learn "to endure with resignation." "If you would endure life," he recommends in "Thoughts for the Times on War and Death," "be prepared for death." In such essays as "An Apology of *Raymond Sebond*" and "That to Philosophize is to Learn How to Die," Montaigne confronted death as nobly and resolutely as Socrates in Plato's *Phaedo,* but without Socrates' eloquent faith in individual resurrection and the afterlife. Since many of us are not Socratics but skeptics, and our problem to adjust not to the dying animal that will be sloughed off to free some eternal spirit, but to the dying animal that becomes putrid meat and nothing else, we might do well to eschew the easy consolations of religion and turn to whatever grimmer satisfactions exist in Freud's stubbornly materialist view. Here we can find not only an Original Sin—the Freudian myth of the expulsion from the Eden of the womb added to the Darwinian myth of the origin of death—in which the modern mind can believe, but some terrestrial hopes for redemption and the good life.

In terms of Greek tragedy, the Oedipus complex is another phrasing of *hybris* (of King Oedipus' own *hybris,* in fact), the child's swollen pride that he is a fitter mate for his mother than the tall stranger. Libido, the blind energy of sexual impulses, is equivalent to the ancient Greek "wild Ate," the daughter of Zeus and Strife, the wrath or madness that seizes the hero and moves him to senseless violence, destruction, or self-destruction. Sublimation is the small moment, the reintroduction of possibility, the birth of art and all human culture out of filth. Sublimation allows St. Francis to create a life of goodness out of an impulse to bestiality, or Bach to compose for an organ that is not the one with which psychoanalysis is preoccupied. Even the curative procedure of analysis itself, the transference, is a scapegoat mechanism, and Freud in his whole life and work is a sacrificial figure, almost a Dying God, even without the benefit of such probably apocryphal anecdotes as the one of Freud dashing out of his office shouting, "Why must I listen to such swinishness!"

If the human condition is ultimately animal, even swinish, man is nevertheless capable of moral action and sometimes of a life of sacrificial good, as Freud himself was. In terms of Ruth Benedict's somewhat oversimple dichotomy between shame cultures and guilt cultures, the Freudian neuroses are our own guilty or introjected equivalents for the public shame of wrongdoing in Attic tragedy, and they motivate an internal symbolic action like the redemptive ritual on the stage. For Freud, the choice is a newer dialectic statement of the old dualism, truly "beyond the pleasure principle": destroy others or turn the destruction inward. The ancient Zoroastrian divinities Ormuzd and Ahriman that Mani brought into Christianity are still locked in mortal combat in Freud's "exquisitely dualistic conception of the instinctive life," now called Eros the life instinct and Thanatos the death instinct. "The death instinct turns into the destructive instinct" when it is directed outward to the external world, Freud writes in "Why War?," and he concludes the grandest of his philosophic works, *Civilization and Its Discontents*, with the extremely moderate hope:

Men have brought their powers of subduing the forces of nature to such a pitch that by using them they could now very easily exterminate one another to the last man. They know this

—hence arises a great part of their current unrest, their dejection, their mood of apprehension. And now it may be expected that the other of the two "heavenly forces," eternal Eros, will put forth his strength so as to maintain himself alongside of his equally immortal adversary.

In essence, this prophetic statement, written as long ago as 1930, asks no more than the old horse player's reasonable prayer, "Lord, let me break even, I need the money."

If Freud produced a climate of opinion in which tragedy could again flourish, an important group of his followers in this country, the neo-Freudians or "revisionists," have done their best to dispel it as quickly as possible. In half a century of existence, psychoanalysis has raced through the whole religious cycle from revolutionary prophetic truth to smug Sunday sermon, and almost as soon as Freud's philosophy began to have an effect on our culture, it was hushed up and denied in his name. The revisionists, principally the late Karen Horney, Erich Fromm, and the late Harry Stack Sullivan, along with a number of others of similar views, have put Freudian psychoanalysis into what Emerson called the "optative mood."

All began by publishing independently, but Horney and Fromm had had some contact in Berlin, where they had been influenced in varying degrees by Wilhelm Reich's "Freudo-Marxist" movement. Horney, who has written most extensively about the causes of her defection, has explained that she could not swallow either the views of feminine psychology Freud published in the *New Introductory Lectures* in 1933, or the death instinct, the former as a woman but the latter as a citizen. "Such an assumption," she writes of the death instinct in *New Ways in Psychoanalysis*, "paralyzes any effort to search in the specific cultural conditions for reasons which make for destructiveness. It must also paralyze efforts to change anything in these conditions. If man is inherently destructive and consequently unhappy, why strive for a better future?" In his more articulate strivings, befitting a social psychologist, Fromm found the gloomy fixities of biological instincts equally incompatible with hopes of improving the human condition by first making over society. Sullivan, from a very different background in clinical psychiatry, primarily with psychotics, came to similar conclusions. All three have influenced one another, first by their publications, later through direct discussion and a kind of uneasy collaboration. Their views and approaches, however, remain different enough so that one can choose to be a Horneyite, a Frommian, or a Sullivanite, and in some cases, like that of Clara Thompson, one can make several of these choices in succession.

The leading neo-Freudians, as well as their shifting followers, appear to be entirely sincere and dedicated psychoanalysts and psychiatrists, convinced by developments in the social sciences or their own clinical experience that Freud was culture-bound, masculine-biased, cancer-morbid, or for some reason blind to what they can see. The result of their revisions has nevertheless, in my opinion, been not to improve or modernize psychoanalysis, but to abandon its key insights both as a science and as a philosophy. Their effect has been to re-repress whatever distasteful or tragic truths Freud dug out of his own unconscious or his patients', and to convert the familiar device of resistance into revisionist theory.

Freud always believed that "prudish America" would welcome his theories and water them down with equal enthusiasm, and his expectation has not been disappointed. The passion of Americans for constant reassurance that they live in the Garden of Eden (which Horney characteristically refers to as "the greater freedom from dogmatic beliefs which I found in this country") was in evidence as far back as 1912, when Jung wrote Freud from America that he was having great success in overcoming resistance to psychoanalysis by playing down sexuality, and Freud wrote back that he need not boast, since "the more he sacrificed of the hard-won truths of psychoanalysis, the less resistance he would encounter." Even predicting this American bowdlerization, however, Freud could hardly have imagined the extent to which it would be done in his name, in books worshipfully acknowledging his teaching or fulsomely dedicated to his memory. Paradoxically, with the aim of making psychoanalysis more scientific, the neo-Freudians have made it less so: where Freud was descriptive, they are hortatory; where he was the humble therapist, they are faith-healers, inspirational preachers, be-glad-you're-neurotic Pollyannas.

The question of whether in fact Horney, Fromm, and Sullivan are Freudians or psychoanalysts at all seems to me of relatively minor importance, and is probably impossible to answer authoritatively anyway. In *The History of the Psychoanalytic Movement* in 1914, Freud reserved the right, as its founder, to say what was and what was not psychoanalysis, but his various statements of the criteria involved shift disconcertingly. In the *History*, he calls the theory of "repression" in the unconscious the pillar on which the edifice rests, "really the most essential part of it," along with the empiric facts of "transference" and "resistance." "Every investigation which recognizes these two facts and makes them the starting-point of its work may call itself psychoanalysis," he writes, "even if it leads to other results than my own." Later in the book he describes the dream as "the shibboleth of psychoanalysis," and a few pages later declares that Jung's approach "no longer has the slightest claim to call itself psychoanalysis," apparently because it discards the sexual nature of the libido and the reality of the Oedipus complex. In other works, Freud makes the infantile sexual etiology of the neuroses the test of psychoanalysis, or remarks "a psychoanalytic, that is, genetic explanation."

If any investigation starting from the mechanisms of the unconscious may call itself psychoanalysis, the theories of Horney, Fromm, and Sullivan are probably psychoanalytic. They certainly recognize the existence of resistance and repression, and Horney even calls the concept of resistance "of paramount value for therapy." On the genesis of the neuroses from infantile sexuality, they are considerably less orthodox, since they recognize early sex frustrations as causative in some cases but insist that factors like "anxiety" or "the current life-situation" are more relevant. They use the term "transference," but mean not a repetition of an infantile attachment, Freud's "cure through love," but, with Sullivan, a significant new sort of interpersonal relation, the first break in the patient's chain of "parataxic" distortions; or, with Horney, simply that human relationship of the patient's easiest to study, control, and explain to him. "As for the transference, it is altogether a curse," Freud wrote in a bleak letter to Pfister in 1910; it never occurred to him that with a little Draconian redefinition he would have no problem.

If we take Freud's sexual concepts, so unattractive to Jung's American contacts in 1912, as basic, there is no likelihood of calling Horney, Fromm, and Sullivan Freudian psychoanalysts. I would take these basic concepts to be: *libido,* the volcanic sexual instinct; *id,* the caged beast of the unconscious ("a cauldron of seething excitement," Freud called it in a different metaphor); and the *Oedipus complex,* the destructive rivalry with one parent and attachment to the other. In varying degrees, the revisionists have denied all three or modified them out of recognition. For Horney, the libido concept is harmful nonsense suggesting discouraging limitations to therapy; the id is a "debatable doctrine" (what she keeps of Freud she calls "findings," what she rejects, "doctrines"); and the Oedipus complex does not exist in healthy adults, but is produced accidentally in neurotics, as Adler had suggested earlier, by parental sex-stimulation or parent-fostered anxiety. For Fromm, as for Jung, the sexual libido is simply an assumption "one does not share"; what Freud called id is largely eradicable drives produced by the culture; and the Oedipus complex is, Fromm agrees, the central phenomenon of psychology and the nucleus of all neuroses, but it is not a nasty sexual attraction to one parent and a murderous rivalry with the other, but merely a normal and healthy struggle against parental authority in the quest for freedom and independence. For Sullivan, sexual difficulties tend to be symptoms rather than causes, so that libido and id simply do not exist, and a variety of interesting interpersonal attachments take the place of the Oedipus complex.

The neo-Freudians insist on the importance of sociology and anthropology for knowledge of the ways in which the culture determines personality and character, or at least limits their possibilities. A good deal of their sociology, however, seems to be about as profound as Fromm's ingenius formulation "the most backward class, the lower middle class," and their anthropology is typified by Thompson's statement that Benedict has shown in the Kwakiutl or the Dobu "a whole society of psychically crippled and unproductive people," and that certain primitive cultures seem to be "predominantly destructive of man's best interests." If Fromm has read more modern anthropology than Freud, he has apparently been less affected by it, and cultural relativism has not laid a glove on him. In *The Sane Society,* Fromm equates all ethics with "Greco-Judaeo-Christian" ethics, a moral absolute, and remarks casually, "natural ethics, the Decalogue," with the engaging footnote: "Minus the first commandment, which bears on man's destiny and not on ethics."

The opportunity, vastly greater than Freud's, that the neo-Freudians have for acquiring some accurate information about the nature of man in society seems to have resulted only in cheerier illusions. Malinowski in *Sex and Repression in Savage Society* would appear to have confirmed the universality of the Oedipus complex by finding among his matriarchal Trobrianders an equivalent—the male child's rivalry with the culture's father-surrogate, the mother's brother. The neo-Freudians have taken it instead to show that, in Horney's words, "the generation of such a complex depends on a whole set of factors operating in family life"; in other words, that all such unwholesome manifestations are socially produced and could be eliminated by social change. If Freud generalized a universal human psyche from an early practice consisting largely of neurotic Jewish middle-class women in turn-of-the-century Vienna, a reading of *The Golden Bough,* and his own self-analysis, all we can say is that the ingredients of that curious stew simmered down to more wisdom than all the resources of American industriousness have brought the neo-Freudians. Socrates sitting on a stone in the market place still knows more about the world than Alexander conquering it.

Ultimately, the differences of Horney, Fromm, and Sullivan with Freud reduce themselves to a contrasting view of human nature, to philosophic disagreement. The revisionists see man as fundamentally good, innocent, and unfallen; thus they inevitably have a different conception of human drives, relationships, and the aims of therapy. In Horney's view of the child, frustration, sibling rivalry, the Oedipus complex, and similar factors are not ultimately determining; the important matters are "such parental attitudes as having real interest in a child, real respect for it, giving it real warmth," and "such qualities as reliability and sincerity." As for adults:

It is so much easier for a woman to think that she is nasty to her husband because, unfortunately, she was born without a penis and envies him for having one than to think, for instance, that she has developed an attitude of righteousness and infallibility which makes it impossible to tolerate any questioning or disagreement. It is so much easier for a patient to think that nature has given her an unfair deal than to realize that she actually makes excessive demands on the environment and is furious whenever they are not complied with.

Horney cannot countenance the Freudian view because it would allow "no liking or disliking of people, no sympathy, no generosity, no feeling of justice, no devotion to a cause, which is not in the last analysis essentially determined by libidinal or destructive drives."

The aim of therapy is not Freud's modest relief from neurotic difficulties, but "true happiness," to which most patients, she says, had never even dared aspire. "The enjoyment of happiness is a faculty to be acquired from within," she adds, and the end of analysis for the patient is "to give him the courage to be himself," or in another formulation, "by rendering a person free from inner bondages make him free for the development of his best potentialities." Horney never doubts that when the patient has the courage to be himself it will be a good self, or that he has best potentialities to develop, because she shares Rousseau's faith that "the spontaneous individual self" is born free and good but is everywhere in environmental chains. Beneath everything there is some sort of ultimate, absolute "genuineness" in the personality, and it is this that gives her her faith, against Freud's "disbelief in human goodness and human growth," that "man has the capacity as well as the desires to develop his potentialities and become a decent human being."

Fromm charges that Freud may have been inspired in his theorizing by "an unsolved problem in the relationship to his own mother," but nothing in Fromm's background has given him cause to doubt "the unconditioned love of the mother for her children *because they are her children*." The slogan of his "humanistic psychoanalysis" is "productive love," which enriches both parties and surpasseth understanding. Fromm's first book, *Escape from Freedom,* carries as its epigraph the unlovely Talmudic saying "If I am not for myself, who will be for me?" His second book, inevitably entitled *Man for Himself,* explains how he got his key term ("Genuine love is rooted in productiveness and may properly be called, therefore, 'productive love' "). Since only a person genuinely capable of loving himself is capable of loving others, self-interest is a social good, as it was for Bernard Mandeville and Adam Smith. Fromm writes:

The failure of modern culture lies not in its principles of individualism, not in the idea that moral virtue is the same as the pursuit of self-interest, but in the deterioration of the meaning of self-interest; not in the fact that people are *too much concerned with their self-interest,* but that they are *not concerned enough with the interest of their real self; not in the fact that they are too selfish, but that they do not love themselves.*

Even the superego in *The Sane Society* is loving and productive, "a voice which tells us to do our duty, and a voice which tells us to love and to forgive—others as well as ourselves."

The aim of therapy is naturally to free this true self for its true productive loving self-interest. "Mental health is characterized by the ability to love and to create," he writes, and "creation" as an ideal is defined rather broadly: "an ever-increasing number of people paint, do gardening, build their own boats or houses, indulge in any number of 'do it yourself' activities." As for the nature of man, "we look upon human nature as essentially historically conditioned," and Freud's Manichaean dualism becomes the Christian certainty of victory for

God's Party: "the forward-going life instinct is stronger and increases in relative strength the more it grows." We know that our redeemers live, even if they are only people in the French Communities of Work with "a resilient spirit of good will," "people who have said 'yes' to life"; not yet the truly "awakened ones" like "Ikhnaton, Moses, Kung Fu-tse, Lao-tse, Buddha, Jesaja, Socrates, Jesus."

Sullivan's underlying philosophy seems essentially similar, although its expression is a good deal more rugged and considerably less inspirational. In *Conceptions of Modern Psychiatry,* Sullivan defines love as a "state of affectional rapport," which has "great adaptive possibilities" and produces "a great increase in the consensual validation of symbols." In *The Interpersonal Theory of Psychiatry,* he redefines it in even clammier terms:

Intimacy is that type of situation involving two people which permits validations of all components of personal worth. Validation of personal worth requires a type of relationship which I call collaboration, by which I mean clearly formulated adjustments of one's behavior to the expressed needs of the other person in the pursuit of increasingly identical—that is, more and more nearly mutual—satisfactions, and the maintenance of increasingly similar security operations.

For Sullivan, perhaps because so much of his clinical experience was with psychotics rather than neurotics, the aim of therapy is less ambitious: better interpersonal relations, better communication, and a positive direction toward goals of collaboration and of mutual satisfaction and security. He is less impressed by the miraculous "unique individual self" that will flower than Horney and Fromm, and his vision of the nature of man is not so much Rousseau's uncorrupted innocent as a neutral network of interpersonal relations, as capable of good, bad, or indifferent functioning as a telephone switchboard. How far it is from a tragic vision we can see in such comments as: "When difficulties in the sex life are presented by a patient as his reason for needing psychiatric help . . . the patient's difficulty in living is best manifested by his very choice of this as his peculiar problem."

Other neo-Freudians show similar optimism. Franz Alexander, the head of the Chicago Psychoanalytic Institute, sponsors a shorter and more directed therapy, in line with his idea that the therapist is not dealing with the stubborn sexual libido, but with three basic human tendencies he has named: to receive or take, to retain, and to give or eliminate. Clara Thompson believes with Fromm in "creative productive love," as a consequence of which she sees the aim of therapy as "calm self-possession," the patient "free to develop his powers." Like Horney, Fromm, and Sullivan, she simply cannot believe in the existence of evil. Surely a child "in a perfectly benign environment" would not show "serious destructiveness," and any child warped by bad parents can be readily redeemed "if a teacher, a Boy Scout leader or some other hero of childhood presents a consistently different attitude." Bruno Bettelheim, the principal of the Orthogenic School at the University of Chicago, calls on psychoanalysis to emphasize "positive human emotions and motivations," and to interpret behavior in terms of "inner freedom and human autonomy" and "man's inherent dignity." Beyond these, there are Fay B. Karpf's "Dynamic Relationship Therapy," and what Patrick Mullahy, a Sullivanite trained in philosophy, describes as "the sense of adequacy, competence, and power which comes from self-respect and respect for others—a rational feeling of power." An inch or two further, and we are lying down in green pastures beside Norman Vincent Peale.

The question is not what degree of therapeutic success these doctrines give, since the evidence suggests that any internally consistent system of interpretation accepted by the patient, from shamanism to the miraculous grottos of Zurich, can cure,[1] but what happens to literature in a culture that has shaped them and is in turn somewhat shaped by them. If tragedy requires Freud's stoic winning through to the perception of harsh truth, and all the influence of our psychology goes directly against it, then perhaps we should be content with comedy or even farce. Unfortunately, the neo-Freudian doctrines could as readily be shown, I think, to be uncongenial to art of any sort. Comedy and farce, like dreams, are the disguised fulfillment of repressed wishes. As the dream is organized in reaction to the commanding injunctions of the superego, so the comic arts get their structuring from a similar ethical conflict, the opposition of accepted what-ought-to-be to what-is. In the cultural determinism of the interpersonalists, where whatever is is no individual's fault, comedy is as impossible as tragedy.

Lionel Trilling, who has been uniquely distinguished among modern literary critics by his defense of Freudian orthodoxy against bowdlerization and revision,[2] has remarked that one of the greatest contributions of psychoanalysis to literature is its image of the mind as a kind of poetry-making machine, so that it constitutes almost a science of tropes. Insofar as literary or artistic form and dream form are the products of similar devices, and operations analogous to condensation, displacement, and the rest shape the poem, Freud has given us one of the great critical tools for literary analysis. Where the revisionists deny genetic and dynamic factors and insist on "the current life situation," here as everywhere they repudiate insight and hobble art. Burke has written in *The Philosophy of Literary Form* that the poem consists of three aspects: dream, prayer, and chart. The neo-Freudian poem has for its dream, The validation of all components of personal worth; for its prayer, Help me to stop making excessive demands on the environment; for its chart, To thine own self-interest be true.

Perhaps a good measure of the fault lies in our country itself. In a paper, "Freud in America: Some Observations," read at the 1954 meeting of the American Psychological Association, Joseph Adelson discussed the resistance to Freud in terms of the deeply entrenched American idea of "the indefinite perfectibility of man" that Tocqueville noted as early as 1835. Adelson writes:

American feeling is animated by a zest for freedom; it cries out against constraint. While men may vary in what they achieve, their destinies are open and infinite. We may fall into error or failure, yet we do so, not because of an inner taint, but through circumstance; and circumstance, the American feels, can be rectified. Original sin, even in its most secular versions, has not attracted our thought. In changing the external, in modifying situations, men, we feel, can make and re-make themselves. It is in the idea of man's perfectibility and in the vision of a tractable world that Americans find their way to life's meaning. Throughout its history American feeling has struggled against the concept of limitation and has been held by the attitudes of hope and optimism.

Adelson summarizes Freud's contrary vision of human life, and adds:

The American mood is substantially different. We experiment enthusiastically, trying this and that, all of our efforts informed by a vigorous faith in the endless plasticity of the human organism. It is my impression that we tend to disregard the dark and archaic components of the personality; at the very least we deprive them, rhetorically, of their vigor. Think of how Freud expressed the intensity of the instincts or of the superego—"oceanic," "surging," "raging." American psychology uses much blander adjectives. We tend to emphasize the ego's resources, its ability, somehow, to drive its way to health. In fact, the systems of Rogers, Horney, and Sullivan have in common the explicit assumption that the organism autonomously moves forward to growth. We incline to see the therapeutic task, then, as involving the strengthening of ego capacities. A friend of mine puts it this way: "We don't try to kill the weeds; we feed the clover and hope that *it* will kill the weeds."

If Freud, *in conjunction with* other intellectual and social forces, succeeded in denting this Emersonian optimism in the period between the two World Wars, many of his most articulate followers have since labored to hammer it back into shape. No one can say that any given work of art is affected by any given body of ideas, but we must assume in general that ideas have consequences. It is instructive to note how many important contemporary writers have followed their earlier tragic work with later mellowings. Hemingway is a classic example. Where *The Sun Also Rises* and *A Farewell to Arms,* if not masterpieces, are authentically tragic, moving from Purpose through Passion to Perception, such later novels as *For Whom the Bell Tolls* and *Across the River and into the Trees* are merely bathetic, and if Robert Jordan or Colonel Cantwell commits *hybris,* the author seems no longer aware of it. Where

"The Undefeated" was a truly cathartic work of art, its recent rewriting as *The Old Man and the Sea* is almost a Frommian parody ("If I am not for myself, who will be for me?"). Faulkner has moved similarly from a fiction of ritual tragedy in *The Sound and the Fury* and *Light in August* to optimistic comedy or fairytale, as have Steinbeck, Caldwell, and so many others. Such dissimilar poets as Frost and Eliot traveled the same route from earlier bleak stoicism to such later chatty affirmations as *A Masque of Mercy* and *The Confidential Clerk,* and if on the whole our poets have been less affected by the retreat from tragic insight, it is perhaps only that, like our dramatists, not many of them were ever there to begin with.

We would all enthusiastically welcome the psychoanalytic good society, where every psyche was well and whole, and no one had impulses that could not or should not be gratified. To the extent that a good part of our literature depends on our being deeply and irremediably sick, renouncing it would be a small price to pay for general psychic health, just as Hegel was prepared to slough off art as an inferior form of communion when the stage of perfect communion was realized. Even within our limited experience at present, we can see how much our great literature depends on and is informed by the patterns of neurosis in our culture. To an unacculturated Cheyenne, King Lear would be simply an old man behaving very badly; to those gentle socialists the Mountain Arapesh, the whole disordered story of ungrateful children and rival claims to power and property would be meaningless. In real life, we are sure, Mr. and Mrs. Othello have no problem that a good marriage counselor couldn't clear up in ten minutes, and any of our clinics would give Iago some useful job around the grounds, allowing him to work off his aggressions in some socially useful fashion.

Unfortunately, Mr. and Mrs. Othello do not exist in real life but in art, where their deadly misunderstanding is essential to our own well-being, and Iago is permanently out of the therapist's clutches. The psychoanalytic good society seems no nearer of achievement now than it did in Vienna in 1900, and to many of us it seems further off. Meanwhile all the Cheyenne are acculturated and apt to behave almost as badly as Lear, given similar provocation. If the Mountain Arapesh have not yet learned the joys of private property and early toilet training from our movies, they soon will, and one day they will all wear pre-faded blue jeans and know what bites sharper than the serpent's tooth. The trouble with the revisionist Freudians is not that they would give up art for the psychoanalytic good society, but that they pretend that it is already here, that we are well when we are in fact desperately ill, and they drive out art when it is almost the only honest doctor who will tell us the truth.

If Freud showed us that human life was nasty, brutish, and short, and had always been, he was only holding the mirror up to our own faces, saying what the great philosophers and the great tragic writers have always said. If we are serious, our reaction to this bitter truth is neither to evade it with one or another anodyne, nor to kill ourselves, but to set out humbly through the great tragic rhythm of pride and fall, so curiously alike in psychoanalysis and literature. At the end of this hard road we can see faintly beckoning that self-knowledge without which, we are assured on good authority, we live as meanly as the ants.

TWELVE

PSYCHOANALYSIS AND THE HISTORY OF ART

E. H. GOMBRICH

When I was honored by the invitation to give this year's Ernest Jones Lecture I felt, of course, the usual mixture of trepidation and pride; trepidation at the thought of having to address an audience of specialists in a field where I am only a trespasser—an audience, moreover, accustomed to listen with the third ear; pride in being allowed thus to pay a public tribute to a great scientist and scholar. I was particularly glad that this should happen in a year in which Ernest Jones has yet again added to the debt of gratitude we owe him by turning historian and biographer in his exciting Life of Sigmund Freud. But what I did not know when I accepted, and what may perhaps also be new to you and to him, is that I would find in Ernest Jones also a dangerous rival in my own proper field—the history of art. I once tried to tell the whole story of art in a mere 450 pages. Imagine my mortification when I found that Ernest Jones had performed the same feat in exactly half a page, and that, perhaps, unconsciously! I must read this rival product to you, because I shall have to come back to it more than once in the course of this lecture. It occurs in Ernest

Jones' classic paper on "The Theory of Symbolism," [1] very near the beginning:

If the word symbolism is taken in its widest sense the sub-ject is seen to comprise almost the whole development of civili-zation. For what is this other than a never-ending series of evolutionary substitutions, a ceaseless replacement of one idea, interest, capacity or tendency by another? The progress of the human mind, when considered genetically, is seen to consist, not—as is commonly thought—merely of a number of ac-cretions, added from without, but of the following two pro-cesses: on the one hand the extension or transference of interest and understanding from earlier, simpler, and more primitive ideas etc., to more difficult and complex ones, which in a cer-tain sense are continuations of and symbolize the former; and on the other hand the constant unmasking of previous symbol-isms, the recognition that these, though previously thought to be literally true, were really only aspects or representations of the truth, the only ones of which our minds were—for either affective or intellectual reasons—at the time capable. One has only to reflect on the development of religion or science, for example, to perceive the truth of this description.

You see how I was saved by a hair's breadth from being put out of business. "Religion or science, for example," says Dr. Jones—and leaves it to me to add art. But psychoanalysis does not believe in accidents of this kind, and maybe it was no com-plete accident that art was not mentioned in the article that was written in 1916. For in these earlier years of psycho-analysis the aspect of art that attracted most attention was not so much the historical progress of modes of representation which is so admirably summed up in this paragraph, as its ex-pressive significance. In most psychoanalytic discussions on art the analogy between the work of art and the dream stands in the foreground of interest. I think it cannot be denied that to this approach literature proved a more rewarding field than painting. True, there are paintings such as some by Goya, Blake, or Fuseli which are dream-like;[2] but if you follow me in your mind on a lightning excursion to the National Gallery with its Madonnas and landscapes, still lifes and portraits, you will realize that the traditional conventional elements often out-weigh the personal ones in many, even of the great masterpieces of the past. Now I would not be here, of course, if I were inclined to deny that a personal determinant must always exist and have always existed; that if you had analysed Hobbema you might have found out why he preferred to make capital of Ruysdael's watermills rather than of Koninck's panoramas; how it came that Wouverman delighted in painting white horses and Paulus Potter cattle.

But does it matter all that much? This may at first seem a very heretical question to ask, yet on its answer depends the whole relationship between Psychoanalysis and the History of Art. For try as we may, we historians just cannot raise the dead and put them on your couch. It is a commonplace that there is no substitute for the psychoanalytic interview. Such attempts as have been made, therefore, to tiptoe across the chasm of centuries on a fragile rope made of stray information can never be more than a *jeu d'esprit,* even if the performance is as dazzling as Freud's Leonardo.[3] We historians could always prove to you that the information you need is not to be had, and you could retort that without such essential information we might just as well pack up and go home. And so I repeat the question whether it really matters all that much if we know what the work of art meant to the artist. It clearly matters on one assumption and on one assumption only: that this private, personal, psychological meaning of the picture is alone the real, the true meaning—the meaning, therefore, which it also conveys if not to the conscious at least to the unconscious mind of the beholder. I know that this assumption underlies a good deal of writing on modern art,[4] but I doubt if it is sound analytical doctrine. I hardly need remind this audience of the letter Freud wrote to André Breton when that leader of Surrealism asked him for a contribution to an anthology of dreams: "a mere collection of dreams without the dreamer's associations, without knowledge of the circumstances in which they occurred, tells me nothing and I can hardly imagine what it could tell anyone." [5] No word of communication here. If the work of art has the character of a shared dream, it becomes urgent to specify more clearly what it is that is being shared. This is the problem to which I should like to direct your attention.

In order to escape from generalities I should like to pose this problem in as concrete a form as possible. I show you here one of Picasso's most popular works—popular at least on the other side of the iron curtain: his so-called peace dove (Fig. 1). What I may call its manifest social or public meaning is quite clear. The dove is an old conventional symbol for peace which owes this meaning to the conviction that it is a very meek bird. Perhaps it is not without significance that Konrad Lorenz has told us that actually doves or pigeons are most savagely aggressive. The psychoanalyst will then want to go beyond this surface meaning. He will ask what other qualities may have contributed to the success of the dove as a symbol. Ernest Jones has drawn attention, in a somewhat different context, to the qualities through which it lends itself as a phallic symbol.[6] Perhaps this meaning is indeed present to reinforce the appeal of the poster as a poster—but this would also be true if a hack rather than Picasso had drawn it.

Now we happen to be able to guess a little at least of the personal meanings that the dove or rather the pigeon must have for Picasso. His friend and companion Sabartés, living in an age made avid for such memories through the influence of psychoanalysis, has recorded episodes from the artist's childhood that center round the pigeons his father used to paint.[7] Picasso's father, Don Pepe Ruiz, was an artist and keeper of the local museum in Majorca, and he used to paint salon pictures of dovecots which Picasso still likes to glamorize. These pictures Don Pepe painted from stuffed pigeons which he carried to his office and back home. Now Picasso remembers having been paralysed with fear when left alone at school, and tells how he used to cling to his father and how he kept his father's walking stick, his paint brushes, and most of all his stuffed pigeon as hostages to make quite sure his father would come back and fetch him. Before this audience I need hardly enlarge further on the symbolic meaning of all these implements of his father's trade. Nor, I suppose, would you consider it far-fetched to imagine that this frantic fear of losing the father screens an obvious oedipal wish. Small wonder, you may say, that the boy took eagerly to helping his father paint

pigeons, that he advertised for these birds in a childish news-
paper that happens to be extant, and that his identification led
him to excel as an infant prodigy in drawing and earn a prize
for academic exercises as a boy of 12. Less wonder even, that
it was this same boy who, as he grew up, eliminated his father's name Ruiz from his signature, called himself Picasso
after his mother, and proceeded to kill his father's academic
standards not only in himself but the world over. So far the
story looks neat enough.[8] But the esthetic question is still un-
answered. Does this private meaning really glow in the work
before you? Could you surmise it from this poster if Sabartés
had not obliged us accidentally with this telling episode?
Frankly I doubt it. Though the pigeon must be charged and
overcharged with meanings and memories for Picasso, though
he cannot but have enjoyed this opportunity of doing a pigeon,
as his father did, but one that would fly over half the world,
I see no evidence that this private meaning reverberates in the
particular work, that it is communicated.

Here, of course, would be a field where psychoanalysis could
help immensely in clearing up the tangle in which the theory
of art as communication has landed us. For if the idea that
the private unconscious meaning of a work communicates itself to the unconscious of the public is more than a misunderstanding of psychoanalytic doctrine, then it should be easy to
test. All you have to do is to compare the reactions, in analysis,
of some of your patients to an identical work of art. If by a
happy chance the artist himself were also in analysis it would
be even better, but it is not a necessary condition. For if the
theory of unconscious communication makes sense, it could be
tested through the recipients alone—if they tally there was a
communication—just as we can be confident that Egyptologists
do read hieroglyphs because, up to a point, they find the same
meaning in the same inscriptions.

But I think one need only formulate this theory in such a
crude manner to appreciate its shortcomings. The relation between an artist and the world at large—between private and
public meaning—are obviously much more complex. Perhaps
we can grope our way a little nearer to the true state of affairs if

we contrast Picasso's peace dove with an earlier work that helped to make his reputation. I mean the *Demoiselles d'Avignon* of 1907 (Fig. 2). Here, too, we are reasonably well-informed about some of its private significance, its manifest content to the artist. We know at any rate that the title I quoted was given to it by an art dealer. What it really represents is a brothel in the Calle de Avignon near Picasso's home in Barcelona.[9] Of course this specific significance would also be hidden from us if we did not happen to have this information. But here we have a work of art which, whether we like it or not, met with a tremendous response. It became the starting-point of Cubism, and thus the origin of much that we call Modern Art. How was this possible?

You need only ask this question to see that if it can be answered at all it cannot be answered in terms of Picasso's personal history alone. It acquired this meaning within a different context: the context of the institution we call art. Now for the psychological history of this institution I must refer you back to Ernest Jones' clandestine history of art which I communicated to you at the beginning of this lecture. It is a history, as you remember, not of external accretions, but of a constant extension and modification of symbols. This is particularly true of what we call representation in art. You know how slowly that skill is acquired in history—how it proceeds from the so-called conceptual symbols of child art or primitive art to a slow approximation to what we call appearances. Indeed, all the mechanisms described by Ernest Jones in his paper on the "Theory of Symbolism" could be illustrated from this history of our peripheral field. The pleasure principle that favors repetition, the recognition of similarities rather than of differences, is exemplified in the representational and ornamental stereotypes of many primitive cultures; the reality principle which proceeds by assimilation of the unknown to the known in the countless instances in which tradition colors perception or expression. Thus it is a familiar fact that the eighteenth century artist who went out to record the beauty of the English countryside was as likely as not to return from his expedition to the Lakelands with a version of Claude Lorrain's Roman

Campagna, just sufficiently modified to pass as a faithful vista of a beauty spot. It is perhaps less familiar but equally true that many a young artist who sets out to record his unconscious images returns from this *descensus ad infernos* with a version of Picasso's penultimate invention just sufficiently modified to pass as self-expression. What matters to us, of course, is not that so much of art or pseudo-art is derivative, but that up to a point all art must be, if Ernest Jones' description applies. It is this fact, I believe, which explains that art has a history, a style, in contrast to perception and to dreaming which have not.[10] And so the fact, for instance, that all eighteenth-century landscapes or twentieth-century dream-paintings have enough in common to allow us art historians to tell, on the whole, where and when they were made, is not due to some mysterious fluid or collective spirit that governs the modes of perception or the images of dreams but rather to the observable fact that symbols developed from a common stock will tend to have a certain family likeness. But I see the *Demoiselles d'Avignon* staring at me fiercely and reproachfully—how did they come to be modified into such a shape? If the genetic approach is right the attempt to answer such a question will always threaten to land us in an infinite regress, or—what is much worse—in an infinite lecture.

I would really have to take you back to Pygmalion, the mythical artist who fashioned the figure of a woman—or rather not a figure, but a woman. For you know from Ernest Jones that in these dim beginnings of art a symbol is not experienced as a symbol. The child's baby doll is not an image of a baby so much as a member of the class "babies"; provided, that is, that you can do with it what babies are for—hug it, bathe it, and throw it on the floor. Pygmalion's statue, we may surmise, was a woman in the sense in which the doll is a baby—it had sufficient characteristics of her sex to be classable as a woman.[11] At least when we enter the light of history we can see that the symbol of a woman is not created by closely imitating the appearance of the female body but more or less in this pseudo-logical process we call conceptual representation. In this case it is the representational formula for

FIG. 1. Picasso: The ' Peace dove.' (Poster.)

FIG. 2. Picasso: *Les Demoiselles d'Avignon.*
Collection The Museum of Modern Art, New York.
(Acquired through the Lillie P. Bliss Bequest.)

FIG. 3. Botticelli: The Birth of Venus. Florence, [Uffizi.]

FIG. 4. Raphael: The Triumph of Galatea. Rome, Villa
Farnesina.

Fig. 5. Titian: The Rape of Europa. (The Isabella Steward Gardner Museum, Boston.)

Fig. 6. Bouguereau: The Birth of Venus. French State Collections.

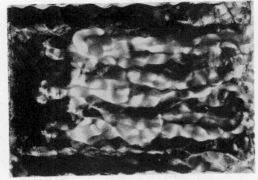

FIG. 8. As 7, seen through rolled glass.

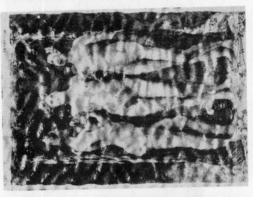

FIG. 9. As 7, seen through rolled glass.

FIG. 7. Bonnencontre: The Three Graces. (Courtesy Soho Gallery, London. Braun et Cie, France.)

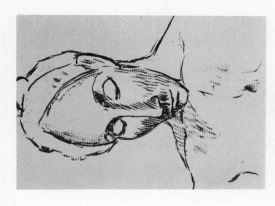

Fig. 10.

Fig. 11.

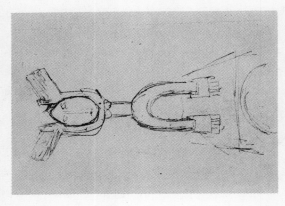

Fig. 13.

Fig. 12.

Picasso: Four Drawings.

Fig. 10. Mother and Child. Courtesy of the Fogg Art Museum, Meta and Paul J. Sachs Collection, Cambridge, Mass. Figs. 11, 12, 13. Studies for the *Demoiselles d'Avignon*.

Fig. 15.

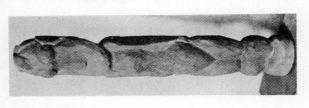

Fig. 14.

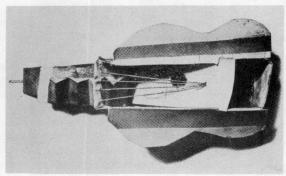

Fig. 17.

Fig. 16.

Picasso: (14) Carving. (15, 16) Still life paintings. (17) Construction.

man which is just sufficiently modified to be acceptable as the symbol of a woman. The reason may be that artists both in archaic Greece and in the Middle Ages (which saw a repetition of this process) were men, and that what Schilder calls the body image, the awareness of the artist's own body, is always a strong compelling force in early attempts at representation. At any rate you can see in such thirteenth-century figures as the Adam and Eve of Bamberg Cathedral that Eve is just distinguished by an addition of two small symbolic breasts. Even when Botticelli painted his Venus (Fig. 3) he had not yet quite mastered the anatomical problem. One can see from his corrections, his *pentimenti,* which remain visible on the canvas, how he shifted the breast about, and how unsure he was of the relative position of arm, shoulder, and breast. One generation later a Raphael, who had absorbed the representational symbols of classical art, had no such difficulties in the painting of his Galatea (Fig. 4). He can and does visualize the body in the round and represent it in the most complex posture. Now it is well to remember that such a complex image is not only more difficult to paint but also more difficult to read than the more primitive representation of Botticelli.[12] Up to a point we have to work from clues and repeat in our mind the imaginative effort of the artist if we are to build up the figure for ourselves. We have to become Pygmalions to this Galatea. It is true that the artist helps us to find these clues. The very symphony of symmetries he builds up helps us in the process of assimilation, for we need not always start afresh; we are being trained while looking, and we cannot but enjoy these correspondences, these visual rhymes which lead our eye around and make it build and re-build the picture. In front of such a painting we may remember the passage from Dr. Jones about the constant unmasking of previous symbolisms. Looking back from here, Botticelli's Venus must have appeared a mere symbol rather than the truth. And yet the same would probably happen to anyone who looked back to Raphael's Galatea a generation later when he had seen Titian's Europa (Fig. 5), which is so obviously a challenge to the former. To people who saw the truth revealed by Titian's painting (now at the

Gardener Museum in Boston), the play of light, the rush of movement, the tangible body, Raphael's nymph may well have seemed contrived. At the same time you see how Titian can rely on a public ready to make even more difficult adjustments. No longer need he rely on overt symmetries. Or look at the arm with its shadow across the foreshortened face. What demands it makes on our imagination! The degree to which Titian can rely on suggestion—on the trained connoisseur meeting him half-way—is particularly revealed in the miraculous landscape of the background with its cloudy forms into which we must—and can—project the figures of Europa's companions rushing to the beach.

Let me pause for a moment to recapitulate what we have observed. In the eighty years between Botticelli and Titian there is clearly an enormous increase in skill; in skill not only of representation but in making sense of representational symbols. This duality, this interplay between the artist and the beholder, is a factor which is often overlooked. We owe its theoretical formulation from the point of view of psychoanalysis to Ernst Kris, who is my guide and mentor in these things. It was Kris who first emphasized that the emergence of what might be called the esthetic attitude to painting—in distinction, that is, from the ritualistic attitude—brings about a new type of reaction, or, as he puts it, of discharge. The connoisseur wants to identify himself with the artist; he must be drawn into the charmed circle and share in his secret. He, too, must become creative under the artist's guidance.[13]

To us historians this psychoanalytic insight is so valuable because without it such rapid developments as the one I described would be inexplicable. Here, as often, a somewhat deeper psychological analysis of what actually takes place has shattered more facile generalizations. The development of style, of modes of representation, is too often treated as the result of organic growth, of real evolution. At the very time that Titian painted, Vasari thought he had discovered the secret of the history of Art. Art grew up like a human being, there was an organic development from childish beginnings to mastery. The conclusion looked only too plausible that art in its turn was just a symptom of a general maturation process—that people who drew like children had a more childish mind. We now see, perhaps, why this plausible view is so superficial. Mature art can only grow within the Institution, as I call it—within the social context of the esthetic attitude. Where this breaks down, representation must soon revert to the more primitive, more readable conceptual image. We can test this theory not only through an analysis of the decline of Western Art in late antiquity, but more strikingly perhaps, by comparing the Venice of Titian with the London of Shakespeare. Nobody would seriously contend, I believe, that the mind of Shakespeare's audience was necessarily more primitive than that of Titian's public. In fact, Shakespeare even provides the proof that the thrills of visual projection were familiar to his audience; think of Hamlet and Polonius talking about the cloud that is shaped like a camel, or of the grandiose image of the changing shape of clouds in *Antony and Cleopatra*. But through lack of opportunity Elizabethans could neither paint nor read such complex pictures. Compared with the miracles of Titian, their portraits look like stuffed dummies.

It cannot have escaped you that within the sphere of painting the esthetic relationship brings about a greater freedom. This *Europa*, painted for Philip II of Spain, is of course more frankly erotic than anything that went before. But the erotic content is neither concealed nor obtruded. It is absorbed, as it were, in that esthetic process of re-creation, of give and take. We can guess that an increase in such active participation, in projective activity, may be accompanied by an easing of conventional taboos. Even the most Christian King could look at such a masterpiece of the brush without guilt feeling, for who could deny that here was art at its highest?

This observation of the compensatory nature of esthetic satisfaction was also suggested to me by the work on the history of caricature I was privileged to undertake with Ernst Kris.[14] For this in a nutshell is really the result at which we arrived by more circuitous paths: Portrait caricature appeared so late in the history of art because of the aggressive component that underlies the distortion of a physiognomy. It could only become acceptable as an art through the premium of the esthetic achievement, the sophisticated game of creating an intentionally dissimilar likeness. This game, in turn, presupposes the trained response of the connoisseur, who repeats the artist's imaginative performance in his own mind. Basically we have, of course, the same mechanism as the one Freud discovered in wit. But visual wit is apparently harder to learn and to appreciate than the verbal anecdote. And so it needed not the evolution of mankind but the development of visual evocation in Italian art to come to fruition.

These examples suggest that there is something like a necessary balance between what one might call esthetic activity and regressive pleasure which would have important consequences for the interpretation of stylistic changes. For if this theory is right the absence of such balance will result in esthetic discomfort. I must apologize if I proceed to test this theory on you, but I see no other way of bringing home to you the truth of this psychological observation. This is a nineteenth-century treatment of our theme of Venus rising from the sea—by that most successful of masters of French nineteenth-century *Art Officiel* Bouguereau (Fig. 6). Let us admit right away that Bouguereau has made further progress in the direction of representational accuracy—beyond Raphael, whom he exploits, and beyond Titian. Aided by the successive conquests of appearance made during two centuries and by the mechanical device of photography, he places before us a most convincing image of a nude model. Why, then, does it make us rather sick? I think the reason is obvious. This is a pin-up girl rather than a work of art. By this we mean that the erotic appeal is on the surface—is not compensated for by this sharing in the artist's imaginative process. The image is painfully easy to read, and we resent being taken for such simpletons. We feel somewhat insulted that we are expected to fall for such cheap bait —good enough, perhaps, to attract the vulgar, but not such sophisticated sharers in the artist's secrets as we pride ourselves on being. But this resentment, I submit, only screens a deeper disturbance; we could hardly feel so ill at ease if we did not have to put up a certain amount of resistance against the

methods of seduction practiced on us. And so it is small wonder that works of this kind coincided with a retrograde movement of taste; the sophisticated looked out for more difficult
gratifications and found them in the cult of the primitive. For
the refined connoisseurs of Bouguereau's age it is Botticelli's
Venus which becomes the haunting image of chaste and childlike appeal. Its very awkwardness in construction endeared it to
the art lover, who wanted to make his own discoveries, his own
conquests, rather than to yield to seduction.[15]

Perhaps this is the moment to remind you of another of
Ernest Jones' papers on art: I mean the essay he published exactly forty years ago about "The Influence of Andrea del Sarto's
Wife on his Art." [16] It is not the historical problem that concerns me. I do not want to yield to the temptation of writing a
del Sarto Resartus and of risking the name of a Teufelsdröckh.
If the biographical facts Vasari tells us about the artist are correct—and that is always a big "if" [17]—Dr. Jones' diagnosis of a
case of suppressed homosexuality will certainly stand, and the
passivity it implies is obviously suggestive in our context. But
what attracted Dr. Jones in his essay was the problem of the
artist whose very virtuosity seems something of a handicap.
Again I resist the temptation of discussing whether we still see
Andrea in that light. For what matters to us is that such a
reaction was not only possible but widespread among the nineteenth-century critics whose verdict forms the starting point for
Dr. Jones' study. I believe it was Robert Browning above all
who reinterpreted Vasari's estimate and created the moving
image of Andrea del Sarto, called the faultless painter—the
artist who suffers from too much facility.

> At any rate, 'tis easy, all of it!
> No sketches first, no studies, that's long past!
> I do what many dream of, all their lives,
> —Dream? strive to do, and agonize to do,
> And fail in doing . . .
> Well, less is more, Lucrezia . . .

And then comes the moment when he takes the charcoal to
show that he could easily correct a false drawn arm of Raphael's; but still, with all its faults—or should I say because of

its faults?—Raphael's is the greater work. This, I dare say, is an idea that could never have entered the mind of Vasari or, for that matter, of the historical Andrea. The fault of faultlessness is a discovery of the nineteenth century.[18] And I think that the question it raises—the question What is wrong with perfection?—has a greater chance of being answered by psychoanalytic thought than the sonorous tautologies often produced by academic esthetics in answer to the question of what is right with perfection. Why do we really abuse the masterpieces of Bouguereau and his school as slick and perhaps revolting? I suspect that when we call such pictures as his soulful *Seur Cadet* insincere, for instance, or untruthful, we are talking nonsense. We screen behind a moral judgment which is quite inapplicable. After all, there *are* pretty children in the world, and even if there weren't the charge would not apply to painting. But this does not mean that our own reaction is not genuine. We do tend to find such things syrupy, saccharine, cloying. With these terms of abuse we are on firmer ground. They describe by synesthetic metaphor our reaction to a surfeit of oral gratifications.

Now it is my conviction, which I should like to submit to you, that the importance of oral gratification as a genetic model for esthetic pleasure is a subject that would reward closer investigation. After all, food is the first thing on which we train our critical faculties from the moment of birth. The very word taste we use to describe a person's esthetic responses points to this model. But so strong is the Platonic prejudice in favor of the spiritual senses, the eye and the ear, that a blanket of social disapproval seems still to cover such animal gratification as eating and drinking. Psychoanalysis cannot be accused of that prejudice, but here the insistence on art as communication and on the model of the dream seems to have worked as a deterrent to investigators. I do not know whether a good cook communicates something through the sauce he makes or invents, but I do think that such an invention need not be all that far removed from esthetic creativity as we are sometimes told. The French, who know most about such things, call an artist's manipulation of paint his *"cuisine,"* and indeed certain paintings are really meant for the dining room —a feast to the eye. I hope you need not be reassured that I do not think that that is all there is to painting. Botticelli's Venus, or a self-portrait by Rembrandt, clearly have other dimensions of meaning and embody different values[19]—but when we speak of the problem of correct balance between too much and too little we do well to remember cookery. For it is here that we learn first that too much of a good thing is repellent. Too much fat, too much sweetness, too much softness—all the qualities, that is, that have an immediate biological appeal—also produce these reaction formations which originally serve as a warning signal to the human animal not to over-indulge. I suppose it could be shown that this warning signal easily shifts from a biological to a psychological plane. I mean that we also develop it as a defence mechanism against attempts to seduce us. We find repellent what yields too obvious, too childish gratification. It invites to regression and we feel not secure enough to yield.

I am afraid I cannot cite much evidence, for if there is psychoanalytical literature about this particular aspect I have failed to spot it; but my impression is that such reaction increases with increasing age and civilization. The child is proverbially fond of sweets and toffees, and so is the primitive, with his Turkish delight and an amount of fat meat that turns a European stomach. We prefer something less obvious, less yielding. My guess is, for instance, that small children and unsophisticated grown-ups will be likely to enjoy a soft milk chocolate, while townified highbrows will find it cloying and seek escape in the more bitter tang or in an admixture of coffee or preferably of crunchy nuts.

Now for the wider psychological interpretation of this distinction between the soft and the crunchy I can quote psychoanalytic authority. Edward Glover, in his study on "The Significance of the Mouth in Psychoanalysis," [20] describes in a masterly fashion how these types of gratification penetrate, as he says:

'. . . every nook and corner of our daily life. All gratifications'
—he says—'are capable of distinction in accordance with the
satisfaction of active or passive aims. They stamp respectively
the biter or the sucker. Study the mouthpiece of pipes, the
stub ends of pencils, offer your friends chocolate caramels, ask
them if they like new bread or stale . . . observe the degree
of partial incorporation of the soup spoon, the preference . . .
for cutlet and sauté or sausages and mashed potatoes, and in a
few minutes you will be able to hazard a guess as to the instinct modifications after birth which may require the deepest
analysis to bring home to the individual. . . .

As you see, Dr. Glover is here concerned with the diagnostic
value of taste, not with its esthetic dynamics. And yet his
analysis has an important bearing on our argument. It links
up the idea of the soft and yielding with passivity, of the hard
and crunchy with activity. It confirms that what makes us sick
in art is an insinuation of passivity which is increasingly re-
sented the higher the brow. For in a way the highbrow, the
sophisticated, the critic is a frustrated artist, and if he cannot
satisfy his standards by creating, he wants at least to project;
this is a craving, it seems, that easily increases with its satisfaction. How much of it is due to narcissism, the need to be able
to enjoy what is inscrutable to the rest, it would be interesting
to know. But one thing is important here. The enjoyment itself is not merely pretended. It is as genuine as the revulsion
from the cheap and vulgar. I should ask your permission to
support this contention with another little experiment *ad homi-
nem*. Again I must beg your forgiveness for inflicting yet another work of Official Art on you. This atrocity is a painting
of the Three Graces by Bonnencontre (Fig. 7).[21] I will spare
you an analysis of all that makes it odious. Let us rather see
whether we can perhaps improve the sloppy mush by adding
a few crunchy breadcrumbs. This is the photograph of the
same picture seen through a wobbly glass (Fig. 8). You will
agree that it looks a little more respectable. We have to become
a little more active in reconstituting the image, and we are less
disgusted. This second image (Fig. 9) shows the same painting
seen at a greater distance through the same glass. By now, I
think, it deserves the epithet "interesting." Our own effort to

reintegrate what has been wrenched apart makes us project a certain vigor into the image which makes it quite crunchy. I'd like to patent that invention, for it has great economic potentialities. In future, when you find a picture in your attic of "The Monarch of the Glen" or of "Innocence in Danger," you need not throw it away or give it to the charwoman. You can put it behind a wobbly glass and make it respectable.[22]

For you must have noticed that this artificial blurring repeats in a rather surprising way the course that painting actually took when the wave of revolt from the Bouguereau phase spread through the art world. Let me just remind you of this mounting crescendo in a few pictures. This Renoir reminds us of the blurring achieved by Impressionism which demands the well-known trained response—you are expected to step back and to see the dabs and patches fall into their place. And then Cézanne, with whom activity is stimulated to even greater efforts, as we are called upon to repeat the artist's strivings to reconcile the demands of representation with obedience to an overriding pattern. It is just because this reconciliation is never complete—because we are constantly brought up against tensions and barbs, as it were, which prevent our eyes from running along smooth lines—that to us Cézanne can never be boring.

But let us not, in pursuance of this one line, forget our formula. The increase in activity permits regression elsewhere. Something like this process of compensation must also find its place in our oral model. The biter who finds the pleasures of passivity barred to him finds his compensation in the indulgence of aggressive impulses. Such a compensation, a redistribution of psychological gratifications, must also take place during the post-Bouguereau period. In a way, I was really over-simplifying when I said that the crudities of *Art Officiel* demand no activity from the beholder. They appeal to him to complete the anecdote, to dream up what happened before and what will come after, as in this painting by Kaulbach called "Before the Catastrophe." I'd like to know why this simple pleasure has also become taboo to the highbrow; why his esthetic super-ego pulls him up not to be childish and to attend to the form—to turn, as it were, from a thematic apperception test to a Rorschach. One could learn a lot in studying such prohibitions. At any rate, Impressionism succeeded in excluding literary association and in confining the give and take to the reading of the scrambled color-patches. But in return for this effort of shared activity, it yields a wonderful premium of regressive pleasure. For the first time in several centuries the public were allowed to see real splashes of loud, bright, luminous colors which had been banned as too crude and primitive by Academic convention. When we speak of the derision encountered by the first impressionist pictures, do not let us forget how quickly the method triumphed and made all earlier paintings look like "mere symbols." [23] Impressionism stands on the watershed between two modes of satisfaction. It can be seen as the summit of the process that leads the pictorial symbol ever closer to be matched with appearances, and as the beginning of openly regressive art, of primitivism. Within the complexities of Cézanne, standards of representational accuracy that had been the norm for centuries could be relaxed; van Gogh and Gauguin forsook them altogether for the sake of an imagery crudely and aggressively regressive. And so at last we are back at the situation within which alone Picasso's *Demoiselles d'Avignon* can be understood.

You remember that Picasso was an infant prodigy, and remained a virtuoso of the easy hand who could outdo his father any time. By 1905 he had developed a distinctive manner of his own, in which he combined a note of social compassion with a predilection for wan, somewhat pre-Raphaelite figures (Fig. 10). There is a touch of *fin de siècle* in these tender mothers and strolling acrobats who so appealed to the imagination of Rilke. And yet one can imagine that the ease with which these insinuating figures came to him must have made the young artist feel a little like Browning's or Ernest Jones' Andrea del Sarto. Imagine the impact on such a nature, first of the Exhibition of the Fauves in 1905, and then of the great show of Cézanne arranged after the master's death in 1907. [24] Like Browning's Andrea, who observes the fault in Raphael's arm, it must have brought home to him that less is more, that the striving and agonizing of Cézanne stood higher than his somewhat fatal ease. What would a gifted and ambitious artist do? He would apply the wobbly glass, but go even further in that direction than Cézanne or the Fauves had ever done. Somewhat like this (Fig. 9)—or rather like this (Fig. 2).

Now psychologically the interesting thing is not that he did what was more or less in the logic of the situation,[25] but how hard he had to struggle to get away from skill and sentiment and meet the demand for more activity and more regression. There is evidence in the sketches that when he first planned the brothel picture it was to have fallen into the category of that compassionate genre Picasso had developed. The artist says at any rate some thirty years later that the man who enters what an American catalog calls "a scene of carnal pleasure" was to have carried a skull.[26] Picasso had doodled erotica before,[27] and maybe his decision to choose such a subject for a monumental canvas was part of his desire for stronger meat—but he still sought contact with tradition. For the moralizing accent reminds us of the Temptation of St. Anthony, which Cézanne had painted several times and which Picasso may have known.[28] The early sketches for the individual women fit this interpretation (Fig. 11). To Picasso, as to many writers of the time, the prostitute symbolized the victim of society, and he endows them with a wistful beauty. It is dramatic to see how he struggles against this pull to paint one more image of graceful outcasts; how he eliminates all trace of the anecdote and sets out to create something more passionate, more savage. And it is important to note that these symbols do not rise spontaneously from his own mind, but can only become articulate through contact with things seen. Sophisticated taste among the Fauves had discovered the enigmatic force of primitive art as seen through Western eyes. And so it is to Negro masks (Fig. 12) and African fetishes (Fig. 13) that he turns. But even in this guise there was still some sentiment. If I am right in my interpretation, it is not before he abandons for a time his own medium, which had become so fatally easy for him, not before he takes to carving where he can exploit his lack of skill (Fig. 14) that he can find the way to the regressive forms from which all trace of Bouguereau had been expelled and which therefore made such an impression on his time.[29]

And now he pours into these regressive forms all the aggression and savagery that was pent up in him. The great smashing begins. He invents the game of Cubism, the art of representing Humpty Dumpty after the fall. In these pictures primitive representational cues turn up, but only to tease and misdirect us—we try to integrate the guitar (Fig. 15) as we integrated Galatea or Europa, but find that we are everywhere brought up against a contradiction, till our mind is set in motion like a squirrel in the cage. But look at the premium of regression that is offered us if we let ourselves be whirled by the merry-go-round. In the dizzy chase after Humpty Dumpty the primary process comes into full play—anything is possible in this crazy world—is not this guitar with its curves and its hollow body (Fig. 17) also a symbol of the female body? And this primitive picture of a bottle beside another guitar (Fig. 16)—is it not also a phallus? Perhaps. Though I readily confess that I put this suggestion to you rather as a premium for all the activity to which I have compelled you. For now, of course, I have nearly done. For, if I am right, the point about such paintings is not that their creator, like all of us, has an unconscious in which these archaic modes of symbolization live on; nor even that like all of us he partakes in his mind of the qualities of Oedipus, Pygmalion, and perhaps of Bluebeard. The point is that thanks to his special conflict situation and his special gifts these perennial private meanings found a specific echo in the situation of art.[30] It is the style, the trend, the demand of the public that creates the sounding board, that makes the particular expression reverberate, and in this reverberation the private meaning is all but swallowed up. What is being shared is not specific contents but what you call dynamic processes, and so we should perhaps not speak of communication but of resonance.

I am afraid I cannot yet quite leave off without showing at least that I do not want to run away from the question that must have obtruded itself on you. If we refuse Bonnencontre our resonance because his paintings are too mushy, does this imply that a Cubist picture that appeals to us for being gritty is therefore good art? I am sure things are not as simple as that. In a way every taste and style can become the instrument of a great artist—though some may be better instruments than others. But while I think that taste may be accessible to psychological analysis, art is possibly not. I am conscious of having oversimplified those shifting urges, the psychological pulls and counterpulls that result in changes of taste and style within the context of civilization;[31] but though a fuller analysis would certainly have to take account of more elements, I do think that such redistributions in the balance of gratification are neither quite so complex nor quite so significant as stylistic movements are sometimes made out to be. For when all is said and done they concern acquired taste, the most malleable part of human nature; the one most easily affected by social pressures and not, as it is sometimes claimed, the inmost soul of what is called "an age." But though I am convinced that art can only become articulate through the symbols presented to the artist by the age, the real work of art clearly achieves more than the satisfaction of a few analysable cravings. Instead of a fairly simple parallelogram of psychological forces we are here confronted with the highest type of organization of countless pulls and counterpulls on a hierarchy of levels that would baffle analysis even if we had greater insight into the kind of elements used. Every square inch of any painting in any style may testify to a yielding to regressive impulses in the color employed and to a domination of such impulse in the disciplined brushwork that husbands its force for the climax.

> *There is a dark*
> *Inscrutable workmanship that reconciles*
> *Discordant elements, makes them cling together*
> *In one society . . .*

Psychoanalytic terminology allows us perhaps at least to discuss these elements, and to indicate the center of what Wordsworth more beautifully describes as "a dark, inscrutable workmanship." It is the ego that acquires the capacity to transmute and canalize the impulses from the id, and to unite them in these multiform crystals of miraculous complexity we call works of art. They are symbols, not symptoms, of such control. It is *our* ego which, in resonance, receives from these configurations the certainty that the resolution of conflict, the achievement of freedom without threat to our inner security, is not wholly beyond the grasp of the aspiring human mind. But, when I come to think of it, I'd like to shirk the question after all, whether the picture on the screen holds all its elements in such a miraculous and reassuring balance. For to answer this question—let it be said in all humility—Psychoanalysis is not really competent; but neither is the History of Art.

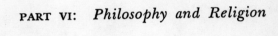

PART VI: *Philosophy and Religion*

THIRTEEN

FREUD AND MODERN PHILOSOPHY[1]
ABRAHAM KAPLAN

Philosophy is culture become self-conscious; the business of philosophy, to rationalize revolutions in culture. The practices of religion, politics, art and science may be carried on with greater or lesser awareness of their presuppositions and principles. To bring them into awareness is to begin to philosophize about them; the end of philosophy is to make them intelligible and acceptable. From time to time, in one or another area of culture changes occur too great and sudden to be assimilated to established patterns of understanding and action. These are the cultural revolutions. It is they which provide the challenge to philosophy—as Greek geometry did for Plato, modern physics for Descartes and Locke, the Reformation for Kant, and Darwinism for Bergson and Dewey. Such a revolution was brought about by Sigmund Freud.

The juxtaposition of Freud and philosophy in this essay does not mark a historical connection, therefore, but one which may yet become a matter of history. I am not concerned with causal relations in either direction—neither the effect of philosophy on Freud's thought, nor the influence of Freud on current philosophizing. Both of these are slight. True, the work of such men as Helmholtz and John Stuart Mill left its mark on

Freud; but those philosophers usually thought to be closest to Freudian perspectives—men like Schopenhauer and Nietzsche —were not read by him till relatively late. And the effect in the reverse direction is, as yet, quite unimportant: academic philosophy is scarcely more informed about psychoanalysis or more sympathetic to it than is academic psychology. My attention focusses on the significance for philosophy of Freud's thought, not on its genesis or historical outcome.

And such significance relates to the scientific substance of his work, not to its speculative efflorescence. It has been suggested, for example, that Freud has provided a new ontology, in which Eros replaces the Logos of the Greeks as the ultimate principle of Being. Now the products of every revolution—in science, art, or whatever—are hard to understand, for understanding is by way of the concepts and categories of the old dispensation. But such talk as this replaces ordinary obscurity by metaphysical impenetrability. My aim is more modest, and it may be, more superficial: to assess the implications of Freudian thought for the main lines of contemporary philosophy—in epistemology, esthetics, ethics, social philosophy, and philosophy of religion. Perhaps only the metaphysical core of his thought would reveal the quintessential Freud. But such a revelation must be left to the psychoanalysts themselves, or to the philosophers of the post-revolutionary era.

EPISTEMOLOGY

The aim of epistemology is to provide a theory of knowledge which accounts for the origin, content, and validity of knowledge, in whatever forms it occurs. This aim has traditionally been conceived as a matter of logic, not psychology, of abstract norms rather than concrete facts. But between the conception and the creation of such a logic falls the shadow of a presupposed psychology. Whether based upon the psychology or only commingled with it, every epistemology is shaped by underlying conceptions of the mind and conduct of which cognition is a product. Thus Locke and Hume theorized about knowledge in the perspectives of associationist psychology, as in our own day Russell made use of behaviorism, Dewey of a functionalist psychology, and the phenomenologists of gestalt. An epistemology which takes account of the depth psychology of Freud and his successors is yet to be written.

Psychoanalysis shares with philosophy the point of view which poses the problem of the theory of knowledge: a distrust of what people think they know. Much of what presents itself as known is projected onto the object from the depths of subjectivity. But an important element even of what is veridical in knowledge is contributed by the knower. Freud provides an empirical refutation of Locke's *tabula rasa* and Baconian induction. His account of the growth and development of the reality-testing functions of the ego renders absurdly superficial any conception of knowledge as resulting from the cumulative force of "objective" facts acting on an empty mind. Knowledge grows by what it feeds on: not "pure" sensation but experiences made significant by present needs and learned patterns of action to satisfy them. What Nietzsche called the dogma of immaculate perception must now be recognized as psychological heresy. The difference between what is "observed" and what is "inferred" or "explained" is no longer a matter of abstract logic but of the concreta of personality and culture.

That knowledge is impossible without a significant contribution from the knowing mind was, of course, already explicit in Kant. But in place of Kant's pure Reason and transcendental categories Freud puts a mind with a determinate history, rooted in the biology of the organism and flowering in the sublimations of culture. Dewey has observed that the classical empiricists were empirical about everything save the concept of "experience" itself, making of it an all-embracing abstraction which miraculously gives birth to both knowledge and existence. But experience is something that happens, an event among other natural events, different for the infant and the mature adult, for the psychotic, the neurotic, and the mind that knows itself, varying in all of these with the constraints imposed by nature and society.

And if empiricists have been unempirical about "experience," rationalists have been equally guilty of irrationality in their conception of "reason." Epistemologies of this type made the senses suspect but accepted intellect without question. Knowledge was held to be genuine and compelling in proportion to the workings of reason in its production. For psychoanalysis, both as clinical practice and as theory, the misuse of reason is as characteristic of the human animal as is its proper employment. Far from being the avenue to truth, reason may serve as a powerful defense against the recognition of truth, masking anxiety by a quest for certainty, perpetuating illusion by elaborate rationalization. Both Hume and Spinoza saw in reason the slave of the passions. It was left to Freud to document this insight with detailed clinical observations. But Hume's scepticism condemned reason to cognitive impotence, while Spinoza's rationalism made it the sole source of truth. Both misconceived the workings of reason by setting it against emotion in its very nature. Not "reason" and "emotion" but rational and irrational emotion are the elements which enter into cognition. Freud's psychology calls for a more subtle appraisal than epistemology has yet made of the passion for truth.

It calls also for a reexamination of the range of cognitive experience. Contemporary scientific philosophy is inclined to restrict knowledge to the highest psychic levels, to what is fully conscious and wholly controlled by logic and the reality principle. In this conception, the paradigm of knowledge is science, but science rationally reconstructed as a product of pure intellectuality. Imagination is denied epistemic significance, and its work identified as "poetry." Thus scientism peoples the mind with children of light and of darkness, and considers only the first to be wise in their generation.

Romanticism acknowledged this image of the poet as being, like the lunatic and lover, a creature of the night. But the philosophers of romanticism insisted on the epistemic importance of the mythopoeic faculty. Though he be of imagination all compact, the poet nevertheless arrives at truth. Poetry is not merely a matter of clothing with feeling a nakedly prosaic cognition. Truth is the very stuff of poetry; fact and fancy are but one. Such a romanticist epistemology obviously courts the danger of obscurantism. When the litterateur preempts the domain of truth, both science and letters are likely to suffer.

Yet the problem for epistemology is a real one. An adequate theory of knowledge must be comprehensive enough to do justice to the whole range of cognitive experience—in art and religion, myth and mysticism, as well as in science. The faculty of imagination which Kant bequeathed to romanticism was, he said, "an art concealed in the depths of the human soul, which nature is unlikely ever to lay open to our gaze." Freud's theory of symbolism and of the workings of fantasy brings this "art" within the purview of science. And in doing so, it provides a challenge for philosophy.

As yet, philosophy has responded to this challenge only by reinstating, in a more subtle form, the classical doctrine of "two truths." What the medievals distinguished as the domains of philosophy and theology, and the moderns as the realms of reason and faith, is formulated today in the dualism of "referential" and "emotive" meaning. Knowledge is in these terms narrowly conceived as "referential" only, and the content of art, religion and morality excluded from the province of epistemology as non-cognitive. But recognition of unconscious processes allows us to trace the affects with which symbols are charged to underlying cognitions, and to see these, in turn, as canalizations of impulse. The possibility thus emerges of a new epistemology, which neither limits reason to make room for faith nor emasculates it to counter the threats against its potency.

Even as an instrument of knowledge, to say nothing of its role in conduct, reason becomes effective only when it draws upon energies not themselves abstractly intellectual and shapes materials not of its own substance. Psychoanalytic therapy, as well as theory, makes central such an employment of reason, called 'insight.' It has a quality of irresistible immediacy which contrasts with the psychic distance of the purely discursive intellect. Modern philosophy has also distinguished two modes of cognition: James, between "knowledge by acquaintance" and "knowledge about"; Russell, between "acquaintance" and "knowledge by description"; Bergson, between "intuition" and "intellect." But in all of these, reason reaches out in vain for direct experience, and the deliverances of sense or intuition become ineffable. Bergson's romantic pragmatism, indeed, defines metaphysics, the area of what is truly cognitive, as the science which dispenses with symbols; and the early Wittgenstein's logical empiricism terminates in the silence of the mystic.

Freud thus poses for epistemology the romantic's problem, while suggesting a solution for it within the realist's framework. Knowledge is not the product of Augustine's light of grace, nor yet does it presuppose Santayana's animal faith. It can be accounted for without appeal either to the supernatural or the subhuman. The resources of the human mind itself will suffice, but only if the mind is seen in its full depth and complexity.

ESTHETICS

It is in esthetics that Freud's thought has probably had the greatest, if not the most direct, influence on technical philosophy. But some of the implications of psychoanalysis for esthetics appear to me to have been often misconceived. And others have scarcely yet established themselves in philosophizing about the arts.

Freud gives art, like mind, a concrete history in the human organism. Art owes its orgin neither to the artistic "soul" nor to a transcendent form of Beauty. Dewey's insistence on the continuity of art with non-esthetic experience, on bringing "ethereal things" into connection with "the live creature," accords wholly with Freud's perspectives. Psychoanalysis is at odds with the idealistic esthetics which conceive of a work of art as an ideal essence produced and contemplated by a correspondingly abstract Mind. Art is created and enjoyed by real people in their concrete individuality, with biological needs and socialized aspirations, acting on materials subject to physical constraints.

To such a naturalistic esthetics Freud makes an important though as yet sketchy contribution: his analysis of creativity provides a beginning for the serious task of dissipating the mystique of inspiration. The Muses are no more than a myth —and no less. That inspiration is as fundamental to art as are the skills of craftsmanship is unexceptionable. But the truism does not imply for the well of inspiration a source outside the psychic life of the artist—only outside his conscious life. The discovery of the unconscious brings within the domain of nature and science much of what traditional esthetics assigned to a transcendent metaphysics.

That psychoanalysis finds the same "primary process" at the core both of the dream and of art has led some to a wholly mistaken identification of art and dream. But surrealism and dada, and the "theories" they have generated, are no closer to Freud than is the purest classicism. For fantasy becomes art only when it is externalized and controlled by the responsible, realistic, and logical ego. The same "primary process" is at work also in the production of science, philosophy, and even mathematics—in short, wherever creative imagination is manifest. But in art as well as in science imagination must submit its work to the scrutiny of the critical faculties. The artistry lies in the care and judgment with which the critical task is performed, as much as in the richness of the creative materials available for criticism. Without both, the work is either as formless and unintelligible as the so-called "art" of the insane, or as mechanical and superficial as the formulas of the skillful hack.

Because the process of creative imagination issues in symbols while the symptoms of neurosis are also symbolic, many literary critics and others have concluded that art is the product of neurosis. The depth meanings of art have been construed out of hand as latent meanings born of the artist's illness. But I cannot see that this conclusion is in any way warranted by psychoanalytic theory. That theory, to be sure, was developed largely from a study of psychopathology. It does not follow that human behavior in all its manifestations is to be understood only in terms of pathology. On the contrary, Freud's theory of neurosis sees illness as impeding the creative impulse. The energies of the neurotic are deflected from realistic problems to cope with inner conflict. If he is unable to master his own emotions he cannot control the affect with which the symbols of his art are to be charged. If he does not understand himself, he cannot attain that understanding of the human condition which his art is to communicate. True, great works of art have been created by neurotic artists. But their achievement testifies to the force of genius triumphing over disease, not to a reward for the endurance of pain and suffering.

Indeed, psychoanalytic theory not only contradicts the conclusion that art springs from neurosis, but even contributes insights into the origin of this mistaken belief. It is not that art is thought to be the reward of neurosis but that neurosis is viewed as a punishment for art. The artist is guilty of the sin of *hubris,* taking unto himself the prerogatives of the divine. The arrogance of his passion to create makes him rival the Creator. What God hath put together he tears asunder, to remold it in his own image, nearer to *his* heart's desire. If his efforts succeed, it is only with God's help; inspiration is the touch of God's hand by which the artist becomes empowered to create. But to look upon God's glory is to be smitten with blindness; and he that wrestles with the angel of the Lord becomes lame. The myth of the blind artist long antedates Freud; but it need not long survive him.

For the blindness of the artist symbolizes only the inwardness of his vision. In enjoying access to his own unconscious he can make manifest to others their common humanity. This approach to art preserves the core of truth in the conception of art as self-expression, while freeing that conception from the infantilisms of romantic individualism. Not Narcissus but Pygmalion is the true artist. He is in love, not with his own image, but with a creation having a form, movement, and substance—in a word, a life—of its own. Only in these terms can art come to have importance for anyone other than the artist and his psychoanalyst. Throughout human history art has developed in intimate association with the most basic concerns of culture—in the institutions of religion, war, food-gathering, the family, and community life. The dehumanization to which art has been subjected in our own time—not least by artists themselves—cannot be made the basis for esthetics. By implication, if not in explicit detail, Freud allows to art a role far more important than a passing release for the artist and a way of passing time for the onlooker. Art brings to artist and audience alike a pulsing awareness both of human desires and of the realities which frustrate and fulfill them.

It is in this sense that art is the fulfillment of a wish: it creates a microcosm in which everything has significance, everything is of value. And it does so by an objective transformation of materials which everyday experience finds recalcitrant. The masterpiece is the work of one who has mastered his materials, forcing them to yield to his will, and who has mastered his impulses, to accord with the real possibilities lying before him. Art is the triumph of the pleasure principle and the reality principle acting in concert. The former lies at the root of Plato's esthetics, for whom the form of Beauty and of the Good are one. The latter is the insight contained in Nietzsche's analysis of art as an expression of the will to power. For contemporary philosophy, Freud poses the challenge of providing an esthetics which does equal justice to both inspiration and skill, inner idea and outer expression, latent content and manifest form—in short, to both wish and reality.

And Freud suggests also the unifying conception which binds together these two moments of the esthetic—it is the symbol. Art as symbol is the distinctive contribution of modern esthetics, from Croce onward. The work of art does not answer to a mysterious "sense of form" nor yet merely to the desire for the delectation of sense: it *makes* sense. Yet its meanings are not to be literalized; the most abstract shapes and sounds can be as rich in content as the most faithful representations. Art, whatever its medium, depends on what is symbolically expressed, not on what is literally represented. An esthetic response to a work is a re-creation of the symbol, an imaginative interpretation in which the audience shares with the artist the shifts in psychic level and in psychic distance through which the work was created. Here, as Croce saw, all the resources of linguistics—or as we would say today, of semantics—can be brought to bear on the problems of esthetics. And the resources of psychoanalysis as well.

ETHICS

Ethics as a branch of philosophy is an abstract theory, not to be confused with the morality embodied in concrete behavior. It is a theory *about* such behavior, which attempts to lay bare the presuppositions and principles of moral conduct. Freud's thought has important bearings on both ethics and morals.

A perennial concern of traditional ethics was the problem of free-will. The determinism presupposed and discovered by science was thought to be incompatible with the genuine acts of choice required by morality. Metaphysicians ranged themselves into two camps, one excluding man from the domain of science, the other excluding objective morality from the domain of action. Kant's resolution of the issue culminates the classical development: free-will falls outside the realm of scientific reality, but is a necessary postulate for the kingdom of ends to which man by his moral nature owes allegiance. Freud's conception of human freedom bypasses these metaphysical controversies altogether.

As a scientist, Freud adheres unswervingly to a deterministic viewpoint. Indeed, the determinism espoused by scientific philosophies in the past went far beyond the actual scientific achievements of their day. Psychoanalysis contributed significantly to an experiential basis for the speculative conviction that causal law was as much at work in the realm of the spirit as in the rest of nature. Not just significant choices, but even the apparently meaningless, trivial, and "accidental" features of psychic life were brought by Freud into determinate connection with events of personal history. There is method in all madness, a meaning derived from causal connection with earlier patterns of impulse and action. The position Spinoza was brought to by his rationalism Freud arrived at empirically: what we call uncaused marks only our ignorance of causes.

But freedom, as Spinoza also insisted, can rest only on knowledge, not ignorance. Slavery to an unknown master is slavery still; and not to know even that we are in bondage is only to deepen it. Metaphysical free-will either puts ethics into irreconcilable conflict with science or can only identify freedom with an illusion. Either we must believe the human psyche too subtle to be caught in the coarse net of scientific causality, or we must analyse freedom in terms of causal agency, not in contradistinction to it.

Such a causal analysis of freedom is at the core of the psychoanalytic theory of its own therapeutic method and aim. Its method is self-knowledge, its aim is self-mastery. Man is free when his choices are the product of full awareness of operative needs and actual constraints. Such needs and constraints, so far as they lie in the self, owe their being to a history of fulfillments and frustrations. But it is a history buried in the unconscious, and what irrationalities it engenders remain invulnerable behind masks of rationality. To remove their masks is not thereby to destroy them but only to reveal them for what they are. To know what he truly wants and what he can truly have—this truth does not make man free, but makes freedom possible. Self-mastery is not antecedently guaranteed, but is something to be achieved.

This conception of freedom accords well with the stoic's formula of "recognition of necessity," Spinoza's "determination by Reason," and Dewey's "reflective choice." For such perspectives Freud provides a greater purchase on the *concreta* of human behavior. Whether and how far man is free need no longer remain a matter for dialectical dispute; it is to be settled by the empirical study of man. And in the course of such study, what freedom we find may be broadened in scope and strengthened in action. Psychoanalysis allots man less freedom than he thought was his, but makes possible more freedom than in fact he had.

Deterministic freedom, however, seems incompatible with moral responsibility. How can we hold a man responsible for what he "could not help doing?" But the question is ill-conceived. Responsibility is not retrospective but prospective. The question to be asked is rather, "Will he act differently for being held responsible?" Causally, the entire pre-history of the universe is "responsible" for every event; ethically, he alone is responsible who can respond to the duties the event calls forth. It is being *held* responsible which is primary; "responsibility" is but a name for that quality of character on which duty takes hold.

What psychoanalysis brings to this viewpoint is the insight that only the self can hold itself morally responsible. Obligations can only be accepted, not imposed. This, indeed, is what binds freedom and responsibility together. So long as a man's duty has another's voice, he is not yet free, and *therefore* not yet responsible. Here again Freud and Kant are at one. Kant's principle of the autonomy of the will is precisely that the moral law is given to the self *by* the self. But Kant grounds his principle on the pure rationality of an abstract noumenal self, while it is, alas, the all-too human phenomenal self which appears on the scene of action. From Plato to the utilitarians morality appealed to "reason"; Freud addresses himself to the problem of the conditions under which the appeal can be made effective.

What is at issue is the conception of the relations between the self which promulgates the moral law, the self which assumes the moral obligations so defined, and the self whose impulses defy those obligations. Traditional ethics was unaware of the depth and complexity of these relations. It failed to recognize that moral integrity—the integration of these diverse selves, indeed, their very acknowledgment—cannot be presupposed. Rationality lies in the realistic unification of this diversity; it is not itself the moral agent which ethics postulates. That morality rests on the injunction "Know thyself" has been acknowledged since Socrates. But only since Freud has ethics been in a position to follow out its implications.

And if the appeal to reason requires revaluation, even more is this true of the appeal to conscience. Freud shares Kant's awe and wonder at the starry heavens above; but as for the moral law within, here, Freud says, God has been guilty of "an uneven and careless piece of work." The critique of conscience as the ground of morality is perhaps the most notable contribution of psychoanalysis to ethics. This critique is not simply a matter of tracing the development of a moral sense to the introjection of parental standards. To disregard conscience because of its origins is to be guilty of the most arrant genetic fallacy. The rational ego also has its history; it does not thereby stand condemned. Such reductionism is a recurrent charge against Freud. In my opinion it is a charge which finds its target only in the vulgarizations of psychoanalytic theory.

What Freud contributes to the critique of conscience is a recognition of its destructive potentialities. A man may be driven by duty as much as by desire, be in bondage to his "principles" as much as to his passions. And under such compulsion he is likely to bring others to perdition and not only himself: more blood has been shed by moral zeal than in the pursuit of pleasure. When the self is brutalized, brutality to others follows quickly. The despot may be his own first victim; he is seldom the last.

Thus, while traditional ethics was content to castigate the passions, Freud invites the attention of the moral philosopher to the immoralities hidden in the castigation itself. Ethics must follow psychology in its exploration of the dark regions that lie beyond the pleasure principle.

All this is not to say that established morality must now go by the board. Psychoanalysis has often been attacked—and not alone by the Pharisees—for weakening moral principles. In part this stems from the detachment of the analyst, as theorist and in therapy. The amorality of objective inquiry is mistaken for the immorality of tacit approval. And the therapeutic aim of achieving "normality" is misconceived as a substitute for moral standards, rather than as a condition for the relevance of moral categories. But only those of little faith fear the outcome of an objective appraisal of their values. Freud is continuing the classical philosophic tradition in holding with Socrates that a life which cannot withstand examination is not worth living.

In part, the fears for morality also stem from another vulgarization of Freud, that the aim of analysis is to encourage the libido to express itself in libertinism. In fact, analysis aims at the resolution of unconscious conflict; and it is explicit in the theory that such conflict is not resolved by supporting one side or the other. Freud does, indeed, criticize conventional morality—and even more, conventional moralization—as futile and dishonest. For the moralizer relies heavily on repression, anxiety, guilt, and the magic of the word, rather than on mature moral insight and conviction. Though it may deplore the sickness, philosophy can only be grateful for the diagnosis: the prevailing moral code is largely a tyranny tempered by hypocrisy.

In short, Freud offers for philosophical consideration a perspective in which morality is seen to be no less complex than is the moral agent himself. Various ethical theories have focussed on one or another element of this complexity—as, say, Kant did on the superego, Nietzsche on the id, and Dewey on the ego. But no ethical theory can be adequate which does not do justice to all these elements, in their relations to one another and to the cultures which provide both setting and significance for moral action. The primary task for a philosophical ethics, as for psychoanalysis, is to understand morality rather than to judge it. Thirty years ago Santayana, writing of the modern conflict of ideals, observed that the "age of controversy" is past, and has been succeeded by "the age of interpretation." In this transition Freud has played a significant role. But it is in the nature of things that we should be better aware of what has already been lost than of what is yet to be won.

SOCIAL SCIENCE AND SOCIAL PHILOSOPHY

Social thought is shaped by its conception of the individual as well as of society. Accordingly, psychoanalytic psychology has profound implications for social science and social philosophy.

As a scientist, Freud posits a human nature sufficiently stable and invariant to make possible scientific generalization beyond individual case histories. Some such posit is presupposed in every study of man, and indeed in every science for its own subject-matter. The kind of order and regularity Newton discerned in the physical world Kant thought Rousseau to have discovered beneath the varying forms of human personality. Contemporary philosophy can find in Freud a more empirical basis for the belief in such regularity.

Now the "deeply concealed essence of man" of which Kant

speaks in this connection need not be understood in Aristotelian terms as a fixed and immutable "nature." Psychoanalysis postulates constancy, not fixity—a regularity of *pattern,* not recurrence of the elements composing the pattern from case to case. For Freud the constancy of human nature is biologically based. But this basis does not preclude—on the contrary, it produces—enormous variation in actual conduct. The plasticity of impulse and the range of its socially conditioned expressions is central to psychoanalytic theory. What is insisted upon is only that the variability is not endless. It occurs within limits, and it is these, rather than a fixed "essence," that make for discernible regularities.

To be sure, the location of the limits cannot be prejudged, but is precisely the object of scientific inquiry. Undoubtedly some social philosophers have drawn them too narrowly, in order to rationalize a *status quo* as all that is humanly possible. But because "human nature" has been ideologically appealed to in defense of privilege, it does not follow that such a concept can be given no scientific standing.

How human nature is conceived obviously affects the formation of broad social policy. In particular, social philosophy has been especially influenced by a belief in a native moral disposition, good or bad. Classically, this belief is embodied in the fiction of the "state of nature"—man considered apart from the institutions of social control. For Locke it was a state of "good-nature"; for Hobbes, life without agencies of socialization would be "nasty, brutish, and short." On this issue Freud stands squarely with Hobbes: the belief in the innate goodness of man he regards as "disastrous." The fictitious "state of nature" can be given empirical anchorage in childhood, if anywhere. And the picture of an innocent childhood corrupted by society is a romanticist myth. Its being so is not simply a matter of infantile sexuality. Far more to the point in psychoanalytic theory are the aggressive impulses which from the outset play so important a role in patterning behavior.

But neither does Freud endorse the myth of the innate depravity of man. The condition of childhood departs from Hobbes' "war of each against all" because as yet the "each" is unformed—the self becomes socialized in the very process of its growth and maturation. And while it is true that Freud reveals the evil impulses in human nature, it is no less true—though less widely remarked upon—that he also reveals the powerful forces within the personality making for their censorship, suppression, or sublimation. In short, human nature for Freud is morally neutral. It is rich in potentialities for good and evil alike. Which is actualized, and to what degree, is not predestined, but depends—within limits—on the wisdom with which society nurtures its human resources.

Such wisdom can be grounded only in knowledge: rational social policy must be based upon the achievement of empirical social science. And social science, for Freud, is nothing other than the study of human nature. Social phenomena are paralleled in individual history, and can be explained by reference to that history. The culture pattern of taboo he interprets in terms of a compulsion neurosis; war, in terms of individual aggression; religion, by reference to father-fixation. The thesis of Plato and Hobbes that the state is "the individual writ large" Freud generalizes to all social institutions. The several social sciences are not autonomous but are all reducible to psychology.

Many critics of Freud have addressed themselves to this generalization, and with some justice. Inferences based on dynamic insights and checked by clinical observations are here too often replaced by sheer speculation, warranted only by extended analogies. Yet even here Freud's scientific genius did not entirely desert him. For indeed, the various social sciences cannot easily be distinguished from one another save, perhaps, as several points of anchorage to which the study of man moors floating anxieties about its scientific status. No institution—political, economic, or "social"—can be understood wholly in its own terms. This does not presuppose an organismic philosophy of culture, but marks only the recognition of empirical interconnections and dependencies among elements which have been abstracted to start with from what is given as unitary.

And what is given are the actions of concrete individuals; it is these on which all the abstractions of social science are ultimately grounded, and to which all observation in social science is at last directed. Empiricism is committed to individualism—as a methodology, not as a social philosophy. It is the rationalists like Hegel who give primacy to the group over its members, to wholes over parts, to History over discrete events. In Freud's perspective, Marx has not stood Hegel back on his feet at all: to account for individual behavior in terms of social classes and social forces is exactly to reverse the order of explanation. It is for this reason that psychoanalysis is often so much more sympathetic to literature than to contemporary "scientific" sociology. Because the novelist, at any rate, presents determinate individuals, and may do so with a consummate sense of psychological realities. It is the student of "movements," "forces," "classes," and "institutions" who runs the risk of writing fiction.

Yet the individual may in turn be analysed socially: not even psychology is autonomous. And such a social analysis is explicit in Freud's own psychology, though its methodological implications are not explicitly assessed. For repression is imposed by man; and surely Freud yields to no one in the importance he assigns to the role of the family as a determinant of the character and action of its individual members. Psychoanalysis thus not only accommodates but requires the distinctively social processes insisted on by Durkheim and Weber. The methodologist is here confronted with a tangle of important questions concerning the interrelations among the human sciences.

But social philosophy is concerned with more than the methodology of social science. It aims at nothing less than an interpretation and appraisal of culture as a whole. Here again Freud raises possibilities for the replacement of speculative by empirical considerations. For to deal with the nature of culture as such is not necessarily to make of it a transcendent reality, but only to detach what is essential in it from the accidents of time and circumstance. But the essence of a thing is only the shadow it casts in the light of some purpose or other; the accidental is what our interests make irrelevant. Social philosophy is interested in social policy. For the philosopher, the essence of culture includes whatever bears upon the realization of human values.

In its full generality, this interest lies beyond the scope of psychoanalytic theory. Yet so far as it goes, that theory has a claim on philosophic attention. For it holds that inner conflict is a product of society as such and not of historical accident. Repression and a heightened sense of guilt is for Freud the price of civilization itself. It is on this basis that he condemns as futile both the cynical denunciations of "modern culture" and the romantic efforts to escape from it. What differentiates man from other species is precisely his capacity for culture, which is to say, his capacity for neurosis. Man is not the rational animal but the repressed animal, and repression and socialization are the same reality viewed from within and without. As in so much nineteenth century thought, here conflict becomes the creative principle. The competition of species, the opposition of thesis and antithesis, and the class struggle are now joined by the antagonisms of id and superego and Eros and Thanatos as providing the dynamics of progress and growth. Through the workings of culture, libido is sublimated into social benevolence, aggression into mastery over nature. And in this transformation culture itself is created.

In his conception of man's place in nature, at bottom Freud belongs to the Age of Enlightenment. But in his view of man's relation to man his sober empiricism sometimes gives way to the dialectic of Romanticism. Freud says somewhere that he proposes to replace metaphysics by metapsychology. For philosophy this may not be an altogether favorable exchange. But the offer must be carefully weighed.

RELIGION

Man's place in nature—this is the preoccupation of the religious philosophies; and it is here that Freud's naturalistic temper is most marked. There is no need to make room for faith conceived as a relation to the supernatural. Lacking an object, faith is not a relation at all, but a condition in the faithful. The psychological understanding of religious belief is to replace the logical analysis of religious truth. Not the semantics but the pragmatics of theology is the proper province of the philosophy of religion.

Freud agrees with James in discerning certain uniformities beneath the variety of religious experience, but differs from him in their interpretation. For Freud they are traceable, not to the presumed identity of the object experienced, but to the shared humanity of the experiencing subjects. The genesis of religious belief is, in Ernest Jones' phrase, the dramatization on a cosmic plane of the child's relations to his parents. Infantile dependency is a cross-cultural invariant under changing patterns of family relationships; and it is this invariant which is abstracted and projected as universal religious truth.

The force of this analysis cannot be met by the easy charge of a genetic fallacy. It is not a question of the genesis of religious belief but of its latent content. Genetic propositions are instruments for interpretation, not premises for demonstrative syllogisms. Freud suggests more than once that scientific interests originate in curiosity about the facts of life; science is not thereby reduced to a state of mind. For science is a matter precisely of curiosity about the *facts;* the scientific interest can develop only with the maturity of a mind capable of sustaining the weight of the reality principle. The question is whether religious belief similarly accords with the norms of maturity. However that question be answered in its generality, religious philosophy cannot overlook the elements of infantilism so often expressed in what is conventionally identified as the religious life.

The psychoanalytic condemnation of religious belief properly extends only so far as faith substitutes for psychotherapy. The peace of mind or soul recurrently promised is not the peace which passeth understanding but one which can very well be understood in psychoanalytic terms. It is the rootless security found in an external source of morality and personal integrity. Such a sense of security is without ground either in a real self or in an external reality. In Freud's perspectives, it is the outlook of a child for whom the world is still a nursery. James' "will to believe" is the imperious claim of a neurotic dependency for its own preservation in the face of what James himself called the robust sense of reality.

Such a condemnation is shared, I am convinced, by the religious spirit. A faith justified by psychological rewards is subtly dependent on a sickness of soul, in which prayer can be only petition, worship only the awe of omnipotence. Not: to be loved though unworthy, but: to find the world worthy of our love—this is surely the religious quest. Security, integrity, and self-respect are its conditions, not its promise.

The mysticism which is the core of the religious experience is thus, to my mind, untouched by Freud's corrosive analysis of its external corruption. Of Bergson's two sources of the religious life, psychoanalysis challenges only the Law, not the Prophets. Perhaps it points to the need even for purification of prophecy—as speaking, not for the god, but out of the fullness of an encompassing self. Such an experience of boundless identification, what Freud calls the "oceanic feeling," he relates to early stages of ego-development. Whether such an account of its genesis also exhausts its content remains problematic. What is beyond doubt is that the philosophy of religion cannot adequately deal with the problem without the fullest exploitation of psychoanalytic insights.

FREUD'S WORLD-VIEW

I cannot conclude this survey of the significance of Freud for philosophy without brief attention to Freud's own philosophy—the *Weltanschauung* grounded in character and temperament, more or less independent of the formulas in which abstract philosophy finds expression.

From this standpoint, Freud is a rationalist, following in the Jewish tradition of Maimonides, Spinoza, and Einstein, closer perhaps to the intellectualism of the first than to the rational mysticism of the other two. With Spinoza's *amor Dei intellectualis* ("intellectual love of God") Freud shares the cathexis, if not the object. Reason itself is for him emotionally charged, and from its own nature, he is convinced, must give the emotions the place they are entitled to. His best hope for the future is that "the intellect—the scientific spirit, reason—

should in time establish a dictatorship over the human mind." On his banner is inscribed "Where id was, there shall ego be."

This rational ideal Freud holds out for everyone, not just Plato's caste of intellectuals. Its attainment is a mark of maturity rather than of philosophical achievement. In an era when political suppression from without reinforces the psychic repression within, Freud remains confident that the voice of intellect, though it speak softly, will persist till it is heard, and heard by all.

Such a conviction is scarcely the credo of the pessimism with which he has been charged. Freud is not so much a pessimist as a realist, possibly the most thoroughgoing realist in western thought. The noblest enterprise of philosophic antiquity Kant saw in the attempt to distinguish appearance from reality. At bottom, this remains the philosophical task, and Freud was occupied with its most basic part: to dispel man's illusions about himself. The rejection of his work he traces to the blow which he delivered to human pride, like those struck by Copernicus and Darwin; and indeed, in that achievement he himself takes pardonable pride.

What is remarkable is that he dispelled illusion without falling into cynicism or groping for new illusions to replace the old. In his own words, he bows to the reproach that he has no consolation to offer. But he is not himself inconsolable; he remains always a yea-sayer to life. The apostle of reason among contemporary academic philosophers is unquestionably Bertrand Russell, whose *Free Man's Worship* hurls defiance at a universe to which human meaning and value is foreign. Freud's rationalism is more resigned: his aim is only "to transform neurotic despair into the general unhappiness which is the usual lot of mankind."

Whether such an appraisal is true of the human condition or only of the life of man in the century since Freud's birth, it is surely impossible to say now. But if in time to come man is secure in a freer, more creative, and more rational existence, not just philosophy and psychology, but human culture as a whole, will owe a debt to Freud's achievement.

FOURTEEN

FREUDIANISM AND PSYCHOANALYSIS: A THOMIST VIEW

JACQUES MARITAIN

To treat the many complex problems posed by Freudianism in one short essay is not an easy thing to do. The matter is further complicated by the fact that interest in Freud's discoveries and theories has not been restricted to psychological and psychiatric circles. On the contrary, it seems to grow greater and more ardent as it extends to less competent groups. Literary men have played an enormous role in the diffusion of Freudianism. It is a formidable trial for a scientific doctrine, or what is presented as such, to owe its success to literary men and the general public. Serious objective discussion of the novelty it imports is confused. In the parasitical din that ensues it is seldom the voice of disinterested intelligence that is heard to advantage. All sorts of obscure desires of justification, vindication and a curiosity more or less pure intervene instead.

Freud lends himself to such confusion because of the passion animating his investigative powers. This is even more true in the case of his disciples. As the abandonment to confusion grows greater on every side, it is the task of the philosopher to attempt all the more persistently to make proper distinctions. I believe that any discussion of this subject is doomed to failure unless at the very beginning *psychoanalysis* as a method of psychological investigation and psychiatric treatment is sharply distinguished from *Freudianism* as a philosophy. Even that is not enough. A threefold division must be made, distinguishing: 1. *The psychoanalytic method;* 2. *Freudian psychology;* 3. *Freudian philosophy.*

Let me state my opinion immediately: on the first plane (psychoanalytic method), Freud shows himself to be an investigator of genius. On the third plane (Freudian philosophy), he seems almost like a man obsessed. On the second plane (Freudian psychology), he appears to be an admirably penetrating psychologist, whose ideas, inspired by his astonishing instinct for discovery, are spoiled by a radical empiricism and an erroneous metaphysics that is unaware of itself.

Since Freud's ideas are more or less known to everybody, there is no point in beginning with an historical and doctrinal exposition that would risk being tiresome.

1

THE PSYCHOANALYTIC METHOD AND THE INVESTIGATION OF THE
UNCONSCIOUS

Freud is well known as a determined defender of the *psychological unconscious*. He refused even to use the word "subconscious," doubtless in order to avoid seeming to favor the tendency to see in the unconscious nothing but a residuum of conscious activity. According to him, it is not the fact of being absolutely inaccessible, but of being inaccessible to *voluntary evocation* that characterizes the unconscious properly so-called. For him, the unconscious comprises *everything* inaccessible to voluntary evocation. For those unconscious elements that can be made conscious by voluntary evocation he reserves the name, *preconscious.*

The question to be raised at the start is whether or not there exists a *psychic life* which eludes consciousness and of which emergences alone reach this luminous zone. In my opinion, a categorical "Yes" must be given in reply to this question and Freud must accordingly be declared right. The problem has been so confused among professional psychologists that some for a long time would not admit anything but a physiological unconscious. Others resorted to the very debatable notion of a plurality of centers of consciousness. The blame for this, however, falls upon the philosophers—and above all, Descartes—who by virtue of an idealist assumption identified *psychological fact* with *fact of consciousness*. In this view, at least with regard to what constitutes psychic life (*le psychisme*), *being* would thus have to be identified with *being known*. In other words, it would be essential for all psychic activity to be aware of itself.

In my opinion, what Émile Meyerson saw as a realist postulate of science and what a Thomistic metaphysician sees as a well established philosophical truth, namely, that things or objects to be known exist independently of the knowledge we have of them, is an axiom of realism as valid for psychology as it is for any other science.

For Saint Thomas Aquinas, it is not just the human soul that is obscure to itself, its concrete existence being known to it only by reflection upon its own acts. Nor are its root tendencies—its powers or faculties—the only realities in us whose inner nature eludes introspection. Instincts, inclinations, acquired tendencies, *habitus* ("states of capacity") or inner perfections of the faculties, virtues and vices and the deep mechanisms of the life of the spirit—all represent a world of reality, only the effects of which reach consciousness. Whether the will is adequate to evoke them or not, it is in a psychic form that a host of memories and images is conserved in us in a latent state. Psychic operations also, even cognitive operations, like those of the senses, can be produced in us without our being conscious of them, that is, without their being explicitly known themselves by intellectual reflection, without the intellect's grasping them for itself to signify them to itself. It is rather primitive and due to an over-simplified form of psychology or to idealist or rationalist prejudices, to believe that there is nothing in us except what we ourselves say of ourselves to ourselves, and that we think and love only what we think we think and love. The least careful observation of our own conduct and the behavior of others should be enough to undeceive us on this score.

In the *Interpretation of Dreams,* Freud writes, "The unconscious is the psychic itself, its essential reality. Its inner nature is as unknown to us as that of the external world, and consciousness informs us about it in a manner as imperfectly as our sense organs about the external world." Taken in itself, this formulation can certainly be endorsed by us.

A qualification, however, must be made immediately. It would undoubtedly be incorrect to state that Freud ignored the efficacy of consciousness. After all, for him, the cure of a neurosis is brought about precisely by the translation of the unconscious to the conscious. What he did ignore, however, is the *proper life* and the *proper energy* of a whole region of psychic life with which consciousness is necessarily connected. I refer to the *rational* part of the soul, to judgments of the intelligence and free choices of the will. These are necessarily conscious by nature, and they are truly of *capital* importance for our conduct. For Freud, however, there is no such thing as free choice. As for functions of the intelligence, for him even the highest of them can be accomplished in the unconscious, along with the rest. If there is any efficacy in consciousness, it consists exclusively in the condition of *becoming known.* For him the unconscious is the main factor in man, if not the sum total of all his energies. Man is led by his unconscious. The light of consciousness, when it functions well, does nothing more than prevent the internal conflicts of unconscious energies from upsetting this leadership too seriously.

But enough of digression. Let us retain the fact of the existence of the psychic unconscious. The question which must now be raised involves the *exploration* of the unconscious. On this head we are indebted to Freud for discoveries whose importance dare not, in justice, be denied.

The first condition for exploring the unconscious is to break down the control and the inhibitions normally exercised by the higher functions over the lower. In other words, it is a question of momentarily putting a stop to this control in order to permit the emergence of the lower psychic life into the field of consciousness. It is what in Freudian language is called *de-repression* or functional liberation. Several stratagems have been employed for this purpose. Some psychiatrists resort to the action of drugs, etherization, for example. Others make use of hypnosis.

Freud's stroke of genius was to have recourse to a voluntary suspension of the exercise of self-criticism and self-control for this purpose. It is well known that this is the essential characteristic of psychoanalysis, or of the technique of free association. It is a matter of momentarily causing the patient to lose his head, as it were. For that purpose the best thing is to obtain his own consent. He then voluntarily delivers himself over to an experience in which his mental life will be decomposed, as it were, or liquified, an experience that will bring him at certain moments to a state very close to hypnosis or dreaming. Stretched out in semi-darkness, he does not see the doctor stationed behind him as an observant witness. The latter simply asks him to associate on a word, then on another given in response, and so on. He abandons himself progressively to the words and images that arise, completely released from logical thought and voluntary self-control. After a certain length of time has elapsed, a whole host of memories and unknown thoughts submerged in the depths of the unconscious begins to mount to the surface.

The process is not unaccompanied by crises and agony, for it is necessary to use violence, as it were, to break down active and tenacious resistances, that have often become automatic, and the mechanisms erected by the neurosis precisely to allow the unconscious the more jealously to guard its secrets.

Interpretation, therefore, has to be joined to the process of de-repression. Interpretation brings the repressive factor to light and transfers it to the field of consciousness. Here it loses its automatic character and disintegrates. The liberation of repressed material and its entrance into consciousness are thereby rendered possible. Lured on by a first de-repression, the psychic unblocking is pursued step by step, de-repression and interpretation mutually conditioning each other. It is in the technique of interpretation, and particularly in the use of symbolism, that Freud and his disciples have allowed themselves to indulge in arbitrary, obsessively dogmatic and pedantic extravagances that risk discrediting psychoanalysis and leave the best jests of Aristophanes and Molière far behind them. This has moved certain wits to declare that the worst enemies of psychoanalysis are the psychoanalysts themselves.

It is likewise true that the diffusion of Freudian interpretations among the general public has had the effect of creating in people the very thing to be discovered in them and poisoning their imagination in the bargain. I refer especially to the lexicon of symbolization that Freud regards as common to all the members of a certain ethnic or linguistic group. A method is not to be judged by the abuses to which men put it, however, but by the positive results it is able to achieve. In my opinion, it must be declared that the principles and laws of Freudian interpretation can be salvaged within an exact and rigorous methodology. The Freudian mechanisms of condensation, displacement, dramatization, symbolization, secondary elaboration, censorship and disguise, obviously provisional in form and subject to revision, represent penetrating insights. But that is not all. Here Freud presents us with a notion of great interest that was almost ignored by professional psychologists before him. It is what Roland Dalbiez,[1] in a book that has since become classic and was the first to elucidate Freudianism in a philosophical way, has called the notion of *psychic expression*. According to this notion, a psychic state is determined not only *from the front,* if I may speak that way, as when I understand it through the object to which it is related, but also *from behind,* as it were, as when I understand it through other states and psychic dispositions of the subject of which it is at once the *effect* and the *sign,* that is to say, the psychic expression. It is something verifiable in a particularly evident way in the case of "dereistic" psychic productions—dreams, hallucination and neurotic symptoms—which are no longer focussed on reality.

Psychoanalysis conducted according to rigorous methodolog-

ical rules is frequently without effect. When it does produce results, they are more often in the order of probability than certitude. In any case, psycho-analytic investigation deals with
knowledge of the singular, explaining individual present by
individual past. All of this means that psychoanalysis does not
pertain to the realm of speculative science, but to the domain
of medicine. It accordingly suffers the imperfections proper
to the logical instruments of such a science. Freud remarks
quite correctly that "a psychoanalysis is not an impartial scientific research, but a therapeutic action. It does not seek by its
essence to prove, but to modify something." Within such
limits, the exploration of the unconscious by the symbolic
method, which plays only a secondary role in psychoanalysis,
moreover, as Freud often repeated, has produced a sufficient
number of well established positive results—the disclosed reality
of memories and traumata buried since childhood has often
been verified from without by inquiry into the patient's past
—to make us regard this technique for exploring the geological
depths of the soul, together with the technique of dream interpretation, as a discovery of the highest value. "The essential
contribution of Freud's work is thus to have created an entirely
new method for exploring the unconscious."

Freud's remark cited a moment ago, however, recalled very
opportunely that it is *in order to cure* that the psychiatrist re-
sorts to psychoanalysis. What then is its therapeutic value?
Without going into a detailed discussion, I shall simply present the conclusions to which it seems a serious study of the
evidence must lead. In my opinion, the psychoanalytic method
—in spite of the logically imperfect form Freud, like almost all
great innovators, has given to his discovery—is not only an
instrument of investigation capable of producing exact results,
but also something that can lead to the cure of neurosis and
perhaps even psychosis. (When it is a question of psychosis,
however, schizophrenia, mental automatism and so on, it would
be preferable to discuss the ideas of Bleuler and Jung instead of
Freud's). It would be absurd to make psychoanalysis the sole
therapeutic instrument for the cure of neuroses. It is *one* of the

therapeutic instruments for the cure of *certain* neuroses, but the mechanism of cure in this case is especially interesting for philosophy.

"As soon as the unconscious processes become conscious," Freud writes, "the symptoms disappear." It is not an abstract notion of the past that de-repression causes to return to the light of day, but the concrete past with the existential certitude proper to the intuition of memory.[2] This is indispensable. It has been said that "the artificial provocation of the phenomena of *hypermnesia* [pathological degree of retention and recall, especially of detail] remains one of the pillars of the psychoanalytic edifice." The patient now has before him his own unconscious, his own past misfortune, his own psychic wounds— inasmuch as they are his, pertain in an ineradicable manner to his own irreversible past and form one body with his own existence. Provocation of hypermnesia is not enough, however. Intelligence must intervene. The interpretation made by the patient or recognized by him as true reveals to him the causal connection between the materials of his past life and the disturbance he is now suffering. It is important to understand that it is a matter of an intellectual act of awareness (*prise de conscience*) that has nothing to do with deduction, but is an intuition bearing upon the very fibers of the subject's psychic tissue. Automatically, through the sole fact of this *prise de conscience,* the automatisms created by the unconscious are made to disappear. The light of the intelligence dispels them. Every cure of a neurotic symptom by psychoanalysis bears testimony to the radical health of intelligence and consciousness.

To indicate how this sort of cure can be spontaneous, I will cite a case of which I have direct knowledge. A young girl experienced symptoms of anxiety, that were becoming more distressing every year, whenever she found herself in an enclosure like a closed room or the compartment of a train. She happened to be an open soul and was accustomed to see herself clearly. One day when she was taking a walk in the country she said to herself, "It is not possible. There must be some explanation for it." She then began to reflect on her past. Suddenly the memory of a *completely forgotten* incident of her early childhood came to mind. When she was about three years old, she was once with her father whom she rarely saw and whom she greatly feared. (The father was separated from her mother.) She wanted to leave the room they were in. The instant she turned the knob on the door, her father put on the lock that was placed too high for the child's hand to reach. She made for the window. But her father closed the window and stood in front of it. The child felt herself imprisoned and overcome with anxiety and humiliation. It was easy to grasp the connection between this event of her early childhood and the anxiety now experienced by the young girl whenever she found herself shut up in a given place. Suddenly the symptoms of the budding neurosis disappeared forever. This young girl, who knew nothing about psychoanalysis, had effected a psychoanalytic cure without knowing it, just as, in Molière's play, M. Jourdain had been speaking prose without knowing it.

Cure by analysis consists essentially in dissolving morbid habits by reducing them to the memory of the events that gave them birth.

Roland Dalbiez notes correctly that "the key to the psychoanalytic cure is the distinction between habit and memory. It has always been observed," he continues,

that the learning of a movement of dexterity, that is, the formation of a motor habit, is achieved only when consciousness has withdrawn from the motor ensemble and the latter is integrated automatically. Inversely, it has been established that the sole fact of attempting consciously to apprehend the separate movements in detail greatly disturbs the motor habit and throws its automatism out of gear. The pianist, the stenographer and the fencer are made by their automatisms. They are lost as soon as they want to analyze them.[3]

It is a well-known fact that it was the Viennese doctor, Joseph Breuer, who in the course of the years 1880-1882, made the discovery that the reintegration of a traumatic memory in the field of consciousness can have a curative effect. He called it a *catharsis* or cleansing of the soul. Breuer's discovery consisted in the application of a general law of psychic dynamism to the domain of morbid affective habits. The personal work of Freud consisted in creating an absolutely original exploratory technique, namely, the analysis of spontaneous associations, dreams and inhibited acts, and in being the first to perceive the pathogenic importance of unsuccessful repressions. As Freud himself always maintained, however, the fundamental therapeutic principle of analysis, namely, the disintegration of habit by recollection, belongs to Breuer.

"It is this fundamental therapeutic principle that distinguishes the Freudian theory of the relations between habit and memory from that maintained by Bergson. The French philosopher would contrast habit as an acquired bodily mechanism with pure memory. Freud also contrasts habit and memory, but in another way. It is impossible for him to grant that habit is purely somatic; that would destroy the foundation of his whole method of treatment. There are psychic, cognitive habits. Automatism can invade the psychic life no less than the organism. The disintegration of morbid affective habits by their reduction to memory demonstrates the psychic character of these habits. We might say that the psychoanalytic cure is the therapeutic refutation of the Bergsonian thesis that restricts habit to the purely organic and sees nothing in it except motor activity." [4]

Psychoanalysis can cure certain neuroses, those whose etiology is not organic but psychodynamic—above all, hysteria (a concept rejected by Babinski, but which played a great role in the genesis of Freud's theories and is at present on the way to being rehabilitated), psychogenic anxiety states and obsessional neurosis. It should immediately be added that it can also aggravate them, and can drag to neurosis or worse unlucky sane people who are well enough, but one day betake themselves to a psychoanalyst's office out of snobbery or imprudent curiosity about themselves. Anyone occupied with these matters knows of examples of men whose mental and moral life have been ruined under such circumstances. It proves that the psychoanalytic method—from the point of view of therapy or the point of view of simple exploration of the unconscious—is a difficult and dangerous method. If it is generally the case of having to choose one good doctor out of a thousand, in this instance it is a case of having to choose one good psychoanalyst out of ten thousand. A discovery can be good in itself, but difficult to handle, dangerous and demanding of exceptional precautions. That is the case with many inventions of the modern world. The psychoanalytic method is risky both for the subject and for the doctor. I should like to give a few brief indications of this fact.

What I mean, in short, is that psychoanalysis—and this is its scientific merit—takes us into forbidden territory. There is always a danger in upsetting the *established relations* between the conscious and the unconscious. There is always a danger involved in entering upon induced states of passivity. A frontier is crossed on the other side of which one can no longer count on the protection of reason. One finds himself in the world of the savage. Who knows whether or not the dreamer off on an adventure will ever again find the door to his own house? The danger referred to already exists in the case of a subject who practices the psychoanalytic method on himself all alone. It is much more serious in the case of psychoanalysis properly so-called, where two people, the doctor and the patient, set out together to enter into the patient's unconscious.

A new feature here not yet sufficiently brought to light is the fact that psychoanalysis transforms the relationship heretofore established between the patient and the doctor. Formerly the doctor was only the *representative* of a certain art which he practiced upon the sick person, disappearing himself as much as possible behind his art. If his personality should make an active appearance (and perhaps therein, as a matter of fact, lay the greatest efficacy of his action), it was *in spite of himself,* as it instrumentally came through his art. The same thing is true in the case of the spiritual director. Here, on the contrary, the medical activity is a single combat between two personalities en route together to the regions of the inner inferno. This duel and entanglement in general sets up an extremely exhausting tension in the physician to maintain his independence and dominant indifference intact. There are risks involved to which his sanity might succumb in the end. As for the patient, he is a patient in a true and more formidable sense than the word formerly conveyed. If the experience turns out badly, he is exposed to disorganization, and to a deeper impairment of his psychic life.

It is sometimes said that psychoanalysis is a kind of substitute for confession. This seems to me to be most incorrect. On the one hand, it would be an illusion to believe that confession has curative power over neuroses and psychoses. Its object and aim are not at all psychotherapeutic. The memories the patient imparts to his confessor are by definition memories that pertain to the sphere of the conscious and the preconscious and depend upon voluntary evocation. If the patient scrutinizes himself and presses his will to probe further, he does not enter for all that the world of the unconscious, he runs the risk of becoming over-scrupulous. When a neurotic or delirious person goes to confession, far from laying bare the root of his neurosis or delirium, he deluges his confessor instead with the effusions of his neurosis and delirium.

On the other hand, confession in itself is an act of reason and will. The two personalities present to each other are cut off from each other as much as possible. The penitent delivers up the secret of his heart to the confessor solely as to an instrument of God. The confessor hides his entire personality behind his role of being a judge.

If we take into account the importance in psychoanalysis of the unique conflict of human personalities just spoken of, two typical features of psychoanalytic treatment begin to take on peculiar significance. The *first* is the fact that it is a rule that in order to avoid certain dangers of nervous disorder, a future psychoanalyst has to begin by being psychoanalyzed himself. It is only after this sort of initiation and preliminary psychic purification that he in turn will be able to undertake the psychoanalysis of others. The *second* typical feature is the law of *transference*. This is the inevitable manifestation at one time or another of the morbid habits of the patient, notably his erotic tendencies, toward the psychoanalyst himself. All whose functions oblige them to accept intimate confidences, confessors, physicians, lawyers, undoubtedly are exposed to becoming the object of the emotions of the neurotic person who may confide in them. But there is a question here of a much deeper and more typical law.

Transference is a necessary stage for a neurotic to go through on the way to psychoanalytic resolution of his difficulties. "A psychodynamic neurosis, according to the schema of Freud, is a system of morbid malrepressed habits expressing themselves in an erratic way. One of the first consequences of the cure (analytic) will be that these morbid habits, instead of manifesting themselves towards the environment, will externalize themselves towards the doctor." [5] Freud declares, "An analysis without transference is an impossibility." If this is necessarily so, is it not due to the fact of the very special relationship in psychoanalysis that links the two personalities of the doctor and the patient together? Is it not a typical manifestation of the intromission of the one into the soul of the other that has been pointed out?

It is this same very special relationship that removes psychoanalysis from the plane of science (practical science) proper to medicine in the classical sense of the term[6] and places it on the level of a conflict between person and person, where individuality and contingency predominate. Perhaps this also explains why psychoanalysts generally have much greater trouble than others in keeping to the laws of objectivity proper to the scientific method. Claparède declared:

Psychoanalysts give one the impression of being the owls of psychology. They can see in the dark. This is certainly a great advantage because many things transpire in the subterranean depths of the subconscious, as in the dark recesses of the primitive soul, and they have discovered a number of connections and facts that have escaped the notice of other psychologists. This advantage has its reverse side, however. Accustomed to the dark, they sometimes seem unable to stand the light and to explain their concepts with clarity, in a rational way convincing to those who, unlike themselves, are not convinced beforehand. They seem also to have lost the sense for nuances and appear to be no longer able to distinguish very well between an abracadabra hypothesis and a likely induction.[7]

The meaning of the observations I have just made should not be misconstrued. They are not meant to condemn the psychoanalytic method. Nor do they presume that it is morally illicit. There is no question of that at all. It is simply a question of the dangers it presents, the reasons of which I have tried to indicate. It is clear that in certain cases it is proper to resort to dangerous medication. When an abnormal connection between the conscious and the unconscious appears in the form of a neurotic symptom that is ravaging a human life, there should be no hesitation about trying psychoanalysis if nosological indications call for it and one is placed in the hands of a good psychoanalyst besides. To have recourse to psychoanalysis as one takes aspirin, however, betokens a very costly naïveté.[8]

Before concluding, and to touch, in passing, upon the question of moral licitness, I would like to mention the way certain investigators proceed on the pretext of being scientific. To verify experimentally the value of Freudian symbolism, Schroetter and Roffenstein would hypnotize their subjects and suggest they dream of some disgusting obscenity whispered into their ear in order to see how the obscene image would be disguised in the dream. Betlheim and Hartmann[9] chose patients affected with certain associative disturbances (Korsakov's syndrome) and made them learn by heart certain prose pieces, offensive in content, in order to see what spontaneous symbolizations could be verified when the subjects later recited the pieces. This sort of experimentation on poor sick people, who are treated as specimens and whose imagination is undoubtedly harmed, raises questions about the moral assumptions animating the experimenters.

2

FREUDIAN PSYCHOLOGY

In my opinion, it is above all for the notion of psychic dynamism that Freudian psychology must be given credit. Other psychologists had already brought this approach to light with greater philosophical force, Bergson in particular. Freud, however, made remarkably fertile use of it in the field of psychiatry and *empiriological* knowledge.[10] The profound life of the unconscious appeared to him to be composed of tendencies, desires, instincts and impulses comparable, not to mechanical forces, but to vital energies directed from within towards an end, each of them working to attain its object with the fierce tenacity, flexibility and artfulness of life. Freud went to extremes in this regard, but the restoration of dynamism and finality has very great value in the eyes of a Thomist. He carried the role of instincts and affectivity to such excess that he seems to see the whole human being in their terms. It remains true, nevertheless, that he forcefully attracted attention to a part of the psychic life of the animal endowed with reason that had generally been neglected because it was masked by higher functions. On the other hand, it is true that he employed a language which was extremely anthropomorphic and mythological. In my opinion, it was the price he had to pay for the correct *methodological feeling,* if I may use the expression, that he had about psychology as an empiriological science. (The unfortunate thing was that he himself wanted to make a philosophy of man out of this empiriological science, and thus succeeded in confusing everything.)

It is a well known fact that with regard to what he calls the *psychopathology of everyday life* his originality consisted in assuming that even occurrences such as lapses, forgetfulness, mistakes, omissions, and the like have a meaning, that is, that they are at the same time effects and signs of hidden affective tendencies. His dream theory is equally well known. To trace every single dream back to a satisfaction of desire in disguise is an assumption so obviously oversimplified that Freud himself felt obliged to modify it. In 1920, in his *Beyond the Pleasure Principle,* he accorded a place to the automatism of repetition and conceded "that in psychic life there exists an inevitable tendency towards reproduction or repetition, a tendency that asserts itself without taking pleasure into account, putting itself above it." It should be noted, incidentally, that in his same theory of the dream as a realization of desire, the desire in question is not, as is so often believed, regarded by Freud as *always* sexual in character. He expressed himself very clearly on this subject.

Enough has been said about this topic. If, in my opinion, the world of dreams is infinitely more complicated and mysterious than Freud maintains and Freud did not succeed in his attempt to master its secrets, it is nevertheless true that he has seen very well that here one must grant a preponderant role to the dynamism of tendencies.

It is in the Freudian theory of neurosis, however, that the role of this dynamism appears to best advantage. I think it has to be acknowledged that both the existence of neuroses of psychodynamic origin and the explanation of them proposed by Freud are well-founded conceptions. Roland Dalbiez has shown in a very profound discussion that the celebrated studies of Pavlov on conditioned reflexes constitute a remarkable confirmation of Freud on this point. For Freud, psychoneuroses "are due to an internal conflict. An instinctive impulse has been repelled into the unconscious and for a certain length of time successfully repressed. The equilibrium then becomes upset. The repression meets with defeat, and the repressed material makes its return in the guise of neuropathological symptoms." Pavlov induced experimental neuroses in a dog, effecting in him a collision of instincts, according to a scheme exactly paralleling the Freudian scheme.

Here is an example of Pavlov's experience. Some food was presented to a dog at the same time that an electric current was applied to a point on his skin. By itself alone, the electric current would produce a reaction of retreat and defense. Associated with the presentation of food, the electric current finally loses the power to arouse a defense reaction and acquires the power to provoke salivation. There is an *inhibition of the defense instinct by a conditioned reflex related to the food instinct.* But the equilibrium thus effected is unstable. If the point of application of the electric current is changed, the equilibrium is destroyed, the current ceases to provoke salivation, and violent manifestations of defense are unleashed. The dog becomes extremely excitable and restless as never before. In the language of Freud, it would be said that there has been a return of what was repressed (the defense instinct) as a consequence of unsuccessful repression.

Another example is very curious because it shows how a conflict of tendencies that disturbs an animal can be related to cognitive phenomena, I mean to the fact that a certain *discernment* has been rendered impossible:

Given a dog in whom there has been established a positive conditioned reflex in response to the appearance of a luminous circle. Food has been presented to the dog each time the circle appears. Thereafter, whenever the circle makes its appearance, the dog salivates. If the animal is now shown an ellipse, the great axis of which is equal to the diameter of the circle and the ratio of whose axes is 1/2, the dog at first salivates. But since the presentation of the circle is accompanied by the food offer, whereas that of the ellipse is not, the dog soon enough comes to distinguish the circle from the ellipse. The experiment is continued with ellipses, the ratio of whose axes is successively 2/3, 3/4, 4/5, 5/6, 6/7, 7/8, and it is found that the dog succeeds in differentiating them. But when it comes to an ellipse the ratio of whose axes is 8/9, which very much resembles a circle, the equilibrium between excitation by the circle and inhibition by the ellipse is destroyed.

There is no means of discerning the circle which says, Food and salivation! from the ellipse which says, Attention! No salivation! "The dog becomes nervous, jumps around on the bench, twists and tears at the apparatus . . ." An experimental neurosis has temporarily been induced in him.

But to come back to Freud. It is remarkable how several of his adversaries with mechanistic or organicist prejudices criticize him for veering, supposedly, towards spiritualism. After all, does he not claim that illnesses, like neuroses and psychoses, and, to speak in the manner of certain of his disciples, even perhaps organic illnesses, can spring from psychic rather than somatic causes? What is one to think of the psychogenic origin of illnesses? To relate this question to metaphysical problems Freud never posed, truthfully speaking, philosophically there is no spiritualism here, neither Cartesian spiritualism nor spiritualism in the genuine sense. Leaving aside the question of the spirituality of the human soul, (of which Freud had no idea), here we have rather an *animism*—one that is very well founded, moreover, in my opinion. If it is true that the soul, conceived of as an entelechy in Aristotle's sense, and the body it informs constitute together a single unique substance, then it becomes clear that every psychic disorder is linked to at least a functional disturbance of the organism. And it becomes no less clear that this same total nosological fact can be considered, if I may say so, from either one side or the other. In certain cases the cause can be altogether psychic, in other cases altogether somatic and in still others again both psychic and somatic at the same time (somatic at least as regards grounding and hereditary dispositions, a thing which Freud never denied). The same thing goes for the cure. This poses no difficulty of a theoretical nature for the philosopher.

There is another aspect of Freudian psychology, a "nocturnal" aspect. This is the aspect, naturally, that has attracted the attention of the general public.

I am thinking particularly of the theory of the libido. Freud has expressed himself on this subject in such opposite terms that sometimes the libido appears to be simply the equivalent of what theologians call concupiscence, the unrestrained desire for what can satisfy the senses and the taste for pleasure, and self-love; sometimes to be a sort of metaphysical eros expressive of the energy of *being* and its striving towards existence and life; and at other times again to be a desire of a sexual nature. The final meaning, however, is so preponderant that the reproach of pansexualism directed at Freudian psychology remains merited in spite of everything. This psychology seems to be dominated itself by a kind of sexual obsession. The preponderance of this last meaning is due either to the fact that sexology was a privileged field of study for Freud or, as will presently be pointed out, because he lacks any philosophical criterion of specification and consequently makes any general notion identical with the most striking example of its realization.

On the other hand, as I have already indicated elsewhere,[11] a general philosophy of a very inferior type prevents Freud from distinguishing potentiality and actuality. He replaces potentiality by a sum total of actualities conflicting among themselves; and for indetermination orientated towards normal actuation but capable of multiple actuations, he substitutes a constellation of opposing actualities in conflict. Hence the normal seems to him to be nothing more than a particular instance of the abnormal, and health a particular case of illness. This is the main reason for the exaggerations contained in his theories on infantile sexuality, the Oedipus complex and the like. In these theories he interprets pathological material, of unexceptionable worth sometimes, in a violent, morose and degrading way. He indulges in the most arbitrary generalizations (as when he considers the existence of the Oedipus complex to be a universal law) and he regards the child as a *polymorphous pervert* (the word, pervert, implying, of course, no moral judgment).

Let us understand, however, that the entire play of the instincts, as numerous and powerful as they are, remains open in man. It possesses a relative indetermination that finds its normal perfection and regulation only in reason. The undifferentiated character of the instincts consequently leaves open the *possibility* of abnormal fixations at any given stage. Let us understand, furthermore, that if certain perversions appear to be a regression to an infantile stage of instinctual development, there is nevertheless an essential difference between "infantile *non-integration* and the *disintegration,* always complicated by anachronistic and discordant reintegration, that is proper to the pathological state." Then we shall understand how absurd the expression of polymorphous pervert is, which Freud uses with regard to the child. Replace this notion of *polymorphous perversion* by the notion of *polymorphous pervertibility,* and the error is corrected, but by the same fact one places oneself outside the pale of Freudianism. Freud declares, "When someone has *become* grossly and manifestly perverted, one can more accurately state that he has been *arrested,* that he represents an arrested stage of development." A formulation like this is typical of the central error of the Freudian psychology here being described.

Finally, with good reason, this psychology aims to be a psychology of a purely empiriological type. It is pervaded and overwhelmed on every side, however, by a pseudometaphysics of the most vulgar character, which Freud is all the less anxious to dispense with as he imagines he has no philosophy or metaphysics at all. I say pseudometaphysics of the most vulgar type, because it combines all the prejudices of deterministic, mechanistic scientism with all the prejudices of irrationalism. A powerful philosophical irrationalism like Bergson's or even Klages' (although the metaphysics of the latter is abominable in my eyes) and an arrogantly rational scientism like Berthelot's, for example, are something noble. But what can be said of a theory of the soul collaborated upon by Caliban become scientist and Monsieur Homais become irrationalist?

The schemata of the psychic apparatus proposed by Freud —especially the second schema: *ego* (comprising the conscious and preconscious), *superego* (comprising the repressing elements of the unconscious), *id* (comprising everything primitive and repressed)—illustrate the confusion just spoken of between the *schemata* of a completely empiriological psychology and the *explanations* of a philosophical psychology, I mean to say when Freud claims he is able to explain with such schemata, say, with the *superego*[12] regarded as "the heir of the Oedipus complex," the origin of morality, for example. The same confusion engenders a sort of explanatory mythology, in which the *life instincts* connected with the libido and the *death instincts* connected with the instinct of individual conservation (that is, for Freud, of a return to the inorganic elements which are the material of the living organism) have as much worth as the Eros and Thanatos of old Heraclitus. It is useless to insist upon so evident a point. I prefer to say a few words about a concept that plays a major role in Freudian psychology, the concept of sublimation.

There is a good discussion of this concept in an essay by Mr. Gustave Thibon (in the *Études Carmélitaines* of April 1936). The first thing to be taken into account is the fact that the notion of the specification of tendencies by their *formal object* is entirely alien to the thought of Freud. Considering tendencies and instincts exclusively from the side of the subject (already a form of materialism as regards the manner of knowing), he is utterly incapable of discovering any difference of essence among them. How could he help, therefore, fusing all of them into one and the same fundamental instinct, of which they supposedly are but various transformations, or rather disguises? On the other hand, his denial of the autonomy of the spiritual and his deeply ingrained taste for taking revenge on man could only serve to push him further in the same direction (a doctrinal materialism this time, if it be true that materialism can be characterized by the reduction of the higher to the lower). The result is that for him the so-called "higher" states, poetic inspiration and mystical love, for example, are simply transformations and masks of instinct, detours by means of which a sensuality inhibited in its normal exercise is satisfied in an insidious and veiled manner. All human inebriation is specifically sensual.

It is only too easy to observe the many mixtures and collusions which can occur by accident in the poor mechanisms of human nature. This very observation, however, attests to the fact that the dynamic structures thus mixed are distinct in essence. The Freudian interpretation is not founded on any necessitating reason, but on the simple and brutal *a priori* denial of an order of realities whose rational certitude is established with the help of the instruments of philosophy, and established solely with the help of such instruments.

Does this mean that the term, sublimation, whose Freudian meaning is unacceptable, has to be rejected in itself? I do not think so. On the contrary, in a quite different sense, it seems susceptible of being used to designate a psychic process of the highest importance.

The inebriation of the poetic or religious soul is specifically spiritual in itself and therefore *specifically distinct* from instinct. Does this mean that it is *divorced* from instinct? It is absurd to absorb the higher into the lower, but it is inhuman to separate the one from the other.

It was suggested a while back that there are typical differences between the instincts as they are to be found in man and the instincts as they are found in animals lacking reason. Instincts have a far greater relative indetermination in man than in animals and require to receive their final regulation at the hands of reason. This is because in man instincts are kindred to the spirit and made for it. "Their true center, their supreme depth lies beyond the finalities of organic life." They possess a secret aspiration to bathe "in those delicate vibrations that communicate with the spirit." This is as true of the typical tonality due to the difference between the sexes as it is of other tonalities of the affective life. This typical tonality—and here we catch up with the Freudian distinction between the *sexual* and the *genital*—greatly overflows in the human being the boundaries of the instinct directed towards procreation. It impregnates the fairest creations of culture and plays an immense role in the genesis of the higher affective states.

With Gustave Thibon, therefore, we can define sublimation —true sublimation—as "a sort of ascendent reflux of instinct in the direction of the immaterial sources of the human being, as the *qualitative* integration of sensible rhythms into the melody of the interior life. Subjectively, it is accompanied by a feeling of equilibrium, peace and inner plenitude, by a sense of liberation from the bondage and discord of the lower appetites and by a spontaneous transparency, as it were," of the depths of nature to the influence of the spirit. If moral progress calls for an ascetic battle of the spirit against the flesh, and knows phases where no sublimation is achieved, in which the lower instincts are vanquished only to become all the more besetting, it also demands to issue in a phase of final integration corresponding to sublimation as just defined, the evangelical name for which is the beatitude of peace.[13]

3

FREUDIAN PHILOSOPHY

I shall devote only a few reflections to Freudian philosophy. There is nothing so unpleasant as to have to speak about a philosophy that does not avow itself to be a philosophy.

The whole of Freudian philosophy rests upon the prejudice of a radical denial of spirituality and freedom. As a result, experimental insights which are often correct, become hardened philosophically into the worst errors. Freud quite rightly saw that human nature bears within itself a plurality of more or less antagonistic forces. For him, however, this pluralism becomes absolute, the human person decomposes and decays before the eyes of the psychologist. He has discovered a powerful instrument for exploring the unconscious and took cognizance of the formidable world, the interior inferno thronged with monsters repressed in the unconscious. But he confuses the unconscious itself with this inferno, which constitutes only a part of it.[14] And because he *divorces* it from the life of reason and spirit, he makes the entire instinctive life, and not just the part that is effectively divorced by repression—or by vice or wickedness—into some kind of pure bestiality crouched in the depths of man's being. He thus disregards the central law of the essentially human character of man's normal instinctive life referred to before. Repressed, active, bestial, infantile, alogical and sexual are the six notes with which Ernest Jones characterizes the unconscious of Freud.

As in the case of Marx, it has to be recognized that in the errors of Freudian philosophy there is an element of grandeur, which pushes a crucial truth to the point of absurdity. Both men recognized the essential importance of what Thomists call material causality. The unfortunate thing is that they made it the whole, or at least the principal thing.

It is hard not to see in Freud's work a punishment for the arrogance of the proud, pharisaical personality which rationalism had erected into an end supreme in itself. The masks drop one after the other; and what was hidden in whited sepulchres comes out into broad daylight.

Man had denied all the evil and the irrational he carries in himself, so as to be able to enjoy the testimony of his own conscience and be pleased with himself and justified through himself. Established in the illusion and deception of a false, nominalist consciousness of self, he made great use of moralism and spiritualism, but emptied of their content.

The effort of Freud was successful in denouncing the lie present in this false consciousness.[15] The latter, to tell the truth, hides and disguises deep unconscious undercurrents—not only economic interests and class interests, as Marx affirmed, but in general the whole world of concupiscence and egoistic love of self, the savage and the demoniacal one wanted to deny. After Freud, a certain type of pharisaism has become impossible. In order to restore his unity, man will have to find a new freshness and attain to a new consciousness of self.

On the other hand—it is a good occasion for speaking of ambivalence—this anxious will to denude human nature and show it its ugliness is accompanied by a strange but undoubted compassion: a compassion for the sick person, a compassion for the child whose first experiences are those of shame and grief, a compassion for man as the prey of many demons and lost in his own misery. Freud sees them all as unfortunate victims tormented by an inexorable fate.

Whatever the worth of these affective dispositions themselves, when they intrude into the intellect and command a philosophy they can wreak nothing but havoc and manias. Freud's larval philosophy appears to be a morbid symptom affecting the intelligence in consequence of an unsuccessful repression of the affective dispositions in question. It is nothing more than a disguise for a deep hatred of the *form of reason*. It is sufficient to note here the failure of the effort of Freud and his school to account for the superior activities of the human being, art, morality and religion, by psychoanalysis and an empiricism or a radical sensualism with sexualist tendencies.

This failure has been established by Jung with regard to art, by Malinowski with regard to the origin of morality and the astonishing theory of the original parricide, which, as Dalbiez puts it, belongs to anthropological romance. Without a smile, in *Totem and Taboo,* Freud explains that one day "the expelled brothers came together and killed and ate the father, thus putting an end to the existence of the paternal horde," and this cannibalistic act is not only the origin of totemic sacrifice and exogamy, but it gives the key to all religions. Freud concludes, "I can therefore terminate and summarize this brief investigation by stating that in the Oedipus complex one finds the beginnings of religion, morality, society and art at the same time." This, on the part of the father of the Oedipus complex, is pushing paternal pride a little too far.

Finally, I think that at the bottom of Freudian metaphysics there is what Max Scheler has called "resentment": the resentment, Freud himself has explained, of a soul insulted and humiliated since childhood, a resentment, as it seems, against human nature itself; a resentment, above all, against all those things—rational, moral and religious forms and regulations—which, according to him, in pretending to subdue the world of instinct in the name of an ideal, only add to men's misfortune and provoke psychic disorders. *Acheronta movebo*.[16] It has already been remarked that this bitter pessimism does not lack a certain greatness. A species of desperate pity, discernible also in the case of Luther, seems to bring Freud, who sees everything from the angle of vision of the clinic for psychoneurotics, to the point of making morality, with its prohibitions, which he considers arbitrary, and the guilt feeling it develops, responsible for a flood of evils and additional tortures that men inflict upon themselves.

Freud bears a special grudge against cultural sexual morality. It is appropriate to point out here that in the first place the human species is a species that cannot live and develop except in a state of culture. In the second place, that the laws of cultural morality precisely tend to lessen the causes of the sufferings and evils to which the species is exposed and to add to its creative tension, but they cannot tend to this end, however, without striking the individual harshly. Consequently morality becomes for humanity a yoke as intolerable as it is indispensable unless love comes to alleviate it and the sway of divine mercy comes to *compensate* for the demands of law, not abolishing them, but superadding other and better requirements to them. This creates for those for whom, through undeserved luck, the fulfillment of the law is less strenuous, unique duties of friendship and fraternal respect towards the others.

This is not the place, however, to begin a discussion of this theme. In conclusion, I would like to point out that in Freud we find an outstanding example of the statistical law according to which great discoveries—especially when they relate to the world of sense—because of the unfortunate condition of man and his lack of strength to sustain the truth, seem to need violent affective stimulation, which, as it inspires and guides research, at the same time inclines the intellect to error. In the ultimate analysis, however, error serves the truth in spite of itself. Thanks to the fact that reason eventually feels obliged to undertake the processes of purification and reintegration it is the truth that will have the last word.

And now, may I be permitted to add two remarks *by way of epilogue?*

The *first* remark has to do with a particularly significant problem, the problem of the relationship between psychotherapy and ethics. Certain passages from an article I have published on the work of Roland Dalbiez can appropriately be reproduced at this point.[17]

In the forceful and suggestive discussion in which he insists upon referring to the specific object and the proper limits of psychotherapy, Dalbiez writes that the education of the will, by reason of the *end* it pursues, is a moral and religious task, and not one for psychotherapy.[18] Psychotherapy is distinguished from moral and religious education not only by its *end,* but also by its *means.* Whereas ethics and religion make use of *freedom,* psychotherapy avails itself of a certain *determinism.* It is absolutely necessary to emphasize this point strongly because it is ignored by many authors in practice and in theory. The phenomena that psychotherapy attempts to modify are pathological phenomena and not moral faults. Its end is not to render people virtuous, but to restore them to health.

"When it is a question of bodily health, its distinction from virtue is completely evident. Nobody declares that palpitations of the heart are moral faults. When it is a question of psychic health, however, it is curious to find how certain people confuse it with virtue. Yet, already in the realm of normal psychic life, the distinction between psychological determinism and morality is easy to grasp. Intellectual and artistic aptitudes are incontestably something psychological, but they do not pertain to morality. Nobody can be blamed morally for his lack of aptitude for mathematics or sculpturing. The most heroic moral efforts run aground trying to overcome the limitations of psychic capacities. *A fortiori* it is the same in the realm of abnormal psychic life. Will-power counts for nothing in the presence of a feeling of depersonalization. Psychic health, far from being confused with virtue, is presupposed by it. It can be appreciated, therefore, that while ethics sets out to realize the total and supreme good of man by means of free will, psychotherapy sets out to realize a human good that is partial and relative, whether psychic or physical, by means of psychological determinism. To introduce the cultivation of the free will into psychotherapy is to be guilty of confusing essences."

Roland Dalbiez pits his characteristically implacable logic against this confusion. He pursues it among the disciples of Jung, as well as those of Jaspers. I am fully in accord with him on the necessity of the distinction. It is desirable, however, that it be not falsely understood and lead to forgetfulness of the fact that psychotherapy, like medicine in general, is not a speculative science, but a practical science, which proceeds *modo compositivo,* and constitutes an art extrinsically related to ethics, since the being this art aims to cure is a man, in whom freedom of choice and natural determinism interact. "The only role of the psychotherapist is to relieve his patient of strictly pathological phenomena and not to furnish him with a metaphysics, a system of ethics or a political theory." That much is understood. It can happen, however, that in order to relieve a certain individual of strictly pathological phenomena, correction of the way he uses his free choice might have to enter into the picture. In the name of what so-called scientific integrity would the doctor be forbidden to point such a thing out to his client? In order to offset dispositions in them unfavorable to the healthy equilibrium of their biological functioning, Dr. Paul Carton used to counsel his patients about rules of dietetic moderation, but in addition, about abstention from lying, resistance to vile speech, etc. Since it is a question in all this of bringing these people back to *good health,* it is in view of an end proper to medicine that these prescriptions, moral in their own nature, are "usurped" by the art of Hippocrates as a means to health.

Likewise, one does not "prescind" from morality, but one acts in conformity with an elementary moral law, when one takes care not to aggravate the condition of a psychopath by offending his convictions through clumsy moralizations or by burdening his will with tasks it cannot carry out (the moralist acts in the same way in cases that are not pathological). On the other hand, let us consider the way in which a physician behaves as a rule. When it is appropriate to administer a purgative or to apply a cupping-glass, the doctor purely and simply prescribes the remedy in question. But if it seems to him that an action forbidden by the moral law, a fault involving sexual morality, for example, would be favorable to the disappearance of a neurosis or mental disorder, he abstains from prescribing such a remedy and contents himself with informing his patient about the state of the question, leaving the decision up to the latter's own free choice and moral code. If he is questioned from that point of view, he even counsels formally against it. What does this signify except that the medical art, in the person of the subject who exercises it and because of its own human purposes, recognizes its subordination to ethics, which forbids the doctor to induce another to commit a moral fault? The additional elucidations here presented in no way lessen the value of the methodological distinctions laid down by the author of a book whose admirable moral wholesomeness as much as its intellectual exactness merit the recognition of the psychologist and the medical man as well as the philosopher and the educated man who is anxious to obtain a sure orientation with regard to problems in which day by day so many incompetents become involved.

My *second* remark has to do with the present essay itself. Since the time it was originally composed, psychotherapy has advanced considerably, and many new ideas have sprung up both outside the Freudian school (Baruk, Stocker, Nodet . . .) and within the different schools related to Freud. A notable effort of reconstruction has thus been undertaken by certain psychiatrists, psychoanalysts and non-psychoanalysts alike. Gregory Zilboorg recently wrote, "Psychoanalysis and religion found themselves largely separated from the beginning. In the course of the last few years, if certain signs of a *rapprochement* between the two can be observed, it is not due to verbal compromise, but, 1) to the fact that moral conscience has become a serious object of study among certain psychoanalysts in

Switzerland and France, and 2) to religious thought that is beginning to consider Freudian discoveries in independence of Freud's atheistic digressions. In other words, Freud's super-ego has begun to be a serious object of investigation and has been revealed as not identical with conscience. In addition, it has become clear to a certain number of thinkers that the philosophical incursions of Freud could have been divorced from his psychiatric, clinical opinions in the same way that the chemistry of Boyle and the physics of Newton can be looked at altogether independently of their theological digressions." [19]

As a philosopher, I particularly appreciate the works of Zilboorg and of Charles Odier for their intellectual value and the elucidations they afford. (The notion of *psychological morality*, in particular, which was introduced by Odier, seems to me to be of great philosophical interest.) On the other hand, it seems to me that Jung and several of those who are called "revisionists," while they indeed are restoring essential values denied by Freud, have aggravated the confusion between the scientific realm and the philosophical and moral realms in an irremediable way, making room for a sort of scientific mythology able to produce some remarkable results in therapeutic practice, but not much healthier for the intelligence than the "philosophy" of Freud. It should also be noted that the cult of adaptation to the cultural milieu is as irrational as that of the individualistic claims of instinct.

FIFTEEN

HUMAN CREATIVITY AND
SELF-CONCERN
IN FREUD'S THOUGHT

REINHOLD NIEBUHR

The position of Sigmund Freud as one of the great scientific innovators of our era is now generally acknowledged. The therapeutic efficacy of his disciplines and discoveries has been amply proved. By laying bare the intricate mechanism of the self's inner debate with itself, and its labyrinthian depths below the level of consciousness, he enlarged or indeed created new methods of healing "mental" diseases. It is not our purpose, for it is beyond the range of our competence, to deal with these thrilling advances in the art of healing. Our purpose is, rather, to examine an ancillary consequence of Freud's theory of the tri-partite division of the self into *id, ego* and *super-ego* upon current conceptions of human nature and behavior, consequences which go far beyond the scope of the practice of psychoanalysis in treating mental illness. For there is a consistent theory of selfhood involved in Freud's scientific views. The question is how this theory has affected the debate on the old problem of the relation of self-concern to human creativity.

The situation before Freud was that the prevailing philosophies of the Enlightenment had practically eliminated the

259

pessimistic conclusions about the inevitability of the egoistic corruption in all forms of human creativity which had been preserved in the Christian doctrine of original sin. From Renaissance to Enlightenment, which was indeed the climax of the Renaissance, the one unifying factor in otherwise diverse philosophies, whether naturalistic or idealistic, was the favorable view of the potentialities of human nature and the confidence that any residual capacity for evil in man could be eliminated progressively if only either nature or reason could be man's guide. The doctrine of "original sin" which had informed the theories of Western Christendom was discredited, partly because it seemed enshrined in outworn dogmas and myths, but chiefly because its pessimism seemed irrelevant in the light of man's new faith in "nature" or in "reason."

Freud entered into this debate in two chief ways: the first was relatively plain to see. His theories seemed to reconstruct the old pessimism about human nature upon the basis of modern science and thus gave modern man a secular view of the inevitability of egoistic corruptions of creativity, which had been asserted for ages before the modern period. The second way was more tangled. Freud's specific account of the tri-partite division of the self into *id, ego* and *super-ego,* and his conception of the internal debate between the *id* and the *super-ego* in which the ego played the part of an uneasy broker between the two, added insights to the wisdom of the therapists. These teachings did not, however, contribute proportionately to moral and political theory, which is concerned with the problem of harnessing, beguiling, and occasionally suppressing the residual egotism in the creative endeavors of good, as well as evil, men.

"The Enlightenment," declares the eminent Harvard historian Crane Brinton, "did not have a leg to stand on" in its conception of human nature. Freud belonged broadly to the spirit of the Enlightenment; but Freud's system broke with the optimism of the Enlightenment and gave us the first scientific realist account of human behavior. The reason for this break was obvious. Freud had no interest in any traditional doctrine and certainly not in the doctrine of original sin; but he drew a picture of the intricate inner relations within the self which shattered the simple mind-body dualism which had in various ways dominated Western thought from Plato and Aristotle to Spinoza and Descartes, not to speak of Kant's version of the intelligible and sensible self. This dualism was informed by the assumption that the mind, if powerful enough or educated sufficiently, would be in control of all of its impulses and it would guide the self to the more inclusive rational ends which constituted the uniquely human aspect of man's life, as distinguished from the animals, who lived merely in the dimension of nature.

Even if the emphasis was not primarily on mind but on nature, as it was during the French Enlightenment, the optimism was not qualified because "nature" simply meant the natural survival impulse which was harmless unless it was frustrated by bad political institutions. It was therefore the business of reason to lead back to nature. Thus the optimism of the physiocrats was based upon the belief that historical events could be equated with natural events and that human society was governed by "laws of nature." These laws were not quite identical with the *lex naturae* of Stoicism. They were not rationally intuited but empirically observed. Therefore modern science would eliminate all the absurdities of political life, which made for inequality and tyranny. It would organize the community upon the principle of *laissez faire,* that is, it would not interfere with man's inclination to "look to his own preservation" and therefore it would prevent the transmutation of the harmless survival impulse into the harmful forms of will to power. Freud was certainly as naturalistic as the physiocrats but the self which he saw was much more complex than that of the physiocrats. The survival impulse was complicated by the "pleasure principle" of the *id.* The self sought satisfaction for its impulses but above all for its sexual impulses; and human society could not be brought back to a simple libertarianism of the physiocrats; for the most primitive society was organized for the purpose of disciplining or frustrating the sexual impulses of the younger males in the interest of the gratification of the father-chief. (*Totem and Taboo*). The Freudian naturalism explained human behavior in terms of the natural impulses and their frustration under the disciplines of the community. But "nature" was not the simple nature to which the physiocrats wished to return. The survival impulse was a more complicated life impulse and it was heavily charged with sexual urges. Later Freudianism amended the emphasis upon sexuality in the description of the libido, but no version of Freudianism came closer than the thought of Freud to the physiocratic picture of "natural" man, who had been corrupted by the ignorance of the rulers, who had not understood the "laws of nature."

Nor was there anything in the thought of Freud which would support the theories of Spencer, a century later than the physiocrats. Spencer derived his optimism and determinism from the application of Darwinian biology to history. He came to the conclusion that historical communities would evolve naturally from primitive to more advanced forms by laws of development, which could not be changed by human contrivance. He thought that the "predatory" habits of society were vestigial survivals of an earlier age of scarcity and would be dissipated in an industrial age of abundance. This was an obvious miscalculation for it did not anticipate the possibility of atomic wars on a global scale in the very heyday of modern technical society. Spencer, like the physiocrats, did not realize that human ends and ambitions are endlessly transmuted with an advancing culture; and that what he regarded as a vestigial predatoriness, was in fact the conflict of particular and parochial ends on every level of civilization.

Freud's *Civilization and its Discontents* was not explicitly concerned with the refutation of Spencer's optimism. But it gave a completely different picture of an advancing civilization. In Freud's version of history the increasing complexities of civilized disciplines placed a greater and greater burden on the self, intent on the lower level of the *id* upon its primary satisfactions. These repressions would create an ever larger measure of "aggressiveness" which, as he confessed in a letter to Einstein, made the idea of a peaceful world community impossible. It may be doubted, whether Freud's version of man's "aggressiveness" is more valid than Spencer's idea of a primitive aggressiveness. For it may be that in each case the fact that men come in conflict with each other on every level of human desire because they betray partial and parochial desires on that level, is obscured. The truth may be that men are neither aggressive because they must fight for goods in a situation of scarcity or because the disciplines of civilization have frustrated their impulses, but because they are simply intent on their own ends which come in conflict with the ends of other men. The comparison between Freud's and Spencer's ideas of conflict may prove the theories of both to be irrelevant to our present political and moral situation. But Freud's pessimism is certainly closer to the facts than Spencer's optimism. The question is whether the pessimism is informed by a realism which can give us the key to the compound of the will to power and utopian dreams which constitute the demonic energy of communism or, for that matter, the compound of arrogance and concern for the "free way of life" which informs the politics of the "Western world." These historical phenomena are "natural" enough but they are not natural in any sense which would make man's unique ambitions identical with the impulses of nature.

If Freud has a more complicated view of the "nature" of man than the Enlightenment, because nature comprehends more than the survival impulse, he certainly has a much more realistic view of the "reason" of man than the rationalists of the Enlightenment. The reason for this superiority lies clearly in the analysis of the relation of the conscious *ego* to the *id* on the one hand, and the *super-ego* on the other. For the conscious or rational *ego* is never the simple master of the self. It engages in "rationalization" in order to dignify the instinctual drives of the *id*. It acts as an uneasy broker between the *id* and the *super-ego*. Everything which the rationalists of the Enlightenment ascribe to the universal and logical demands of reason upon the self, is regarded by Freud as the consequences of the *super-ego* and the cultural-super-ego's pressure upon the self. While he would strengthen the rational *ego* so that it would assume more power than either the *id* and the *super-ego* he has no dreams of the rational self achieving perspectives of universal validity. He does not expect the mind to create a universal and therefore virtuous self.

The Freudian psychology certainly challenges the Kantian conception of the "intelligible" and the sensible self. Freud's science has invalidated the idea of a god-like reason, which can and does impose duty on inclination. He has also invalidated the more pretentious Hegelian conception of the self's extricating itself from its condition of particularity by rational discipline until it achieves identity with the universal reason itself. Whatever may be the defects of the Freudian view of human nature, it has permanently refuted the pretensions of Hegelianism. Freud did not engage in explicit debate with Comte, any more than with Kant and Hegel. But it is significant for our cultural situation that Freudian analyses of selfhood challenge the rationalistic and voluntaristic theories, derived from Auguste Comte, as definitely as they challenge the more philosophic rationalism.

It is more significant than generally realized that social theory should be variously indebted to the contradictory theories of Spencer and Comte. For Spencer's social Darwinism was in a sense an elaboration of the physiocratic theory in evolutionary terms. But Comte's voluntarism challenged this determinism. Comte aspired to control human destiny by scientific power. He thought we were living in the third world period, after the theological and metaphysical ages; and that in this third period men would master historical destiny in the same way in which they once mastered nature. It was significant that Spencer's determinism should be matched by Comte's voluntarism, for between them they prove that it is difficult to comprehend the human situation, because man is at once the creature and the creator of historical events. It is because he can never be purely creator but pretends to be, that he is corrupted by "original sin," or the pretension which defies and denies creaturely limitations. Comte had a simple solution for this dilemma. He would place historical destiny under the management of scientifically competent managers, who have mastered the laws of history. These superhuman members of the elite would of course manage other human beings who would be less than human, for if they were not, they would not be the malleable stuff which could be managed so easily. Comte, in short, gives a liberal version of the communist dream of a managed historical destiny. He lacks only the dangerous apocalyptic vision of a particular climax of history in which a particular class has the mission to catapult mankind from the realm of necessity to the realm of freedom.

The voluntarism of Comte has certainly had more influence on the modern mind than the Spencerian determinism. All men have the inclination to assert their freedom and power over the flow of events, because they have some evidence that man is at least in partial control of his destiny. An absolutely deterministic doctrine is too contrary to common experience to be plausible. But a combination of determinism and voluntarism in the fashion of either Comte or Marx seems plausible, at least to the reflective. For if it debases some men to subhuman status, it does not include the "intelligent classes" among them. And if it lifts an elite to a superhuman status it only exaggerates a power over historical destiny which we constantly experience.

The Freudian psychology has made nonsense of the Comtean pretensions. For the man whom Freud analyzes is certainly not capable of the God-like disinterestedness and of the universally valid viewpoint which the Comtean scheme demands. Yet Freud did not engage in explicit debate with the followers of Comte; and Julian Huxley is able to maintain (in *Man in the Modern World*) that the bias in historical judgments can be eliminated by only slightly more complicated procedures than were needed to eliminate bias in the natural sciences. We must study the reason for this failure of the Freudian realism to challenge the rationalistic utopianism, ultimately derived from Comte, which informs so much social and political theory in the modern era.

The fact is, that the theory of human nature which broke with the sentimentalities of the Enlightenment and with its confidence in the virtue of "reason" or of "nature" had remarkably little direct influence on social and political theory, which could not come to terms with actual realities without assuming the perennial and universal nature of man's self-regard, with what Jeremy Bentham described as the inclination "to prefer his own happiness to that of all other human beings." Yet this same theory became the basis of a remarkable therapeutic process for healing the inner maladjustments of the self. What is the reason for this therapeutic efficacy and political irrelevance?

To answer that question we must examine Freud's theory of the tri-partite division of the self into *id, ego* and *super-ego*. It was this theory which challenged the traditional mind-body dualism upon which the optimism was based. Freud insists that there is no sharp dividing line between the *id* and the *ego*. He describes them as analogous to two nations with indiscernible boundaries. Nor is there a sharp distinction between the unconscious instinctual drives of the *id* and those parts of the unconscious which have been dismissed from consciousness, and the fear of the eruption of which creates neuroses. In short, he describes the lower part of the self which is intent upon the satisfaction of immediate ends, chiefly sexual satisfaction, though "sexual" includes all family relations. He describes the dynamic stuff which is not yet properly organized by conscious purpose; and it is significant that the cause of mental illness is usually found in childhood. Possibly some traumatic experience has caused the difficulty. The healing art consists in the effort to bring the repressed portions of the self into full consciousness, so that the conscious and coherent self will be emancipated from its anxieties due to repression. In his *Civilization and Its Discontents* he draws the pessimistic conclusion that the disciplines of an advancing civilization, without any untoward experiences of childhood are bound to cause neurotic anxieties and increase consequent "aggressiveness," though there is always the possibility that science can arm the conscious self with the capacity for relating itself to the "reality principle" rather than the "pleasure principle."

The *super-ego* is obviously not an integral part of the self. It does not represent the self's freedom to stand above itself, either to "accuse or else excuse itself." It is the pressure of the communal discipline upon the self. Freud regards the "cultural super-ego" with particular pessimism. It represents the moral demands which transcend the necessities of the immediate community and is typified by the universal ethical principles which are contained, for instance, in the ethics of Stoicism, of Christianity and in the moral code of the "Bill of Rights," as projected by the idealism of the Enlightenment.

Self-regard, in Freud, does not mean the organized and calculated designs of the organized and rationally coherent *ego*. It means the confusion of desires below the level of consciousness. The *id* is described as a "cauldron of seething excitement." What is described, in short, is the confusion of "passion" below the level of conscious purpose and not the confusion of ambitions and ends which conscious selves elaborate and which the refinements of reason may both mitigate and aggravate. Freud's pessimism must be compared with the pessimism of that other great dissenter from the optimism of the Enlightenment, Thomas Hobbes. Hobbes places the root of the inordinateness of human ambitions in precisely those faculties of reason which are regarded as emancipating by both the orthodox Enlightenment and by Freud. Hobbes thinks that human desires have no limit precisely because men have "reason." Men's reason is not for Hobbes the instrument for lifting them above themselves and viewing their interests from some universally valid perspective. It is the servant of the self's interests and passions. Obviously Hobbes has just as one-sided an interpretation of the function of reason as the Enlightenment. For reason in the individual and the collective self is more ambiguous than either realizes. The rational faculties may function in two ways in the same person. They may enlarge the field of interest and concern and force the self to view its interests as merely one factor in a whole field of interests. But they may also prompt the self, beginning with its own interests, to justify them to itself so that they become more inordinate than the mere survival impulses of nature. Hobbes, in short, defines as "reason," what could more accurately be defined as man's freedom. That freedom has both creative and destructive possibilities; and Hobbes sees only the destructive possibilities. But Hobbes recognizes that the freedom of man has potentialities of inordinateness on every level of culture. He saw what is very apparent in modern history: that there is no simple redemption in the growth of rationality, because reason is never completely emancipated from the particular and parochial interests of the individual and collective particular. The pessimism of Hobbes was so consistent that it led to political absolutism, to the projection of an absolute political authority which would be capable of suppressing the anarchy of particular and parochial interests. Democracy could not prosper until Locke and others saw that reason could not only be the instrument of man's capacity for injustice but also of his disposition to do justice.

But the Hobbesian realism is politically relevant, while the Freudian realism is not. Its lack of relevance is due to the fact that it pictures an ego, which is bedeviled, not by organized and coherent ambitions in conflict with other interests and ambitions, but with the anarchy of passions within and below the level of selfhood. The self is really the *id-ego* in the Freudian scheme. It does not calculate upon the level of every advancing historical situation but is increasingly threatened by the tension between the primitive, i.e., the childhood condition and the increasing demands of a complex society. Since the psychiatric problems arise chiefly from childhood experiences before the self is fully organized, this very view of the self which makes for its inadequacy in political and social affairs becomes the basis for its relevance in the healing art.

The depth of Freud's pessimism in regard to the progress of civilization is succinctly expressed in words which are in sharp contrast with all historical optimism, but which also make his theories irrelevant to the problems of an advancing civilization. He declares:

The process (of culture) proves to be in the service of Eros, which aims at binding together single individuals, then families, then tribes, races and nations into one great unity, that of humanity. Why this has to be done we do not know. It is simply the work of Eros. These masses of men must be bound together libidinally. Necessity alone, the advantages of common work, would not hold them together. The natural instinct of aggressiveness in man, the hostility of each against all, and all against each, opposes this program of civilization. This instinct is the main representative and derivative of the death instinct, which we have found along side of Eros, sharing the rule over the earth. And now it seems to me that the meaning of the evolution of culture is no longer a riddle to us. It presents us with the struggle between Eros and Thanatos, between the instinct of life and the instincts of destruction, as it works itself out in the human species. This struggle is what life consists of essentially and so the evolution of civilization may be described as the struggle of the human species for existence. It is this battle of Titans which our nurses and governesses try to compose with lullaby songs of heaven." (*Civilization and Its Discontents,* p. 102-3)

If Hobbes equated the freedom and self-transcendence of the self too simply with "reason," Freud's mistake was to equate the bond of the self to its own interests too simply with its natural impulses and necessities. But the organized and coherent self may be "normal" in the sense that it is not subject to neurotic anxieties and psychic maladjustments and may yet be too consistent in seeking its own ends at the expense of the community.

If the *id* is too closely identified with the *ego,* the *super-ego* is on the other hand not sufficiently identified with the structure of selfhood. For the *super-ego* represents the demands of the community upon the self. This social interpretation of conscience makes the ability of the self to defy the community inexplicable, whether it does so in its own interests or in the name of a higher value than that which the community embodies. Since Freud's system is a consistently naturalistic one, it can not, despite the subtleties of its analyses of the intricacies of human selfhood, do full justice to the transcendent freedom of spirit of which the self is capable and it cannot survey the creative and destructive possibilities of that freedom. For the capacity of transcending every social situation and its own self bears within it all the possibilities of creativity. It enables the self to make a critical survey of its own actions and of its culture, and to project a different end and goal from the traditionally established one. No doubt the self uses all of its ra-

tional faculties as instruments of this freedom. The freedom
is however more than the capacity for discursive reason and the
creative capacities of this freedom do not prevent it from being
used destructively or egoistically. The self can rise above a situation for the purpose of arranging any common enterprise so
that it will be more in accord with its interests. That is why
the rational self is not necessarily more virtuous than the self
which is unreflectively engaged and immersed in some communal loyalty or creative devotion.

The self in its self-transcendence can always use its freedom
both to justify and to accuse itself. This freedom is of course
not absolute. Retrospectively it is always possible to establish
scientifically what pressures prompted the self to certain actions. It is only prospectively that the self is free. The moment
it has acted its actions become one in a chain of cause and
effect. Freud is not to be criticized for his determinism as such,
though probably for the consistency of his deterministic assumptions. But the primary problem of his determinism is that
he finds the causative factors in a too narrow range of subconscious motives. Meanwhile, the self acts in a large arena of
events and forces in which the action may be prompted by any
combination of causes on many levels of economic, cultural,
ethnic and other interests. The freedom of the self is in fact
partly due to its ability to choose between the pressures which
seek to prompt its actions. If the self is determined after it has
acted, it is because it is possible to chart the particular cause
which prompted its action. But the freedom of the self, as self-
determining agent, is always hidden from view.

It is not therefore the determinism of Freudian psychology as
such which is subject to criticism but the narrow view of the
causative factors which eliminates all genuinely historical causes
of human behavior. This narrowness has tempted some Freudians to explain modern totalitarianism by attributing the political ineptitude of Germans, Russians, or Japanese to faulty
child training methods of the mothers of Japan, Germany or
Russia. Freud cannot, of course, be held responsible for these
aberrations.

The Neo-Freudians have sought to correct what was regarded as a too purely "biological" approach of Freud. They have emphasized the lack of love and security in the home as the cause of neuroses (Harry Stack Sullivan: *Interpersonal Psychiatry*). Or they have found the cause of mental illness in the cultural situation, as for instance in the insecurities of a capitalistic order. (Karen Horney: *The Neurotic Personality of Our Time* and *Neurosis and Human Growth*). Or they have taken Freud's dim attitude toward the *super-ego* so seriously that they derived human ills from the moral demand made upon the self and thus reduced Freudianism to another version of the physiocratic thesis that human egotism would be harmless if not repressed. (Erich Fromm: *Man for Himself*).

These Neo-Freudian theories may have enlarged the scope of causes but at the price of eliminating the virtue of the Freud concept of the universality of the self-seeking or pleasure seeking inclination of the self. Thus they capitulated to the error of the Enlightenment and sought particular causes for universal phenomena. There are of course always specific causes for specific forms of self-regard or the will to power or human vanity. The self-regard of a German general, a Japanese Buddhist abbot and an American go-getter are different and have different historical causes. But it would be ill-advised to have a completely nominalistic attitude toward these phenomena and to assume that we could eliminate these forms of self-regard by progressively eliminating the specific causes of specific forms of it.

It would be even more erroneous to find a specific cause for all forms of egotism after the fashion of Marxism, which attributed "greed" to the institution of property and identified covetousness with egotism *per se*. Consequently it hoped for the elimination of egoistic forces in history through the abolition of a social institution. Significantly the Marxist effort to eliminate evil from history involved a supposedly destined proletarian class to commit the most vivid expression of a general human inclination by pretending to an omniscience and grasping after an omnipotence which is not within reach of man as creature. Nothing can alter the ambiguous situation of man as both creature and creator in history. The most plausible form of the doctrine of original sin is to define this persistent and universal tendency to forget and to defy man's creaturely limitations as "original sin."

Thus we return to the presumably discredited traditional doctrine of original sin for which the realism of Freud was regarded by many as a welcome scientific substitute. The doctrine was discredited in modern culture for many reasons. It was part of an outmoded religious tradition. It rested upon a primitive myth, that of the "Fall of Adam"; and it availed itself of an even more dubious dogma, the dogma that Adam's sin was inherited from generation. Since Augustine the inheritance was presumably transmitted through the sin of lust in the act of procreation. Neither the myth nor the dogma has much relevance today though it is worth observing that the primitive myth contains an insight which has not been vouchsafed to much more sophisticated ages. That insight is contained in the idea that the first man's sin was in transgressing the limits set for the creature and desiring to be "like God." The Promethean myth of Greek tragedy expresses the same insight but with the difference that transgressing the limits of the creature is regarded as the necessary and tragic price of human creativity. In the Biblical myth the defiance of creaturely limitations is not the necessary precondition of creativity, but a fortuitous corruption of that creativity.

But even if the myth and the dogma are not taken seriously the modern still has cause to reject the doctrine because it asserts that a fortuitous corruption of self-concern is inevitable and universal. This logical absurdity is not plausible unless we can prove that it accords with the facts of experience. It is possible to prove this if we carefully analyze the detailed facts of man's self-transcendence, his creativity and self-concern. Such an analysis will reveal that there is always a possibility of creativity in human freedom, but that the self which transcends itself is never a universal or rational self. It is always a particular self and this anxious particular self universally insinuates concern for its power and prestige, for its glory and approbation into its creative responsibilities and loyalties. The fact that this concern is universal does not mean that it is universally and equally harmful. Self-concern may express itself in harmless vanities or in harmful forms of will to power. It may or may not come between the artist and his art. It may be harmless if not inordinate though no one has ever given a measure for ordinacy and inordinacy. Modern psychiatry has taught us to regard the egoistic motives not only as universal but as useful, if not inordinate.

Religious thought may therefore have been morbid in defining every form of self-concern as sinful. But if it is recognized that a valid religious view is an existential one, it can be realized why the self is not in a position to absolve itself of blame because it regards its self-concern as ordinate. It is not in a position to judge. In any case it is inclined to judge itself leniently except in cases of religious awareness. Man, in short, is bound to have an uneasy conscience about his egotism, though he knows it to be a universal characteristic. He feels himself responsible, despite the inevitability of the corruption, because he always envisages a purer deed in prospect than it appears in retrospect. For in an honest retrospect the self will always be proved to have insinuated itself into the creative effort.

Perhaps it is well that modern culture should have been engaged in a debate between the religious traditions and the presuppositions of the Enlightenment. For the religious traditions without challenge tend to produce morbidity in regard to the universality of the egoistic impulse and to lack discrimination between ordinate and inordinate forms of it, since there is no objective standard for ordinacy, at least not one which can be applied universally. The Enlightenment, on the other hand, denied the facts which gave rise to the uneasy conscience, for it denied the fact that human freedom is ambiguous and it sought the root of evil either in the inertia of natural impulse and regarded reason as the source of all virtue; or it attributed the perennial emergence of self-regard to specific historical causes which would be progressively eliminated. In this debate Freudianism entered with a new realism, which challenged the rationalism and optimism of the Enlightenment, without however consciously or explicitly supporting a pessimistic realism, which was imbedded in the Christian tradition.

The relation between Freudian and Christian pessimism has been universally observed. Usually the Freudian account of the situation has been given preference in modern culture simply because it was "scientifically" established, while the Christian view is derived from an incredible myth and an equally incredible dogma.

If the claim is made that the traditional Christian view is superior to the Freudian one, this claim can only be validated by adducing proof that it explains more facts in regard to human behavior. Perhaps an explanation is also in order why the discredited religious view should be superior in explaining the facts. Our thesis has been that Freudian realism is defective in explaining the facts of the emergence of self-regard on every level of civilization and in doing justice to the fact that these forms did not represent the inertia of a primitive *id* but the corruption of the freedom of a coherent and organized *ego*. It must be added that the Freudian account of the matter is even more defective in explaining collective forms of self-regard. There is no explanation of the power of alter-egoism expressing itself on the level of family, nation or empire, which is probably a greater hazard to justice than individualistic types of egotism. The Christian explanation of human behavior is sometimes equally individualistic and therefore irrelevant to the collective evils and the problem of the conflict of collective interests.

We can approach the problem of the collective expression of particular interest in contrast to "universal" values, whatever these may be, without entering the debate about the validity of the concept of "personality" for a collective, whether race, nation or other community. Organized communities have one similarity with individuals. They have an organ of will, insofar as they have an organ of government. They are different from individuals because they have no sharply defined organ of self-transcendence. No one in the nation is destined to view the total situation and to place the national interest in some coherent scheme of values. This function is performed by all reflective individuals and groups of individuals who have the ability to survey a larger scene and a more inclusive system of values than those dictated by the survival impulse or the collective pride of the community. But the very fact that these expressions of freedom are not as coherent and organized as the nation's will, makes it inevitable that the collective will should always prove more potent than the freedom, which expresses the conscience of the nation. It is one of the many reasons why collective egotism should be more powerful than the egotism of the individual. It is quite irrelevant to define any form of collective self-regard in terms derived from Freudian psychology. Freud did not attempt this himself and those Freudians who have attempted it have usually defined forms of collective egotism and extravagant nationalism as "infantilism."

The greater inadequacy of Freudian realism in interpreting collective, rather than individual forms of self-regard, is derived from the basic defect of the realism. It is not sufficiently historical, it fails to consider man as an historical creature. It knows him to be involved in history but it regards the increasing demands of civilization as sources of increasing tension upon the nature-bound self.

The self is of course always rooted in nature and does not escape any of the impulses and needs which Freud describes. But all of these impulses are subject to historical elaboration, individually and collectively; and probably they are more obviously historical in their collective expressions. The expression of particular interest and desire, and the rationalization of that interest in the pretension of principles of universal validity takes place within the context of these historical elaborations of initial vitalities. Therefore a realism which ascribes the expression of particular interest and vitality to a nature which is too non-historical is bound to be oblivious to all the complexities of creativity and self-concern, which historical development constantly elaborates. For this reason any form of historical empiricism is superior to an empiricism which is too closely bound to "nature."

Insofar as the myths of the Bible contain the stuff of history and illumine man's perennial problem arising from his position as creator and creature of history, they are bound to illumine some facets of the human situation which the most rigorous science, too closely bound to a non-historical nature, fails to il-lumine. In that sense the doctrine of original sin surveys a broader aspect of human nature and behavior than the Freud-ian pessimism. For it suggests a corruption of self-regard in human nature, which is historical rather than natural because it is a corruption of man's freedom and not some inertia of nature operating against that freedom. A realistic political sci-ence assumes the facts implied in the doctrine though it may know nothing of the doctrine.

The analyses of Freud have consequently been much more successful in laying the foundation for the art of healing mental disorders than in giving us new insights into the po-litical realities of this or any age. Freud did not pretend to be a political scientist. We can not quarrel with him if some fol-lowers sought to draw political and moral conclusions from his system of thought. For it was a total system of thought which in principle transcended the bounds of psychoanalysis. It is im-portant however to make a sharp distinction between the therapeutic efficacy and the political and moral relevance of Freud's great discoveries.

SIXTEEN

FREUD AND THE IMAGE OF MAN
JEROME S. BRUNER

By the dawn of the sixth century before Christ, the Greek physicist-philosophers had formulated a bold conception of the physical world as a unitary material phenomenon. The Ionians had set forth a conception of matter as fundamental substance, transformation of which accounted for the myriad forms and substances of the physical world. Anaximander was subtle enough to recognize that matter must be viewed as a generalized substance, free of any particular sensuous properties. Air, iron, water or bone were only elaborated forms, derived from a more general stuff. Since that time, the phenomena of the physical world have been conceived as continuous and monistic, as governed by the common laws of matter. The view was a bold one, bold in the sense of running counter to the immediate testimony of the senses. It has served as an axiomatic basis of physics for more than two millennia. The bold view eventually became the obvious view, and it gave shape to our common understanding of the physical world. Even the alchemists rested their case upon this doctrine of material continuity and, indeed, had they known about neutron bombardment, they might even have hit upon the proper philosopher's stone.

The good fortune of the physicist—and these matters are always relative, for the material monism of physics may have impeded nineteenth-century thinking and delayed insights into the nature of complementarity in modern physical theory—this early good fortune or happy insight has no counterpart in the sciences of man. Lawful continuity between man and the animal kingdom, between dreams and unreason on one side and waking rationality on the other, between madness and sanity, between consciousness and unconsciousness, between the mind of the child and the adult mind, between primitive and civilized man—each of these has been a cherished discontinuity preserved in doctrinal canons. There were voices in each generation, to be sure, urging the exploration of continuities. Anaximander had a passing good approximation to a theory of evolution based on natural selection; Cornelius Agrippa offered a plausible theory of the continuity of mental health and disease in terms of bottled-up sexuality. But Anaximander did not prevail against Greek conceptions of man's creation nor did Cornelius Agrippa against the demonopathy of the *Malleus Maleficarum*. Neither in establishing the continuity between the varied states of man nor in pursuing the continuity between man and animal was there conspicuous success until the nineteenth century.

I need not insist upon the social, ethical, and political significance of an age's image of man, for it is patent that the view one takes of man affects profoundly one's standard of dignity and the humanly possible. And it is in the light of such a standard that we establish our laws, set our aspirations for learning, and judge the fitness of men's acts. Those who govern, then, must perforce be jealous guardians of man's ideas about man, for the structure of government rests upon an uneasy consensus about human nature and human wants. Since the idea of man is of the order of *res publica,* it is an idea not subject to change without public debate. Nor is it simply a matter of public concern. For man as individual has a deep and emotional investment in his image of himself. If we have learned anything in the last half-century of psychology, it is that man has powerful and exquisite capacities for defending himself against violation of his cherished self-image. This is not to say that Western man has not persistently asked: "What is man that thou art mindful of him?" It is only that the question, when pressed, brings us to the edge of anxiety where inquiry is no longer free.

Two figures stand out massively as the architects of our present-day conception of man: Darwin and Freud. Freud's was the more daring, the more revolutionary, and in a deep sense, the more poetic insight. But Freud is inconceivable without Darwin. It is both timely and perhaps historically just to center our inquiry on Freud's contribution to the modern image of man. Darwin I shall treat as a necessary condition for Freud and for his success, recognizing, of course, that this is a form of psychological license. Not only is it the centenary of Freud's birth; it is also a year in which the current of popular thought expressed in commemoration of the date quickens one's awareness of Freud's impact on our times.

Rear-guard fundamentalism did not require a Darwin to slay it in an age of technology. He helped, but this contribution was trivial in comparison with another. What Darwin had done was to propose a set of principles unified around the conception that all organic species had their origins and took their form from a common set of circumstances—the requirements of biological survival. All living creatures were on a common footing. When the post-Darwin era of exaggeration had passed and religious literalism had abated into a new nominalism, what remained was a broad, orderly, and unitary conception of organic nature, a vast continuity from the monocellular protozoans to man. Biology had at last found its unifying principle in the doctrine of evolution. Man was not unique but the inheritor of an organic legacy.

As the summit of an evolutionary process, man could still view himself with smug satisfaction, indeed proclaim that God or Nature had shown a persistent wisdom in its effort to produce a final, perfect product. It remained for Freud to present the image of man as the unfinished product of nature: struggling against unreason, impelled by driving inner vicissitudes and urges that had to be contained if man were to live in society, host alike to seeds of madness and majesty, never fully free from an infancy anything but innocent. What Freud was proposing was that man at his best and man at his worst is subject to a common set of explanations: that good and evil grow from a common process.

Freud was strangely yet appropriately fitted for his role as architect of a new conception of man. We must pause to examine his qualifications, for the image of man that he created was in no small measure founded on his painfully achieved image of himself and of his times. We are concerned not so much with his psychodynamics, as with the intellectual traditions he embodies. A child of his century's materialism, he was wedded to the determinism and the classical physicalism of nineteenth-century physiology so boldly represented by Helmholtz. Indeed, the young Freud's devotion to the exploration of anatomical structures was a measure of the strength of this inheritance. But at the same time, as both Lionel Trilling and W. H. Auden have recognized with much sensitivity, there was a deep current of romanticism in Freud—a sense of the role of impulse, of the drama of life, of the power of symbolism, of ways of knowing that were more poetic than rational in spirit, of the poet's cultural alienation. It was perhaps this romantic's sense of drama that led to his gullibility about parental seduction and to his generous susceptibility to the fallacy of the dramatic instance.

Freud also embodies two traditions almost as antithetical as romanticism and nineteenth-century scientism. He was profoundly a Jew, not in a doctrinal sense but in his conception of morality, in his love of the skeptical play of reason, in his distrust of illusion, in the form of his prophetic talent, even in his conception of mature eroticism. His prophetic talent was antithetic to a Utopianism either of innocence or of social control. Nor did it lead to a counsel of renunciation. Free oneself of illusion, of neurotic infantilism, and "the soft voice of intellect" would prevail. Wisdom for Freud was neither doctrine nor formula, but the achievement of maturity. The patient who is cured is the one who is now free enough of neurosis to decide intelligently about his own destiny. As for his conception of mature love, it has always seemed to me that its blend of tenderness and sensuality combined the uxorious imagery of the Chassidic tradition and the sensual quality of the Song of Songs. And might it not have been Freud rather than a commentator of the Haftorahs who said, "In children it was taught, God gives humanity a chance to make good its mistakes." For the modern trend of permissiveness toward children is surely a feature of the Freudian legacy.

But for all the Hebraic quality, Freud is also in the classical tradition—combining the Stoics and the great Greek dramatists. For Freud as for the Stoics, there is no possibility of man disobeying the laws of nature. And yet, it is in this lawfulness that for him the human drama inheres. His love for Greek drama and his use of it in his formulation are patent. The sense of the human tragedy, the inevitable working out of the human plight—these are the hallmarks of Freud's case histories. When Freud, the tragic dramatist, becomes a therapist, it is not to intervene as a directive authority. The therapist enters the drama of the patient's life, makes possible a play within a play, the transference, and when the patient has "worked through" and understood the drama, he has achieved the wisdom necessary for freedom. Again, like the Stoics, it is in the recognition of one's own nature and in the acceptance of the laws that govern it that the good life is to be found.

Freud's contribution lies in the continuities of which he made us aware. The first of these is the continuity of organic lawfulness. Accident in human affairs was no more to be brooked as "explanation" than accident in nature. The basis for accepting such an "obvious" proposition had, of course, been well prepared by a burgeoning nineteenth-century scientific naturalism. It remained for Freud to extend naturalistic explanation to the heart of human affairs. The *Psychopathology of Everyday Life* is not one of Freud's deeper works, but "the Freudian slip" has contributed more to the common acceptance of lawfulness in human behavior than perhaps any of the more rigorous and academic formulations from Wundt to the present day. The forgotten lunch engagement, the slip of the tongue, the barked shin could no longer be dismissed as accident. Why

Freud should have succeeded where the novelists, philosophers, and academic psychologists had failed we will consider in a moment.

Freud's extension of Darwinian doctrine beyond Haeckel's theorem that ontogeny recapitulates phylogeny is another contribution to continuity. It is the conception that in the human mind, the primitive, infantile, and archaic exist side-by-side with the civilized and evolved.

> Where animals are concerned we hold the view that the most highly developed have arisen from the lowest. . . . In the realm of mind, on the other hand, the primitive type is so commonly preserved alongside the transformations which have developed out of it that it is superfluous to give instances in proof of it. When this happens, it is usually the result of a bifurcation in development. One quantitative part of an attitude or an impulse has survived unchanged while another has undergone further development. This brings us very close to the more general problem of conservation in the mind. . . . Since the time when we recognized the error of supposing that ordinary forgetting signified destruction or annihilation of the memory-trace, we have been inclined to the opposite view that nothing once formed in the mind could ever perish, that everything survives in some way or other, and is capable under certain conditions of being brought to light again . . . (Freud, *Civilization and Its Discontents*, pp. 14-15).

What has now come to be common sense is that in everyman there is the potentiality for criminality, and that these are neither accidents nor visitations of degeneracy, but products of a delicate balance of forces that, under different circumstances, might have produced normality or even saintliness. Good and evil, in short, grow from a common root.

Freud's genius was in his resolution of polarities. The distinction of child and adult was one such. It did not suffice to reiterate that the child was father to the man. The theory of infantile sexuality and the stages of psychosexual development were an effort to fill the gap, the latter clumsy, the former elegant. Though the alleged progression of sexual expression from the oral, to the anal, to the phallic, and finally to the genital has not found a secure place either in common sense or in general psychology, the developmental continuity of sexuality has been recognized by both. Common sense honors the continuity in the baby-books and in the permissiveness with which young parents of today resolve their doubts. And the research of Beach and others has shown the profound effects of infantile experience on adult sexual behavior—even in lower organisms.

If today people are reluctant to report their dreams with the innocence once attached to such recitals, it is again because Freud brought into common question the discontinuity between the rational purposefulness of waking life and the seemingly irrational purposelessness of fantasy and dream. While the crude symbolism of Freud's early efforts at dream interpretation has come increasingly to be abandoned—that telephone poles and tunnels have an invariant sexual reference—the conception of the dream as representing disguised wishes and fears has become common coin. And Freud's recognition of deep unconscious processes in the creative act, let it also be said, has gone far toward enriching our understanding of the kinship between the artist, the humanist, and the man of science.

Finally, it is our heritage from Freud that the all-or-none distinction between mental illness and mental health has been replaced by a more humane conception of the continuity of these states. The view that neurosis is a severe reaction to human trouble is as revolutionary in its implications for social practice as it is daring in formulation. The "bad seed" theories, the nosologies of the nineteenth century, the demonologies and doctrines of divine punishment—none of these provided a basis for compassion toward human suffering comparable to that of our time.

One may argue, at last, that Freud's sense of the continuity of human conditions, of the likeness of the human plight, has made possible a deeper sense of the brotherhood of man. It has in any case tempered the spirit of punitiveness toward what once we took as evil and what we now see as sick. We have not yet resolved the dilemma posed by these two ways of viewing. Its resolution is one of the great moral challenges of our age.

Why, after such initial resistance, were Freud's views so phenomenally successful in transforming common conceptions of man?

One reason we have already considered: the readiness of the Western world to accept a naturalistic explanation of organic phenomena and, concurrently, to be readier for such explanation in the mental sphere. There had been at least four centuries of uninterrupted scientific progress, recently capped by a theory of evolution that brought man into continuity with the rest of the animal kingdom. The rise of naturalism as a way of understanding nature and man witnessed a corresponding decline in the explanatory aspirations of religion. By the close of the nineteenth century, religion, to use Morton White's phrase, "too often agreed to accept the role of a non-scientific spiritual grab-bag, or an ideological know-nothing." The elucidation of the human plight had been abandoned by religion and not yet adopted by science.

It was the inspired imagery, the proto-theory of Freud that was to fill the gap. Its success in transforming the common conception of man was not simply its recourse to the "cause-and-effect" discourse of science. Rather it is Freud's imagery, I think, that provides the clue to this ideological power. It is an imagery of necessity, one that combines the dramatic, the tragic, and the scientific views of necessity. It is here that Freud's intellectual heritage matters so deeply. Freud's is a theory or a proto-theory peopled with actors. The characters are from life: the blind, energic, pleasure-seeking id; the priggish and punitive super-ego; the ego, battling for its being by diverting the energy of the others to its own use. The drama has an economy and a terseness. The ego develops canny mechanisms for dealing with the threat of id impulses: denial, projection, and the rest. Balances are struck between the actors, and in the balance is character and neurosis. Freud was using the dramatic technique of decomposition, the play whose actors are parts of a single life. It is a technique that he himself had recognized in fantasies and dreams, one he honored in "The Poet and the Daydream."

The imagery of the theory, moreover, has an immediate

resonance with the dialectic of experience. True, it is not the stuff of superficial conscious experience. But it fits the human plight, its conflictedness, its private torment, its impulsiveness, its secret and frightening urges, its tragic quality.

Concerning its scientific imagery, it is marked by the necessity of the classical mechanics. At times the imagery is hydraulic: suppress this stream of impulses, and perforce it breaks out in a displacement elsewhere. The system is a closed and mechanical one. At times it is electrical, as when cathexes are formed and withdrawn like electrical charges. The way of thought fitted well the common-sense physics of its age.

Finally, the image of man presented was thoroughly secular; its ideal type was the mature man free of infantile neuroticism, capable of finding his own way. This freedom from both Utopianism and asceticism has earned Freud the contempt of ideological totalitarians of the Right and the Left. But the image has found a ready home in the rising, liberal intellectual middle class. For them, the Freudian ideal type has become a rallying point in the struggle against spiritual regimentation.

I have said virtually nothing about Freud's equation of sexuality and impulse. It was surely and still is a stimulus to resistance. But to say that Freud's success lay in forcing a reluctant Victorian world to accept the importance of sexuality is as empty as hailing Darwin for his victory over fundamentalism. Each had a far more profound effect.

Can Freud's contribution to the common understanding of man in the twentieth century be likened to the impact of such great physical and biological theories as Newtonian physics and Darwin's conception of evolution? The question is an empty one. Freud's mode of thought is not a theory in the conventional sense, it is a metaphor, an analogy, a way of conceiving man, a drama. I would propose that Anaximander is the proper parallel: his view of the connectedness of physical nature was also an analogy—and a powerful one. Freud is the ground from which theory will grow, and he has prepared the twentieth century to nurture the growth. But far more important, he has provided an image of man that has made him comprehensible without at the same time making him contemptible.

A NEW COPERNICUS?: *Walker*

[1] Exception was taken by Dr. Ernest Jones to an earlier version of this passage concerning Freud's estimate of himself and his claim to be compared to Copernicus. Dr. Jones wrote: "nothing would have been more unlike Freud." In reply to an inquiry from the present editor, Dr. Walker cites "Lecture XVIII of *The Introductory Lectures*, pp. 351-56 of Vol. IV and p. 173 of Vol. V of Freud's *Collected Papers*." Dr. Walker further explains: "The comparison has become a *cliché* of his (Freud's) adulators, which is the reason why I have taken it as my text." Cf. Walker, "Freud and Copernicus," *The Listener* (London), June 7, 1956, p. 764. [EDITOR]

[2] The major works of Groddeck (1866-1934) are now available in translations by V. M. E. Collins. See, especially, the biographical appreciation and the translator's note in *The World of Man* (New York: Funk and Wagnalls, 1951). Other writings by Groddeck include: *The Unknown Self, Exploring the Unconscious,* and *The Book of the It*. [EDITOR]

A PREFACE (*1917*): *Freud*

[1] This constitutes the Preface to Theodor Reik, *Ritual: Psychoanalytic Studies (The Psychoanalytic Problems of Religion, I),* tr. from the 2d German edition by Douglas Bryan (New York: Farrar, Straus, & Cudahy, Inc., 1946), 7-12. [EDITOR]

[2] Otto Rank and Hanns Sachs, *Die Bedeutung der Psychoanalyse für die Geisteswissenschaften* (Wiesbaden, 1913), tr. under the title, *The Significance of Psychoanalysis for the Mental Sciences* (New York, 1915). [EDITOR]

[3] See O. Rank, *Das Inzest-Motiv in Dichtung und Sage* (Leipzig and Vienna, 1912).

[4] W. Robertson Smith's *The Religion of the Semites* is now available in the Meridian Library (New York: Meridian Books, 1956). [EDITOR]

REMINISCENCES OF FREUD AND JUNG: *von Weizsaecker*

[1] From Viktor von Weizsaecker, *Natur und Geist* (Goettingen: Van denhoeck & Ruprecht, 1954), 172-87. The original reads: "27.5.1939" (May 27, 1939), but Freud's death did not occur until September 23, 1939. The explanation for this slip and for a number of others which the present editor has taken the liberty of correcting may lie in the fact that these reminiscences appear to have been written down during the author's internment in Festung Breslau in 1944. [EDITOR]

[2] The author seems here to pre-date the origin of psychoanalysis as a distinctive technique or doctrine. According to Dr. Ernst Kris, who has carefully studied Freud's long-lost, remarkable series of early letters, drafts, and notes from this particular point of view, the introduction of "the psychoanalytic technique proper" belongs to the years 1895-1898. See Dr. Kris' learned introduction to Sigmund Freud, *The Origins of Psychoanalysis: Letters to Wilhelm Fliess, Drafts and Notes (1887-1902)*. (New York: Basic Books, 1954), 3-47, esp. at p. 21. [EDITOR]

[3] The original reads: ". . . the *Interpretation of Dreams*, the quantum theory and the theory of relativity appeared in 1900." Actually, the quantum theory was announced in 1901 and the theory of relativity in 1905. Indeed, the *Interpretation of Dreams* was available toward the close of 1899 but its publication was postdated 1900 by the firm of Deuticke in Leipzig. [EDITOR]

[4] These remarks refer—it will be noted with favorable interest—to the researches of Malinowski; cf. the latter's *Sex and Repression in Savage Society* newly issued by Meridian Books in 1955. [EDITOR]

[5] The original reads: "only a few years later." The *Future of an Illusion* was initially published in 1927 at Vienna, Leipzig, and Zürich by the Internationaler Psychoanalytischer Verlag. A second edition appeared in the following year. [EDITOR]

[6] For Lou Andreas-Salomé, see now her autobiographical sketches, *Lebensrueckblick: Grundriss einiger Lebenserrinerungen* (Zürich: Max Niehans Verlag, 1951). Her correspondence with Rilke is also an invaluable source: cf. the edition by Ernst Pfeiffer (Zürich: Max Niehans Verlag, 1953). [EDITOR]

[7] From Viktor von Weizsaecker, *Natur und Geist*, 159-64.

[8] In a letter dated June 17, 1956 to the present editor, Dr. Jung mentions the following writings as clues to his own evaluations of his relations to Freud: two essays from his pen in *Character and Personality*, I.1(1932) and the *Basler Nachrichten* for October 1, 1939 and ch. vi, entitled "Freud and Jung: Contrasts" in *Modern Man in Search of a Soul* (New York: Harcourt, Brace, 1933); also, the recent volume by Friedrich Seifert, *Tiefenpsychologie: Die Ent-*

wicklung der Lehre von Unbewussten (Jena: Diederichs Verlag, 1955). Other aspects of the relations between the two men and their views will be found in numerous writings mentioned below in the Selected References, notably those by Martin Buber, E. Glover, J. Jacobi, L. Marcuse, I. Progoff, and V. White. [EDITOR]

THE FIRST PSYCHOANALYST: *Erikson*

¹ See Sigmund Freud, *The Origins of Psychoanalysis. Letters to Wilhelm Fliess, Drafts and Notes (1887-1902)*, ed. Maria Bonaparte, Anna Freud and Ernst Kris, tr. Eric Mosbacher and James Strachey (New York: Basic Books, 1954). Dr. Erikson has reviewed this publication in *The International Journal of Psychoanalysis*, Vol. XXXVı (1955), 1-15. [EDITOR]

² See Freud, *The Origins of Psychoanalysis*, 336-445, where it is entitled "Project for a Scientific Psychology." [EDITOR]

THE CURRENT IMPACT OF FREUD ON
AMERICAN PSYCHOLOGY: *Murphy*

¹ Address to the Division of Clinical Psychology, American Psychological Association, Hotel Sherman, Chicago, Illinois, August 30, 1956. Readers who care to survey the lives and works of psychologists mentioned in this essay may wish to consult the following volumes: Edwin G. Boring, *History of Experimental Psychology*, 2d ed. (New York: Appleton-Century-Crofts, 1950); E. R. Hilgard, *Theories of Learning*, 2d ed. (New York: Appleton-Century-Crofts, 1956); Gardner Murphy, *Historical Introduction to Modern Psychology*, rev. ed. (New York: Harcourt, Brace, 1949); Gardner Lindzey, ed., *Handbook of Social Psychology*, 2 vols. (Cambridge, Mass.: Addison-Wesley, 1954); Ruth L. Munroe, *Schools of Psychoanalytic Thought* (New York: Dryden, 1955); R. S. Woodworth, *Contemporary Schools of Psychology*, rev. ed. (New York: Ronald, 1948). [EDITOR]

FREUD, MARX, AND KIERKEGAARD: *Hacker*

¹ See, especially, *The Sickness unto Death,* tr. W. Lowrie (Princeton: Princeton University Press, 1941), and *The Concept of Dread*, tr. W. Lowrie (Princeton: Princeton University Press, 1944); also both the long and short biographies by Lowrie: *Kierkegaard* (New York: Oxford University Press, 1938); *A Short Life of Kierkegaard* (Princeton: Princeton University Press, 1942). [EDITOR]

² This statement, comparing Freud to Hegel, needs to be read alongside of Freud's insistence on what he calls the "law of bifurcated mental development" and the "special capacity of the mind," which is found in human evolution, for retroversion or retrogression. "The primitive mind is, in the fullest meaning of the word, imperishable," Freud writes. "Thoughts for the Times on War and Death (1915)" *Collected Papers*, IV, pp. 288-317, esp. at 300-01. [EDITOR]

FREUD, THE REVISIONISTS, AND SOCIAL REALITY: *Herberg*

¹ "In the deepest sense, our debt is to the work of the great founders of modern social science, among whom we may single out Durkheim, Freud, and Max Weber," Talcott Parsons and Edward A. Shils, *Toward a General Theory of Action* (Harvard, 1951), p. 52.

² Sigmund Freud, *An Outline of Psychoanalysis* (1949), p. 14.

³ Sigmund Freud, *New Introductory Lectures on Psychoanalysis* (1933), p. 105.

⁴ *An Outline of Psychoanalysis*, p. 109. "The pleasure principle . . . reigns supreme in the id." *The Ego and the Id* (1927), p. 30.

⁵ "The power of the id expresses the true purpose of the individual organism's life. This consists of the satisfaction of its innate needs," *An Outline of Psychoanalysis*, p. 19.

⁶ *Ibid.*, p. 15.

⁷ *Ibid.*, p. 19.

⁸ *The Question of Lay Analysis*, p. 43.

⁹ "The ego has the task of bringing the influence of the external world to bear upon the id and its tendencies, and endeavors to substitute the reality principle for the pleasure principle which reigns supreme in the id. The ego represents what we call reason and sanity, in contrast to the id, which contains the passions." *The Ego and the Id*, pp. 29-30.

¹⁰ *New Introductory Lectures on Psychoanalysis*, p. 107.

¹¹ Sigmund Freud, *Moses and Monotheism* (1937), p. 183.

¹² *The Ego and the Id*, p. 30.

¹³ *Moses and Monotheism*, p. 183.

¹⁴ "The gratification of instincts is happiness . . ." Sigmund Freud, *Civilization and Its Discontents* (1930), pp. 31-32. "This [the true purpose of the individual organism's life] consists of the satisfaction of its innate needs." *An Outline of Psychoanalysis*, p. 19.

¹⁵ *Civilization and Its Discontents*, p. 66; see also pp. 65, 68.

¹⁶ *Ibid.*, p. 73.

¹⁷ *Ibid.*, p. 74.

¹⁸ *Ibid.*, p. 80.

¹⁹ *Ibid.*, pp. 86-87.

²⁰ *Ibid.*, p. 102.

21 Gregory Zilboorg, *Mind, Medicine, and Man* (1943), p. 235.

22 *Civilization and Its Discontents*, p. 105.

23 Sigmund Freud, *Group Psychology and the Analysis of the Ego* (New York, 1940) esp. pp. 49, 52, 66, 100, 102.

24 "This danger [a state one may call *'la misère psychologique'* of groups] is most menacing where the social forces of cohesion consist predominantly of identifications of the individuals in the group with one another, whilst leading personalities fail to acquire the significance that should fall to them in the process of group formation. The state of civilization in America at the present day offers a good opportunity for studying this injurious effect of civilization which we have reason to dread. But I will resist the temptation to enter upon a criticism of American culture. I have no desire to give the impression that I would employ American methods myself." *Civilization and Its Discontents*, p. 93.

25 *Civilization and Its Discontents*, p. 93.

26 *The Future of an Illusion*, p. 11.

27 *Civilization and Its Discontents*, pp. 61, 143-144.

28 Erich Fromm, *Escape from Freedom* (1941), pp. 205-206; *The Sane Society* (1955), p. 69.

29 *The Sane Society*, p. 275.

30 Paul Kecskemeti, "The All-Powerful 'I'," *Commentary*, February 1956.

31 *The Sane Society*, pp. 20-21.

32 *Ibid.*, p. 361.

33 *The Future of an Illusion*, p. 11.

34 *Civilization and Its Discontents*, p. 92.

35 *Ibid.*, p. 102.

36 David Riesman, *Individualism Reconsidered* (1954), p. 340.

37 *New Introductory Lectures on Psychoanalysis*, p. 108.

38 *Escape from Freedom*, p. 35. Freud himself explains: "[The task of psychoanalysis is] to strengthen the ego, to widen its vision and extend its field of organization, so that it can take over portions of the id. Where the id is, there shall ego be." *New Introductory Lectures on Psychoanalysis*, p. 112.

39 *The Future of an Illusion*, pp. 73, 77.

40 Lionel Trilling, *Freud and the Crisis of Our Culture* (1956), p. 40.

41 *The Sane Society*, p. 69.

42 Reinhold Niebuhr, *The Self and the Dramas of History* (1955), p. 128.

43 Paul Tillich, *The Courage to Be* (1952), p. 85.

44 Robert K. Merton, *Social Theory and Social Structure* (1949), p. 578. See also Zilboorg: "Even the concept of original sin or of the original fall of man finds its empirical counterpart in the findings of psychoanalysis." *Mind, Medicine, and Man*, p. 326.

45 *Mind, Medicine, and Man*, p. 326.

⁴⁶ *The Future of an Illusion*, pp. 32, 76.
⁴⁷ *Civilization and Its Discontents*, p. 24.

PSYCHOANALYSIS AND THE CLIMATE OF TRAGEDY: *Hyman*

¹ In *The New Statesman and Nation* for January 7, 1956, Dr. H. J. Eysenck of the University of London printed some disconcerting figures on psychoanalytic cure, based on a review of the published material. Of neurotic patients treated by means of any kind of psychotherapy, approximately two out of three recover. Of neurotics who receive no therapy whatsoever, approximately two out of three recover. In other words, two out of three is apparently the percentage of spontaneous recovery. Since then, none of the letters in *The New Statesman* taking issue with Dr. Eysenck's conclusions has challenged these figures.
² Since this was written, Trilling has published his 1955 Freud Anniversary Lecture, *Freud and the Crisis of Our Culture*, with its bold and brilliant vision of Freud's biological limitation as a sanctuary against the omnipotent tyranny of culture.

PSYCHOANALYSIS AND THE HISTORY OF ART: *Gombrich*

¹ Reprinted in *Papers on Psycho-Analysis*, 5th ed. (London: Baillière, Tindall and Cox, 1948), pp. 87 ff.
² I have discussed one aspect of this dream-style (as applied to satire) in "Art and Imagery in the Romantic Period," *Burlington Magazine*, June 1949.
³ Giuseppina Fumagalli, *Eros di Leonardo* (Milan: Garzanti, 1952). The romantic tone and tendency of this book (which is to vindicate Leonardo's sexual normality) need not blind us to the fact that much of the author's criticism of Freud's data (which were mainly derived from Marie Herzfeld's studies) must be accepted as philologically sound.
⁴ For a vigorous criticism of this view from a different angle cf. G. Boas, "Communication in Dewey's Aesthetics," *Journal of Aesthetics and Art Criticism*, December 1953.
⁵ For a facsimile of this letter cf. *Transformation*, 1951, I. The translation published alongside it hardly brings out the charm and force of Freud's reply.
⁶ "The Madonna's Conception through the Ear," *Essays in Applied Psycho-Analysis* (London: Hogarth Press, 1951) pp. 326 ff.
⁷ Jaime Sabartés, *Picasso* (London: W. H. Allen, 1949).
⁸ Daniel Schneider, *The Psychoanalyst and the Artist* (New York:

Farrar, Strauss & Co., 1950), pp. 113 ff. and 208 ff., looks at the same material from a slightly different angle.

⁹ C. Zervos, *Pablo Picasso* (Paris: Édition Cahiers d'Art, 1942), Vol. II, 1, p. 10.

¹⁰ cf. H. Hartmann, E. Kris and R. M. Loewenstein, "Some Psychoanalytic Comments on Culture and Personality," in *Psychoanalysis and Culture,* edited by G. B. Wilbur and W. Muensterberger, (New York: International Universities Press, 1951). The interpretation of the relevant data by these authors appears to me more fruitful than the one given by A. Ehrenzweig, *The Psycho-Analysis of Artistic Vision and Hearing,* (London: Routledge & Kegan Paul, 1953). For the methodological aspect of this question cf. K. R. Popper, "The Poverty of Historicism," *Economica,* 1944/45; esp. section 26.

¹¹ For this aspect of representation as a creation of "substitutes" cf. my "Meditations on a Hobby Horse" in *Aspects of Form,* edited by L. L. Whyte (London: Lund Humphries, 1951).

¹² For a test concerning the difficulty of interpreting foreshortened images cf. D. Katz, *Gestalt Psychology,* (New York: Ronald Press Company, 1950), p. 63.

¹³ E. Kris, *Psychoanalytic Explorations in Art* (New York: International Universities Press, 1952), p. 56, and, the same, "Psychoanalysis and the Study of Creative Imagination," *Bulletin of the New York Academy of Medicine,* April 1953, second series, Vol. 29, No. 4, esp. p. 348.

¹⁴ Now reprinted in E. Kris, *Psychoanalytic Explorations in Art.*

¹⁵ cf. L. Rosenthal, *Sandro Botticelli et sa réputation à l'heure présente* (Dijon, 1897), and my article, "Botticelli's Mythologies," *Journal of the Warburg and Courtauld Institutes,* VIII, 1945, esp. p. 11 note.

¹⁶ *Essays in Applied Psycho-Analysis, op. cit.,* I, pp. 22 ff.

¹⁷ Dr. Jones was, of course, aware of the fact that Andrea's near-contemporary biographer is not always a reliable witness, but it is only in the last few decades that we have learned to see the purpose and degree of Vasari's distortions. Briefly, his book must be read as a series of inspiring examples and cautionary tales for young artists. Within this moralizing context Andrea is cast for the role of the hen-pecked weakling who does not get anywhere despite his undoubted gifts. He must have had character-traits that lent themselves to such interpretation, but it is likely that Vasari fastened on them for two reasons: first, because he knew Andrea to have left the service of the French king, quite an unforgivable act in the eyes of the courtier Vasari; and secondly, because of his unwillingness to jump on the bandwagon of Michelangelo's followers, an equally serious blunder to his arch-mannerist biogra-

pher. If we add to this that Vasari may well have been bossed by del Sarto's wife (as apprentices were apt to be bossed in those days) when he stayed in the master's house as a poor and rootless beginner, the personal motives which guided his literary revenge become only too apparent. How far this account, in its turn, then prejudiced an objective appreciation of del Sarto's art this is hardly the place to discuss.

[18] This is not to imply that it has no roots in traditional esthetics. For those who are interested in these roots Longinus' comparison between the faultlessly fluent Hypereides and the rugged grandeur of Demosthenes (*On the Sublime*, XXXIV) may be relevant.

[19] For Botticelli cf. my article quoted above and "Icones Symbolicae, The Visual Image in Neo-Platonic Thought," *Journal of the Warburg and Courtauld Institutes*, XI, 1948.

[20] *British Journal of Medical Psychology*, IV, 1924.

[21] The example is taken from F. Jourdain, "L'Art Officiel," *Le Point* (Revue artistique), VII.

[22] I wish to thank Mr. Otto Fein of the Warburg Institute who applied his unfailing photographic skill to my problem and produced a series of photographs of which Figs. 8 and 9 are examples.

[23] Even J. Rewald's *History of Impressionism* (New York: Museum of Modern Art, 1946), the standard work on the movement, to which all histories of modern art will remain indebted, should not be read uncritically by those who are interested in the psychological implications of this story. The Romantic image of the lonely artist facing a hostile world had taken such deep roots in the nineteenth century that success smacked of compromise and threatened a painter's self-respect. E. Kris (*Psychoanalytic Explorations in Art*, ch. 2) has shown how hard it is in such cases to disentangle myth from reality. But even where hostility was genuinely widespread (and not overdramatized by the artists and their friends) a psychological analysis of such situations will fail as long as we see it exclusively in terms of "progress" versus philistines. For resistance is not only due to the lazy attitude of those who shun a greater effort (though this, too, plays its part) but also to what might be called the regressive component which seems to threaten the inner security of those not ready to yield. I have attempted to discuss some of the "moral" aspects of this question in a paper on "Visual Metaphors of Value in Art" in *Symbols and Values: An Initial Study*. Thirteenth Symposium of the Conference on Science, Philosophy and Religion. Ed. L. Bryson and others. (New York: Harper and Brothers, 1954.)

[24] cf. A. H. Barr Jr., *Picasso* (New York: Museum of Modern Art, 1939).

[25] For the concept of the "logic of the situation" cf. K. R. Popper, *op. cit.*, section 31.

²⁶ cf. A. H. Barr Jr., *op. cit.*

²⁷ e.g. Zervos, *op. cit.*, Vol. I, pl. 70.

²⁸ L. Venturi, *Cézanne* (Paris: Paul Rosenberg, 1936), Nos. 103, 240, 241, 880, 1214. One of these versions was apparently in the possession of Mr. Kahnweiler, Picasso's dealer.

²⁹ How hard it was for Picasso to achieve this regression also appears from the report, quoted by D. Schneider, *op. cit.*, p. 223, that the artist is said to have taken hashish at the time "to induce a primitive mood." The element of aggressive caricature, also referred to by the author, fits into the picture.

³⁰ For a most illuminating discussion of the complex relationship between private meaning and public response cf. the interpretation of F. X. Messerschmidt's busts of character types, by E. Kris, reprinted in *Psychoanalytic Explorations in Art.*

³¹ cf. my paper on "Visual Metaphors of Value in Art," *op. cit.*, which supplements the present paper in certain respects while it may be superseded by it in others.

FREUD AND MODERN PHILOSOPHY: *Kaplan*

¹ Based on the Freud Centenary Lecture delivered before the Society of Psychoanalytic Medicine of Southern California, May 18, 1956.

FREUDIANISM AND PSYCHOANALYSIS— A THOMIST VIEW: *Maritain*

¹ Roland Dalbiez, *La méthode psychanalytique et la doctrine freudienne* (Paris: Desclée De Brouwer, 1936; 2d ed., 1949). *Ed. note:* There is an English translation by T. F. Lindsay (2 vols., New York, Toronto and London: Longmans, Green, 1941). Unless otherwise specified, references are to the second French edition.

² What memory presents to us is a formal sign. Through it and in it, we know not an image of our past, but our past itself—that which has been and is no more. Cf. my critical studies, *La Philosophie Bergsonienne*, 2d ed., pp. 273-77 and *Les Degrés du Savoir*, pp. 231-33.

³ In English tr., II, 221-22.

⁴ *op. cit.*, II, 222.

⁵ *op. cit.*

⁶ On the intrinsically practical character of medical science (something that is totally different from an applied speculative science), I made some remarks in a brief report ("Le discernement médical du merveilleux") at the *Journées de Psychologie Religieuse d'Avon*, in 1936 (*Études Carmélitaines*, April 1937).

[7] *Ed. note:* For Claparède's views on Freud, see his "Freud et la psychanalyse," an introduction to the French translation of Freud's Clark University Lectures, entitled, "Origine et dévelopment de la psychanalyse," *La Revue de Genève* for 1920 and 1921; cf. Freud, *Cinq Leçons sur la Psychanalyse.* (Paris: Payot, 1926.) An autobiographical sketch by Claparède will be found in C. Murchison, *A History of Psychology in Autobiography,* I (Worcester, Mass.: Clark University Press, 1930).

[8] It should be noted here that conscientious psychoanalysts are the first to proclaim that psychoanalytic treatment is not to be recommended without reservations. Cf. for example, Dr. Michel Gressot, "Les indications et la techniques de la cure psychanalytique," in *Médecine et Hygiène,* Geneva, 15 November 1952, p. 17: "Finally the indication must be weighed with prudence when it is surmised that the process depends on a conflictual situation, but that the *prise de conscience* of that dependence, or a reversal in the pathogenic situation, would make the patient incur a risk of more serious disequilibrium or depression, for example, in the case of dislocation of irreplaceable family ties, however neurotic as they might nevertheless be. . . . However, contra-indication is not equivalent in these matters to therapeutic nihilism, for the alternative posed in general is not psychoanalysis or abstention, but psychoanalysis or psychotherapy of another type—a radical treatment or, by default, a symptomatic treatment. And in doubtful cases, one can resort for a time to a 'trial-psychoanalysis' aimed at clarifying the prognostication."

[9] For a translation of this paper, which originally appeared in German in 1924, see now Stefan Betlheim and Heinz Hartmann, "On Parapraxes in the Korsakow Psychosis," in *Organization and Pathology of Thought,* ed. David Rapaport (New York: Columbia University Press, 1951), ch. 13, pp. 288-310. The experimental studies by Karl Schroetter and Gaston Roffenstein, mentioned above by the author, as well as others by Herbert Silberer and M. Nachmansohn, are provided in Part Three of this book. [EDITOR]

[10] On the distinction between empiriological and ontological knowledge, see my book *The Degrees of Knowledge,* ch. 4.

[11] *Religion et Culture,* p. 16.

[12] Concerning the notion of the superego and the authentic interpretation of this notion, see the important remarks of Dr. Odier in his work, *Les deux sources, consciente et inconsciente, de la vie morale,* 2d ed., Neuchâtel, 1947.

[13] "Our interpretation of sublimation," writes M. T. L. Penido, in *La conscience religieuse, Essai systématique suivi d'illustrations* (Paris: Téqui, 1936), p. 111, "differs from that of the Freudians on two fundamental points: 1) We do not admit that spirituality is

sublimated sexuality; 2) we admit a sublimation which functions under the domination of spiritual forces, and which consequently involves a certain purification or spiritualization of sensibility." The author cites Charles Baudouin, "Sublimation et Synthèse," *Revue de théologie et de philosophie,* January 1935, pp. 46-56: "When it is shown that a higher tendency proceeds from a displacement of a certain crude instinct, one is no more reducing the first to the second than one would pretend to be reducing man to lower organisms when he assumes the evolution of living beings. The reality of sublimation must all the more be affirmed as there exist cases of precisely false sublimation, and one sees very well that then he has to do with an entirely different thing (eroticization of the religious life, for example). We have the right to speak of a real sublimation when the whole of actual conduct is in conformity with motives set up by consciousness. On the contrary, we shall speak of rationalization and disguise when there is a flagrant discrepancy and conduct continues to be governed by the lower movements which the subject pretends to be renouncing."

[14] He particularly neglects to recognize the spiritual unconscious, distinct by nature from the instinctual unconscious. On the essential distinction between these two forms of the unconscious, see my book, *Creative Intuition in Art and Poetry,* (New York: Meridian Books, 1955), ch. 3.

[15] Pointing out to an audience of theologians the domain of this false consciousness, which adorns itself with the fairest pretexts, Doctor Charles-Henri Nodet says quite rightly: "If you affirm, in the name of theology, the existence in all human behavior, and still more in every engagement in the religious life, of a reality that is *mysterious because supernatural,* psychoanalysis requires of you a complementary affirmation, namely, the existence, in all human behavior, of a reality *mysterious because unconscious.* Two domains, therefore, elude immediate, current, rational observation, two mysterious, extrarational domains, the supernatural, where your discernment of spirits maintains rights I do not wish to contest, and unconscious life, where psychoanalytic investigation maintains rights that I ask you in turn not to contest." *Considérations psychanalytiques à propos des attraits névrotiques pour la vocation religieuse* (Bourges: Imprimerie Tardy, 1950) p. 6. Cf. the same author, *Psychiatrie et vie religieuse* in the Encyclopédie Médico-Chirurgicale, 1955.

[16] Virgil, *Aeneid,* VII.312. The full passage reads: "Flectere si nequeo superos Acheronta movebo—If I cannot bend the Higher Powers, I will move the Infernal regions." Freud twice used this line with evident stress in *The Interpretation of Dreams,* first on the title page as the book's motto and then in the closing paragraphs. For Freud's attraction to this text, see *The Interpretation*

of Dreams, tr. and ed. James Strachey (New York: Basic Books, 1955), 608, n.1. It has recently been suggested that Freud's attention to this passage may have been drawn by the significant and different use of it made by Ferdinand Lassalle. [EDITOR]

[17] In my "Notes sur le freudisme, à propos de l'ouvrage de Roland Dalbiez," *Études Carmélitaines,* April 1938.

[18] Dalbiez, II, 406 ff.

[19] G. Zilboorg, "L'amour de Dieu chez Freud," in *Supplément* of *La Vie Spirituelle,* 1953, p. 8.

SELECTED REFERENCES

●

* A vast literature on Freudian and other "dynamic psychologies" has poured from presses in recent years. Many of these works deserve to be better known outside professional circles than they now are. In the interest of achieving economy in this present section, works cited elsewhere in this volume, especially in the footnotes, or in the "Notes on Contributors," are generally omitted below.

●

BIBLIOGRAPHIES AND DICTIONARIES

FROSCH, JOHN, ed. *The Annual Survey of Psychoanalysis: A Comprehensive Survey of Current Theory and Practice.* New York: International Universities Press, 1950–. In progress.

Vol. III (1956) covers the publications of 1952.

GRINSTEIN, ALEXANDER. *The Index of Psychoanalytic Writings.* 5 Vols. In progress. New York: International Universities Press, 1956.

Vol. I of this now essential work has 10714 entries and ranges from Aall through Freud.

MENNINGER, KARL A. *A Guide to Psychiatric Books.* 2d ed. rev. New York: Grune & Stratton, 1956.

HINSIE, LELAND E. AND JACOB SHATSKY. *Psychiatric Dictionary.* Rev. ed. with supplement. New York: Oxford University Press, 1953.

FREUD'S WRITINGS

A. COLLECTIONS AND ANTHOLOGIES

The Basic Writings of Sigmund Freud. Ed. by A. A. Brill. New York: Modern Library, 1938. Includes *Psychopathology of Everyday Life; The Interpretation of Dreams; Three Contributions to the Theory of Sex; Wit and Its Relation to the Unconscious; Totem and Taboo; The History of the Psychoanalytic Movement.*

Collected Papers, 5 vols. Ed. by Joan Riviere and James Strachey. New York, London, Vienna: International Psychoanalytic Press, 1924–50.

　Includes basic technical and theoretical essays.

Gesammelte Schriften, 12 vols. Leipzig, Vienna, Zurich: Internationaler Psychoanalytischer Verlag, 1924–34.

Gesammelte Werke, 18 vols. London: International Psychoanalytic Press, 1940–52.

The Standard Edition of the Complete Psychological Works of Sigmund Freud. In progress. 24 vols. Ed. by James Strachey and others. London: Hogarth Press and Institute of Psychoanalysis, 1953–.

　The masterly edition of *The Interpretation of Dreams* in this series supersedes all previous versions.

On War, Sex and Neurosis. Ed. by Sander Katz, with a preface and glossary by Paul Goodman. New York: Arts and Science Press, 1947.

B. INDIVIDUAL WORKS

The works which deal principally with cultural themes comprise:

1907. *Delusion and Dream in Jensen's "Gradiva,"* newly edited with introduction by P. Rieff (Boston: Beacon Press, 1956).
1910. *Leonardo da Vinci.*
1912–13. *Totem and Taboo.*
1921. *Group Psychology and the Analysis of the Ego.*
1927. *The Future of An Illusion.*
1930. *Civilization and Its Discontents.*
1937–39. *Moses and Monotheism.*

Many basic statements will also be found in the *Collected Papers (CP).* Especially notable are:

1908. "Civilized Sexual Morality and Modern Nervousness" in *CP,* II, 76–99.
1908. "The Relation of the Poet to Day-Dreaming" in *CP,* II, 173–83.

1914. "The Moses of Michelangelo" in *CP*, IV (1925), 257–87.
1915. "Thoughts for the Times on War and Death" in *CP*, IV (1925), 288–317.
1923. "A Neurosis of Demoniacal Possession in the Seventeenth Century" in *CP*, IV (1925), 436–72.
1928. "Dostoyevsky and Parricide" in *CP*, V (1950), 222–44.
1933. "Why War" in *CP*, V (1950), 273–87. An exchange with Albert Einstein.

SERIAL PUBLICATIONS

International Psycho-analytical Library. Edited by Ernest Jones. In progress. London: The Hogarth Press and the Institute of Psycho-analysis.

> Includes the basic monographs and collections of papers of Karl Abraham, Sandor Ferenczi, Ernest Jones, Melanie Klein, Theodor Reik, Ella Freeman Sharpe, and others.

Nervous and Mental Disease Monograph Series. New York: *Journal of Nervous and Mental Diseases,* 1913–.

The Psychoanalytic Study of the Child. Ed. by Ruth S. Eissler, Anna Freud, Heinz Hartmann, and Ernst Kris. In progress. New York: International Universities Press, 1945–.

> Includes many notable papers of broad clinical and theoretical significance.

Psychoanalysis and the Social Sciences. Ed. by Géza Róheim, Warner Muensterberger, and Sidney Axelrad. In progress. New York: International Universities Press, 1947–.

Yearbook of Psychoanalysis. Ed. by Sandor Lorand. In progress. New York: International Universities Press, 1945–.

JOURNALS

The American Imago, American Journal of Orthopsychiatry, American Journal of Psychiatry, British Journal of Medical Psychology, Bulletin of the Menninger Clinic, Complex, Contemporary Psychologist, Imago (Vienna), *International Journal of Psycho-analysis* (London), *Journal of Abnormal and Social Psychology, Journal of American Psychoanalytic Association, Journal of Analytical Psychology, Pastoral Psychology, Psychiatry, Psyché* (Paris), *Psyche* (Heidelberg, Stuttgart), *Psychoanalysis, Psychoanalytic Quarterly, Revue française de psychanalyse.*

Special notices, including original documents on Freud's life and work, will be found in many of these Journals for the years 1939–40 and 1956–57.

FREUD'S LIFE AND TIMES

ARLOW, JACOB. *The Legacy of Sigmund Freud.* New York: International Universities Press, 1956.

BINSWANGER, LUDWIG. *Erinnerungen an Sigmund Freud.* Berne: A. Francke Verlag AG, 1956.

    Excerpts numerous letters from Freud.

FREUD, SIGMUND. *An Autobiographical Study* (1934). London: Hogarth, 1935.

————. *History of the Psychoanalytic Movement* (1914). In *Basic Writings.*

————. *The Origins of Psychoanalysis. Letters to Wilhelm Fliess, Drafts and Notes: 1887–1902.* Ed. by Maria Bonaparte, Anna Freud, and Ernst Kris. Introduction by Ernst Kris. New York: Basic Books, 1954.

DOOLITTLE, HILDA *(pseud. H.D.). Tribute to Freud.* New York: Pantheon Books, 1956.

    Unpublished Letters by Freud to the Author, the noted poet ("H. D.").

JONES, ERNEST. *The Life and Work of Sigmund Freud.* In progress. 3 vols. New York: Basic Books, 1955–.

————. *Four Centenary Addresses.* New York: Basic Books, 1956.

KATCHER, NAOMI, ed. *The Catalogue of the Freud Centenary Exhibit of the American Psychoanalytic Association.* New York: International Universities Press, 1956.

MARCUSE, LUDWIG. *Sigmund Freud: Sein Bild vom Menschen.* Hamburg: Rowohlt, 1956.

REIK, THEODOR. *The Search Within.* New York: Farrar, Straus and Cudahy, 1956.

    Selections from the author's *Thirty Years with Freud, Listening with the Third Ear, Fragment of A Great Confession.* The last section discloses hitherto unpublished letters from Freud to Reik.

SACHS, HANNS. *Freud: Master and Friend.* Cambridge: Harvard University Press, 1944.

WITTELS, FRITZ. *Freud and His Time.* New York: Liveright, 1931.

WORTIS, JOSEPH. *Fragments of an Analysis with Freud.* New York: Simon & Schuster, 1954.

ZILBOORG, GREGORY. *Sigmund Freud.* New York: Scribner's, 1951.

DISSENTING SCHOOLS

ADLER, ALFRED. *The Individual Psychology of Alfred Adler. A Systematic Presentation in Selections from His Writings.* Ed. and annotated by Heinz L. Ansbacher and Rowena R. Ansbacher. New York: Basic Books, 1956.

ALLERS, RUDOLF. *The Successful Error.* New York: Sheed and Ward, 1941.

BINSWANGER, LUDWIG. *Ausgewahlte Vortraege und Aufsaetze,* 2 vols. Berne: A. G. Francke Verlag, 1947–1955.

BUBER, MARTIN. *The Eclipse of God.* New York: Harper, 1954.

———. *Pointing the Way.* New York: Harper, 1957. Forthcoming.

> The first indicates Buber's objections to Jung's views as "Gnostic" in character; the second will print Buber's essay on "healing through encounter."

FROMM, ERICH. *The Art of Loving.* New York: Harper, 1956.

GLOVER, EDWARD. *Freud or Jung?* New York: Meridian Books, 1956.

JACOBI, JOLANDE. "Versuch einer Abgrenzung der wichtigsten Konzeptionen C. G. Jung's von der S. Freuds." *Psyche* (Stuttgart), IX.5 (August 1955), 261–78.

JUNG, CARL. *Collected Works.* Edited by Herbert Read, Michael Fordham, and Gerhard Adler. 18 vols. In progress. New York: Pantheon Books.

> See, especially, *Symbols of Transformation* (previously translated as *Psychology of the Unconscious*).

MARCUSE, LUDWIG. "Der Fall C. G. Jung." *Aufbau* (New York) December 30, 1955.

———. "Ein Vorläufiges Schlusswort," *Ibid.,* April 27, 1956.

> This issue contains a separate section entitled "Für und gegen C. G. Jung" with numerous letters from notable correspondents.

MULLAHY, PATRICK. *Oedipus—Myth and Complex.* New York: Grove Press, 1955.

> Reviews the theories of Freud, Adler, Jung, Rank, Horney, Fromm, and Sullivan.

MUNROE, RUTH L. *Schools of Psychoanalytic Thought.* New York: Dryden, 1955.

PERLS, FREDERICK S., RALPH F. HEFFERLINE AND PAUL GOODMAN. *Gestalt Therapy.* New York: Julian Press, 1951.

PROGOFF, IRA. *Death and Rebirth of Psychology.* New York: Julian Press, 1956.

———. *Jung's Psychology and its Social Meaning.* New York: Julian Press, 1953.

The more recent volume espouses the final teachings of Otto Rank.

RADO, SANDOR. *Psychoanalysis of Behavior. Collected Papers.* New York: Grune & Stratton, 1956.

————— and GEORGE E. DANIELS, eds. *Changing Concepts of Psychoanalytic Medicine.* New York: Grune & Stratton, 1956.

SARTRE, JEAN-PAUL. *Existential Psychoanalysis.* Tr. by Hazel E. Barnes. New York: Philosophical Library, 1953.

DEVELOPMENTS OF DOCTRINE AND TECHNIQUE

ALEXANDER, FRANZ. *Psychoanalysis and Psychotherapy: Developments in Theory, Technique and Training.* New York: W. W. Norton, 1956.

————— and FRENCH, T. M. *Psychoanalytic Therapy, Principles and Application.* New York: Ronald, 1946.

————— and ROSS, HELEN. *Dynamic Psychiatry.* Chicago: University of Chicago Press, 1952.

AMERICAN PSYCHOLOGICAL ASSOCIATION. *Psychoanalysis as seen by Analyzed Psychologists: A Symposium.* Washington, D.C.: American Psychological Association, 1953.

Includes pungent autobiographical statements by Edwin Boring, Hanns Sachs, Henry Murray, and Franz Alexander.

BRENNER, CHARLES. *An Elementary Textbook of Psychoanalysis.* New York: International Universities Press, 1955.

BROMBERG, WALTER. *Man Above Humanity: A History of Psychotherapy.* New York: Lippincott, 1954.

DEVEREUX, GEORGE, ed. *Psychoanalysis and the Occult.* New York: International Universities Press, 1953.

EHRENWALD, JAN. *From Medicine Man to Freud.* New York: Dell, 1956.

FAIRBAIRN, W. R. *Psychoanalytic Studies of the Personality.* London: Tavistock Publications, 1952.

FEIGL, HEBERT and MICHAEL SCRIVEN, eds. *The Foundations of Science and the Concepts of Psychology and Psychoanalysis.* Minneapolis: University of Minnesota Press, 1956.

The essay by Albert Ellis attempts a so-called "operational reformulation of psychoanalysis."

FENICHEL, OTTO. *Collected Papers.* 2 vols. New York: W. W. Norton, 1953–54.

—————. *The Psychoanalytic Theory of Neurosis.* New York: W. W. Norton, 1945.

FLIESS, ROBERT. *The Psychoanalytic Reader.* New York: International Universities Press, 1948. Vol. I. Only one published.

FRENKL-BRUNSWICK, ELSE and others. "Psychoanalysis and the Scientific Method." *Scientific Monthly,* November, 1954, pp. 293 ff.

> Includes papers and comments by B. F. Skinner, Michael Scriven, and J. Richfield.

FREUD, ANNA. *The Ego and the Mechanisms of Defense.* New York: International Universities Press, 1946.

GLOVER, EDWARD. *The Technique of Psycho-analysis.* New York: International Universities Press, 1955.

HALL, CALVIN and GARDNER LINDZEY. *Theories of Personality.* New York: John Wiley, 1957.

> Includes chapters on Freud, Jung, Adler and the "neo-Adlerians," Henry A. Murray, Kurt Lewin, Gordon Allport, Carl Rogers, Gardner Murphy, and many recent American researchers.

HEALY, WILLIAM, AUGUSTA F. BRONNER and ANNA MAE BOWERS. *The Structure and Meaning of Psychoanalysis.* New York: Alfred A. Knopf, 1953.

KLEIN, MELANIE, PAULA HEIMAN, and R. E. MONEY-KYRLE. *New Trends in Psychoanalysis.* New York: Basic Books, 1955. With a Preface by E. Jones.

KLUCKHOHN, CLYDE and HENRY A. MURRAY. *Personality in Nature, Society, and Culture.* 2d ed. New York: Alfred A. Knopf, 1955.

KNIGHT, ROBERT P. *Psychoanalytic Psychiatry and Psychology: Clinical and Theoretical Papers.* Austen Riggs Center, Vol. I. New York: International Universities Press, 1954.

REICH, WILHELM. *Character-Analysis.* 3rd enlarged ed. New York: Orgone Institute Press, 1949.

SCHILDER, PAUL. *The Image and Appearance of the Human Body.* New York: International Universities Press, 1950.

THOMPSON, CLARA, MILTON MAZER, and EARL WITTENBURG, eds. *An Outline of Psychoanalysis.* Revised ed. New York: Modern Library, 1955.

> 34 essays and excerpts.

TOMPKINS, SYLVAN S., ed. *Contemporary Psychopathology: A Source Book.* Cambridge: Harvard University Press, 1947.

> The 45 papers emphasize experimental research.

WOLBERG, LOUIS. *The Technique of Psychotherapy.* New York: Grune & Stratton, 1954.

ZILBOORG, GREGORY. *A History of Medical Psychology.* New York: W. W. Norton, 1941.

FREUD, DYNAMIC PSYCHOLOGIES, AND CULTURE

ALEXANDER, FRANZ. *Our Age of Unreason: A Study of the Irrational Forces in Social Life.* Philadelphia: Lippincott, 1942, reprinted 1951.

American Journal of Sociology. Various writers. Vol. XLV, no. 3. Nov. 1939.

Notable essays and book reviews by Havelock Ellis, A. A. Brill, Smith Ely Jelliffe, Gregory Zilboorg, Ernest W. Burgess, Harold Lasswell, Kenneth Burke, William Healy, Karen Horney, Fritz Wittels, A. L. Kroeber, and Salo W. Baron. Kroeber's paper is entitled "Totem and Taboo in Retrospect." Baron reviews *Moses and Monotheism.*

Aufbau (New York). Friday, May 25, 1956.

Articles by William G. Niederland, L. Marcuse, W. C. Hulse, Heinrich Meng.

BEHARRIELL, FREDERICK J. "Freud's Debts to Literature." *Psychoanalysis and the Future,* edited by Board of Editors of *Psychoanalysis.* New York: Liberal Press, 1957. In press.

Discusses the recently printed correspondence of Freud and Arthur Schnitzler.

BRACELAND, FRANCES J., ed. *Faith, Reason, and Modern Psychiatry.* New York: P. J. Kenedy, 1956.

Important essays by Roman Catholic writers. The essay by Allers surveys the relations of Freud and continental existentialist psychiatries.

BROSIN, HENRY W. "A Review of the Influence of Psychoanalysis and Current Thought." In *Dynamic Psychiatry,* ed. F. Alexander and H. Ross (Chicago, 1952), 508–53.

This learned article concludes with a bibliography of 150 items.

CHOISY, MARYSE. *Le chrétien devant le psychanalyse.* Paris: Téqui, 1955.

FEUER, LEWIS S. *Psychoanalysis and Ethics.* Springfield, Illinois: Charles C. Thomas, 1955.

FINGARETTE, HERBERT. "Psychoanalytic Perspectives on Moral Guilt and Responsibility." *Psychoanalysis,* IV. 2 (1955–56), 46–66.

FRANK, JEROME. *Law and the Modern Mind.* New York: Howard-McCann, 1949.

FROMM, ERICH. "A Counter-Rebuttal (to H. Marcuse)." *Dissent.* Winter, 1956.

——. "The Human Implication of Instinctive Radicalism." *Dissent.* Fall, 1955. 142–49.

————. "The Present Human Condition." *The American Scholar.* Winter, 1955–56.

HOFFMANN, FREDERICK J. *Freudianism and the Literary Imagination.* Baton Rouge: Louisiana University Press, 1944.

International Journal of Psycho-analysis. Various writers. Vol. XXXVII. Pt. 1 (Jan.–Feb. 1956).

> This exemplary centenary number includes: Alan Tyson and James Strachey, "A Chronological Hand-List of Freud's Works"; Franz Baumeyer, "The Schreber Case"; Louis Fraiberg, "Freud's Writings on Art"; Thomas Mann, "Freud and the Future."

JONES, ERNEST. *Hamlet and Oedipus.* New York: Anchor Books, 1954.

LASSWELL, HAROLD D. *World Politics and Personal Insecurity.* Glencoe, Illinois: The Free Press, 1950.

LINDNER, ROBERT and CLEMENT STAFF, eds. *Explorations in Psychoanalysis: Essays in Honor of Theodor Reik.* New York: Julian Press, 1953.

MARCUSE, HERBERT. *Eros and Civilization: A Philosophical Inquiry into Freud.* Boston: Beacon Press, 1951.

————. "A Reply to Erich Fromm." *Dissent.* Winter 1956.

————. "The Social Implications of Freudian Revisionism." *Dissent.* Summer 1955.

MAY, ROLLO. *The Meaning of Anxiety.* New York: Ronald, 1950.

MENNINGER, KARL. *Love Against Hate.* With the collaboration of Jeannette Lyle Menninger. New York: Harcourt, 1942.

MCNEILL, JOHN T. *A History of the Cure of Souls.* New York: Harper, 1951.

NELSON, BENJAMIN. "The Future of Illusions." *Man in Contemporary Society,* ed. Contemporary Civilization Staff of Columbia College (New York: Columbia University Press 1956), II (1956), pp. 958–79.

PARSONS, TALCOTT. *Essays in Sociological Theory.* Glencoe, Illinois: The Free Press, 1956.

PFISTER, OSKAR. *Christianity and Fear.* London: Allen and Unwin, 1948.

PUMPIAN-MINDLIN, EUGENE, ed. *Psychoanalysis As Science.* Palo Alto: Stanford University Press, 1952. With Lawrence S. Kubie and Ernest R. Hilgard.

RANK, OTTO. *Art and Artist: Creative Urge and Personality Development.* New York: Alfred A. Knopf, 1948. With a Preface by Ludwig Lewisohn.

REDL, FRITZ and D. WINEMAN. *Children Who Hate.* Glencoe, Illinois: The Free Press, 1951.

RIESMAN, DAVID. *The Lonely Crowd.* New Haven: Yale University Press, 1950. New York: Anchor Books, 1956. In collaboration with Reuel Denney and Nathan Glazer.

————. *Individualism Reconsidered*. Glencoe, Illinois: The Free Press, 1954. Abridged ed. New York: Anchor Books, 1955.

RÓHEIM, GÉZA. *The Origin and Function of Culture*. New York: Nervous and Mental Disease Monographs, no. 69, 1941.

SCHAPIRO, MEYER. "Leonardo and Freud: An Art-Historical Study." *Journal of the History of Ideas*. April, 1956.

————. "Two Slips of Leonardo and a Slip of Freud." *Psychoanalysis*. Vol. IV, no. 2 (1955–56), 3–5.

SCHILDER, PAUL. *Psychoanalysis, Man, and Society*. New York: W. W. Norton, 1951.

SEARS, ROBERT. *Survey of Objective Studies of Psychoanalytic Concepts*. New York: Social Science Research Council, 1947.

SIEVERS, W. DAVID. *Freud on Broadway: A History of Psychoanalysis and the American Drama*. New York: Thomas Nelson, 1955.

STERN, KARL. *The Third Revolution: A Study of Psychiatry and Religion*. New York: Harcourt, Brace, 1954.

WELLISCH, ERICH. *Isaac and Oedipus*. New York: Humanities Press, 1956.

WHITE, VICTOR, O. P. *God and the Unconscious*. Chicago: Regnery, 1953. Foreword by C. G. Jung. Appendix by G. Frei.

WILBUR, GEORGE and WARNER MUENSTERBERGER, eds. *Psychoanalysis and Culture*. New York: International Universities Press, 1951.

   Includes essays by H. Hartmann, E. Kris, R. Loewenstein, R. Spitz, K. Menninger, G. Devereux, Maria Bonaparte, K. R. Eissler, J. Campbell, H. A. Bunker, B. Lewin, G. Bychowski, M. Grotjahn, and bibliography of Géza Róheim's writings.

310 Notes on Contributors

Department of Philosophy at the University of California at

NOTES ON CONTRIBUTORS

JEROME S. BRUNER is currently Professor of Psychology,
Harvard University. He has been a visiting member of the In-
stitute of Advanced Study, as well as visiting lecturer at the
University of Cambridge and University College, London. His
publications include: *Opinions and Personality; A Study of
Thinking; Mandate from the People.*

ERIK H. ERIKSON is a psychoanalyst at the Austen Riggs
Center at Stockbridge, Massachusetts and Professor of Psychology at the University of Pittsburgh School of Medicine. His
publications include *Childhood and Society* and numerous articles on psychology and sociology.

E. H. GOMBRICH is currently Professor in the History of
Renaissance Art at the University of London at the Warburg
Institute. From 1950 to 1953 he was Slade Professor of Fine
Arts at the University of Oxford. His publications include:
Caricature (with Ernst Kris), *The Story of Art,* and numerous
essays in learned journals.

FREDERICK J. HACKER is the Director of the Hacker Psychiatric Clinic in Beverly Hills, California and a member of the
teaching staff of the Menninger Clinic. His publications include
numerous articles on the cultural aspects of psychoanalysis and
forensic psychiatry.

WILL HERBERG is Adjunct Professor of Judaic Studies and
Social Philosophy at Drew University, and has been a visiting
lecturer at many American universities. His publications in-

clude *Judaism and Modern Man; Protestant-Catholic-Jew;* and *The Writings of Martin Buber.*

STANLEY EDGAR HYMAN is a member of the literature faculty at Bennington College and a staff writer for *The New Yorker.* His publications include *The Armed Vision* and *The Critical Performance.*

ABRAHAM KAPLAN is Professor and Chairman of the Department of Philosophy at the University of California at Los Angeles. His publications include *Power and Society* (with H. D. Lasswell), and numerous papers in philosophical journals.

ABRAM KARDINER is Clinical Professor of Psychiatry and Director of the Psychoanalytic Clinic of Columbia University. His publications include: *The Individual and Society; The Psychological Frontiers of Society; The Mark of Oppression;* and *Sex and Morality.*

ALFRED KAZIN is Professor of American Studies at Amherst College. His publications include: *On Native Grounds; A Walker in the City; The Stature of Theodore Dreiser* (Editor) and many other works.

JACQUES MARITAIN now resides in Princeton, New Jersey. His works include: *Creative Intuition in Art and Poetry; Art and Scholasticism; The Degrees of Knowledge;* and many other works in philosophy and theology.

GARDNER MURPHY is Director of Research at the Menninger Clinic and past President of the American Psychological Association. His publications include: *Historical Introduction to Modern Psychology* and *Personality: A Bio-Social Approach to Origins and Structure.*

BENJAMIN NELSON is the editor of this volume.

REINHOLD NIEBUHR is Charles A. Briggs Graduate Professor and Vice-President of the Union Theological Seminary. His publications include: *The Self and the Dramas of History; The Irony of American History; The Nature and Destiny of Man; An Interpretation of Christian Ethics.*

NIGEL WALKER received his Ph. D. from the University of Edinburgh, and is associated with the Davidson Clinic in Edinburgh. His publications include numerous articles in British journals on the logical aspects of psychology and psychotherapy.

VIKTOR VON WEIZSAECKER is an outstanding German physician, psychoanalyst, and philosopher. From 1926-1930, he edited with Martin Buber and Joseph Wittig, the journal *Die Kreatur*. His publications include: *Artz und Kranke; Pathosophie;* and *Natur und Geist.*

GREGORY ZILBOORG is Clinical Professor of Psychiatry at the New York State University College of Medicine and Associate Editor of the *Psychoanalytic Quarterly.* His publications include: *A History of Medical Psychology; Mind, Medicine, and Man; Psychology of the Criminal Act and Punishment.*

PERMISSIONS AND
ACKNOWLEDGMENTS

1. KAZIN, ALFRED: *The Freudian Revolution Analyzed*. Reprinted from the *New York Times Magazine*, May 6, 1956 with the permission of the author.

2. WALKER, NIGEL: *A New Copernicus?* Reprinted, with minor changes, from *Listener* with the permission of the author.

3. ZILBOORG, GREGORY: *The Changing Concept of Man in Present-Day Psychiatry*. Reprinted from the *American Journal of Psychiatry*, Vol. III, with the permission of the author and the editor.

4. FREUD, SIGMUND: *A Preface: 1917*. Reprinted from *Ritual: The Psychological Problems of Religion* by Theodore Reik, Farrar, Straus, and Cudahy, Inc. New York, 1946, with the permission of Farrar, Straus, and Cudahy, Inc.

5. KARDINER, ABRAM: *Freud: The Man I Knew, The Scientist, and His Influence*. This essay was prepared for the present volume and is published with the permission of the author.

6. VON WEIZSAECKER, VIKTOR: *Reminiscences of Freud and Jung*. Excerpted from *Natur und Geist* by Viktor von Weizsaecker, Vandenhoeck and Ruprecht, Göttingen, 1954, with the permission of Vandenhoeck and Ruprecht. Translated by Hugo Knoepfmacher.

7. ERIKSON, ERIK: *The First Psychoanalyst*. Reprinted with the permission of the author. This essay appeared in the *Yale Review*, September, 1956.

8. MURPHY, GARDNER: *The Current Impact of Freud on American Psychology*. Reprinted with the permission of the author and with the cooperation of Dr. George A. Kelly of Ohio State University and other members of the Executive Committee of the American Psychological Association.

9. HACKER, FREDERICK J.: *Freud, Marx, and Kierkegaard*. This essay was prepared for the present volume and is published with the permission of the author. Dr. Hacker writes in acknowledgment: "Many of the ideas contained in this essay were developed as a result of the author's close cooperation with Ludwig Marcuse, Ph.D., Professor of Philosophy at the University of Southern California, Los Angeles, California. Although an acknowledgment of each specific contribution by Dr. Marcuse will not be attempted, the author wishes to state his general and over-all indebtedness. Several of the formulations appearing here were originally used by Dr. Marcuse in his recent book *Sigmund Freud: Sein Bild vom Menschen* (Rowohlt, Hamburg, 1956), which was also based on our cooperation."

10. HERBERG, WILL: *Freud, the Revisionists, and Social Reality*. This essay was prepared for the present volume and is published with the permission of the author.

11. HYMAN, STANLEY EDGAR: *Psychoanalysis and the Climate of Tragedy*. Reprinted with the permission of the author from the *Partisan Review*, where it appeared in Spring, 1956 under the title "Freud and the Climate of Tragedy."

12. GOMBRICH, E. H.: *Psychoanalysis and the History of Art*. Reprinted with the permission of the author from the *International Journal of Psycho-analysis*, Vol. XXXV, (1954), 401–411.

13. KAPLAN, ABRAHAM: *Freud and Modern Philosophy*. This essay was prepared for the present volume and is published with the permission of the author.

14. MARITAIN, JACQUES: *Freudianism and Psychoanalysis: A Thomist View*. The original essay, on which the present text is based, appeared in *Scholasticism and Politics* and is utilized with the permission of Geoffrey Bles, Ltd., London. The present text was translated by Dr. Bernard Gilligan of Fordham University and revised for this edition by the author and editor.

15. NIEBUHR, REINHOLD: *Human Creativity and Self-Concern in Freud's Thought*. This essay was prepared for the present volume and is published with the permission of the author.

16. BRUNER, JEROME: *Freud and the Image of Man*. Reprinted, with the permission of the author, from the *Partisan Review*, where it appeared in the Summer issue of 1956.

Anticipating the centenary of Freud's birth (May 6, 1856), Benjamin Nelson began gathering materials for *Freud and the Twentieth Century* in the Fall of 1955. Editor and publisher were agreed upon a single resolve: to provide a forum wherein outstanding contemporary thinkers might express their minds, from their diverse points of view, on the meaning of Freud and his work for all aspects of contemporary culture. Many of the essays included in *Freud and the Twentieth Century* were undertaken especially for this volume and many others, which were inaccessible heretofore, were edited and, in some cases, translated.

The manuscript was completed in the Fall of 1956; composed in December, 1956; and released in the spring of 1957.

MERIDIAN BOOKS

17 Union Square West, New York 3, New York

If you have enjoyed this book, you will want these titles of related interest. Ask your bookseller for them.

Titles listed here are not necessarily available in the British Empire.

MERIDIAN BOOKS

17 Union Square West, New York 3, New York

If you have enjoyed this book, you will want these
titles of related interest. Ask your bookseller for them.

ANTHROPOLOGY

M15 SEX AND REPRESSION IN SAVAGE SOCIETY
by Bronislaw Malinowski

ART AND ART HISTORY

M7 THE PHILOSOPHY OF MODERN ART *by Herbert Read*
M8 CREATIVE INTUITION IN ART AND POETRY
by Jacques Maritain
M18 NEW DIRECTIONS 15: An anthology of new directions in prose
and poetry. International issue
M33 VISION AND DESIGN *by Roger Fry*. Illustrations
M38 THE ESSENCE OF LAUGHTER AND OTHER ESSAYS ON ART AND LITERA-
TURE *by Charles Baudelaire. Edited, selected, and introduced
by Peter Quennell. Meridian Original*
ML2 A DICTIONARY OF CLASSICAL ANTIQUITIES *by Oskar Seyffert. Re-
vised and edited by Henry Nettleship and J. E. Sandys. More
than 450 illustrations. Meridian Library*

CLASSICS

M9 OUTLINES OF THE HISTORY OF GREEK PHILOSOPHY
by Edward Zeller
M23 BYZANTINE CIVILIZATION *by Steven Runciman*
MG3 PROLEGOMENA TO THE STUDY OF GREEK RELIGION
by Jane Harrison. Meridian Giant
MG7 PLATO: The Man and His Work *by A. E. Taylor.*
Meridian Giant
ML1 ROMAN SOCIETY FROM NERO TO MARCUS AURELIUS *by Samuel
Dill.* Meridian Library
ML2 A DICTIONARY OF CLASSICAL ANTIQUITIES *by Oskar Seyffert. Re-
vised and edited by Henry Nettleship and J. E. Sandys. More
than 450 illustrations. Meridian Library*

DRAMA AND THEATER

M6 THE PLAYWRIGHT AS THINKER *by Eric Bentley*
MG4 MY LIFE IN ART *by Constantin Stanislavski.*
Meridian Giant
MG5 THE ROMANTIC AGONY *by Mario Praz.* Meridian Giant

EDUCATION

M31 FREEDOM, EDUCATION AND THE FUND: Essays and Addresses,
1946–1956 *by Robert M. Hutchins.* Meridian Original
MG4 MY LIFE IN ART *by Constantin Stanislavski.*
Meridian Giant

Titles listed here are not necessarily available in the British Empire.

MERIDIAN BOOKS

MERIDIAN BOOKS

LIVING AGE BOOKS, also published by MERIDIAN BOOKS, INC., is the original paper cover series of outstanding general contemporary religious writing in history, art, literature, theology, and Biblical studies. Ask your bookseller for catalog.